HANDBOOK OF KEY ECONOMIC INDICATORS

R. Mark Rogers

IRWIN
Professional Publishing
Burr Ridge, Illinois
New York, New York

This publication is designed to provide accurate and authoritative information in regard to the subject matter covered. It is sold with the understanding that neither the author nor the publisher is engaged in rendering legal, accounting, or other professional service. If legal advice or other expert assistance is required, the services of a competent professional person should be sought.

From a Declaration of Principles jointly adopted by a Committee of the American Bar Association and a Committee of Publishers.

Senior sponsoring editor: Amy Hollands Gaber
Project editor: Mary Conzachi
Production supervisor: Bob Lange
Interior designer: Mercedes Santos
Cover designer: Tim Kaage
Compositor: BookMasters, Inc.
Typeface: 10/12 Times Roman
Printer: Kingsport Press

Library of Congress Cataloging-in-Publication Data

Rogers R. Mark.
    Handbook of key economic indicators / R. Mark Rogers.
        p.   cm.
    Includes index.
    ISBN 0-7863-0193-7
    1. Economic indicators—United States.   2. Business cycles—United States—Statistics.   3. United States—Economic conditions
—Statistics.   I. Title.
HC103.R64   1994
330.973'0021—dc20   94–9328

Printed in the United States of America
2 3 4 5 6 7 8 9 0   1 0 9 8 7 6 5

To Graceann and Alexander

PREFACE

Why is following economic releases important? For investors and traders, the answer is obvious: economic releases move markets. And the markets—including bonds, stocks, foreign exchange, and commodities—usually move quickly. However, markets sometimes make mistakes initially focusing on wrong interpretations of economic news. Markets want a quick buy or sell verdict based on some hurried rule-of-thumb analysis. Yet the data are complex and initial impressions can be at odds with more in-depth analysis. The problem for traders and investors is that markets can turn on a dime once they realize that for a given economic release the initial, superficial interpretation is wrong. Of course, the change in reaction to the data can be for a number of reasons: a minor, unimportant subcomponent may have experienced a large monthly change and affected the overall number; a "technical factor" may have affected the overall number; a definition could have changed; previous data were revised; or there may have been problems seasonally adjusting the data.

Markets crave rules-of-thumb for quick buy or sell directions. But rules-of-thumb make mistakes; there is no substitute for in-depth knowledge and experience for learning what to look for in economic indicators to portray the current health of the economy.

This book is written to meet the needs of market watchers—traders, investors, and financial analysts—and even academics who want to move beyond the superficial to become knowledgeable in understanding the true content of each month's economic news. Academics often get caught up in simply using data as inputs for statistical models without a clear understanding of definitions, methodologies, or changes in methodologies. In turn, many studies misuse data or ignore key facets that can have a significant bearing on empirical analysis. This book is also written to be useful to researchers seeking to avoid such pitfalls.

While there are numerous books explaining financial instruments, there are only a handful of quality books that explain nonfinancial economic indicators. Since these books take a "dictionary" approach—many indicators but with only very basic information—the *Handbook of Key Economic Indicators* focuses on the nonfinancial economic indicators most closely followed by financial markets. In-depth methodologies and analytics are detailed for each indicator. In particular, this book concentrates on explaining the nonfinancial economic indicators that can move financial markets on a regular basis. Those chosen are generally acknowledged by the financial community as the key economic indicators. These are mostly government-produced indicators that cover all of the major segments of the economy. The breadth of coverage is seen in the table of contents with sections on employment, personal income, and consumer spending; monthly inflation indicators; the manufacturing sector; international trade; construction activity; gross domestic product; and the Commerce Department's composite indicators.

This book is written primarily for market analysts and investors who want to improve their expertise and ability to correctly gauge the strength and direction of the economy. In essence, to fully understand financial markets, one must be knowledgeable about key economic series. As already noted, the series chosen cover all major real sectors plus key inflation measures. It is the combination of real sector developments and inflation news together with monetary and fiscal policy changes that move financial markets. Additionally, it is often news about inflation or the real sector (e.g., unemployment) that leads to changes in monetary policy. The bottom line is that financial market behavior cannot be fully understood without a broad awareness of nonfinancial economic indicators. Some basic approaches to using the data are discussed later in the introduction.

This work is based on many years of experience as an analyst and economist at the Federal Reserve Bank of Atlanta, tracking the data and watching market reactions to the numbers. It is also based on reading hundreds of pages of technical papers on methodologies and talking with dozens of government economists and statisticians in person and over the telephone.

Because many economic indicators are interrelated, this book is best used through more than one reading, making cross references between chapters. Each month, news about key economic indicators that move the markets can be compared with each chapter's key features about the data. This book helps to develop an analyst's knowledge and experience about a given economic indicator by developing an analyst's awareness of key as well as subtle features of the data. Each chapter explains not only methodologies behind the indicators but also what to look for each month.

At the end of the chapters are key questions for analyzing each monthly economic report. These questions get to the heart of the issue of how economic indicators are currently portraying the economy. Each chapter provides the methodologies, the basic characteristics, and even some quirks in the data to provide insight into the answers for these questions each month. Over time, as one relates the methodologies to actual news releases and to the key questions, properly thinking about and analyzing economic indicators will become second nature.

This book reflects the work of many dedicated professionals who work for or have been associated with various government statistical agencies or policy institutions or have worked with the data extensively in the private sector. The author thanks them for their many considerations over the years and hopes that this publication does justice to their work. Many have indirectly contributed to the author's effort, and this is appreciated. The author would particularly like to thank those who commented specifically on earlier drafts or offered suggestions. Of course, the author accepts full responsibility for any errors within the manuscript.

Special thanks are due to Steve Andrews, Cynthia Bansak, Steve Berman, Janice Breuer, Mary Cho, Gerald Donahoe, David Fondalier, Charles Gilbert, Daniel Ginsburg, George Green, Harvey Hamel, Ethan Harris, Steve Haugen, Steven Henderson, Craig Howell, Linda Hoyle, Curt Hunter, Robert Keleher,

James Kennedy, Frank King, Don Luery, Haydn Mearkle, Patricia Nielsen, Ronald Piencykoski, Lois Plunkert, Brooks Robinson, Charles Robinson, George Roff, Mary Rosenbaum, Mary Lee Seifert, Dixon Tranum, Irving True, and Sheila Tschinkel.

The views in this book are the sole responsibility of the author and do not necessarily reflect the views of the Federal Reserve Bank of Atlanta or the Board of Governors of the Federal Reserve System.

R. Mark Rogers

CONTENTS

INTRODUCTION

THE MONTHLY FORECAST CYCLE

Each month financial markets make judgments on the strength of the economy and base many of their positions in the markets on these interpretations. Over the course of the month, with each release of economic data, new information is added to the "databanks" (whether actual or intuitive) of market analysts. Due to the intensively competitive nature of the primary financial markets, data is assimilated rapidly. In turn, market perceptions change—sometimes quite sharply. For example, a significantly stronger-than-expected employment or consumer price index (CPI) report can cause the financial markets to change from having priced bonds and stocks with the expectation of a near-term ease by the Federal Reserve System to one where expectations are that interest rates are unlikely to change soon. As such, bonds and stocks are immediately repriced.

Prior to the release of economic indicators, participants take positions in the market based on their expectation of what the data for various indicators suggest is the direction of the economy, bond prices, and prices for other financial assets. Sophisticated participants explicitly prepare forecasts for the indicators and then determine their market position of either "going long" or "going short" in (that is, buying or selling) various financial instruments.

Financial markets use every piece of readily available data to try to determine the current state of the economy. First, analysts take advantage of the fact that various statistical agencies sometimes use earlier released data from other agencies to derive portions of their own series. For example, the Bureau of Economic Analysis (BEA) uses employment and earnings data from the Bureau of Labor Statistics (BLS) to derive large segments of the wages and salaries component in personal income.

Second, a number of earlier released data series have a usefully significant statistical, behavioral relationship to later released data. A prime example of this is that the producer price index (PPI) for a given month is generally released about a week before that month's consumer price index is made public. Finally, analysts try to understand long-term relationships between economic data in order to better project trends in the economy and in financial markets.

The following section summarizes how financial markets use monthly data to forecast concurrent, later released data in that month. *Forecast* is somewhat of an awkward word to use since the forecast here is generally for data of the same month. Still, given the differences in the timing of releases and the rapid assimilation of information in the financial markets, the term does apply. A typical calendar of the most watched economic data is included in the subsequent table to give a good idea of the timing involved in this forecast cycle. Various bond houses and investment firms regularly compile and publish calendars for upcoming releases. These newsletters are often free subscriptions. Also, the Commerce Department puts a schedule of releases on its Electronic Bulletin Board (EBB). In later chapters, the specific links between the various series are discussed in more detail. Long-term considerations are discussed later.

MONTHLY INDICATORS AND THEIR USE
IN CONCURRENT FORECASTING

Construction Expenditures

These Census Bureau data are modified by the BEA and are then used as major inputs in the BEA's estimates for residential and nonresidential fixed investment in the gross domestic product (GDP) accounts. Market analysts use these monthly series to help project the above-mentioned components of GDP for the upcoming release.

Purchasing Managers' Index

The indicator and the components of the Purchasing Managers' Index—compiled by the National Association of Purchasing Management (NAPM)—are basically ordinal net measures of "better," "worse," or "same" conditions by respondents and are not quantitative (dollar value) in the same sense that surveys by the Census Bureau are. However, the total index and components provide some insight for:

1. The manufacturing component of industrial production.
2. Manufacturing employment.
3. Producer prices.
4. Manufacturers inventories.
5. New factory orders.

Specifically, simple regression models use NAPM data for forecasting the upcoming releases for manufacturing employment and for industrial production.

Also, the vendor performance component of the NAPM index is one of the eleven series parts in the Commerce Department's index of leading indicators.

Manufacturers' Shipments, Inventories, and Orders

Since the nondefense capital goods component of manufacturers' shipments provides a key input into the GDP component for investment in producers' durable equipment, money market economists use this indicator to project that component in GDP for that month's gross national product (GNP) release. Also, the inventory number provides some initial insight into the strength in inventories prior to the release of overall business inventories. A portion of the orders data goes into the Commerce Department's index of leading indicators.

Employment Report

The Employment Report released by the Labor Department provides the first broad measure on the state of the economy for any given month and is probably the most closely watched of all reports. The key forecast information is the following:

1. Aggregate production hours in manufacturing (based on production employment and the average workweek) are used to project the manufacturing component of industrial production.
2. Average hourly earnings, payroll employment, and average weekly hours are used to estimate major portions of the wages and salaries component of personal income.
3. The average manufacturing workweek enters the Commerce Department's index of leading indicators and payroll employment also enters Commerce's coincident indicators index.

Both of the first two sets of data are followed because in the predicted series they are actual methodological components used by the source agencies for their figures—at least for the initial estimates. The Federal Reserve Board uses labor hours models for initial estimates of a significant number of the components in industrial production. Also, the BEA directly derives much of their wage income data from the payroll data.

Unit New Auto Sales by the American Automobile Manufacturers Association (AAMA)

These industry data are used by market analysts to estimate the auto component within retail sales. Also, this series more closely correlates with the auto component of durables within personal consumption expenditures as derived for the personal consumption expenditures that is part of the personal income report produced by the BEA.

Retail Sales

Data are generally used to project major subcomponents of personal consumption expenditures for durables and nondurables for the personal income report. The retail sales data are also used as a proxies for the missing months of personal consumption data in GDP.

Producer Prices

Market analysts use regression analysis (or even simple estimates) based on producer prices to project the consumer price index for the latest release. There is no tie between the BLS methodologies in terms of inputs for producer prices and consumer prices. The connection is simply statistical. In other words, the BLS does not use the PPI in its estimates for the CPI, but market analysts try to use historical patterns between the two to make forecasts.

Business Inventories

Most estimates for the inventory component of GDP are based on monthly business inventory figures. The inventory data are taken from the Census Bureau for use by the BEA in the GDP accounts. Various adjustments to put data in current value and the deflation from current dollars to constant dollars—both of which are done at fine levels of detail—make the statistical relationship of the overall monthly figures to the quarterly inventory number to be very loose.

Monthly International Trade

The Census Bureau and BEA data on monthly international trade are used to help estimate real net exports (goods and services) for the upcoming GDP release. Prior to March 1994, the monthly report was for merchandise trade only.

The Monthly Release Schedule

Schedule for July 1993		
Date	Indicator	For Month/Quarter
1	Construction expenditures	May
1	Purchasing managers' index, National	
	Association of Purchasing Managers	June
	Manufacturers' shipments, inventories,	
	and orders	May
2	Employment situation	June
6	Auto sales, AAMA (American Automobile	
	Manufacturers Association)	June
7	Wholesale trade	May
13	Producer price index	June
14	Consumer price index	June
14	Advance monthly retail sales	June
15	Business inventories and sales	May
16	Advance report on US merchandise	
	trade	May
16	Industrial production and capacity	
	utilization rate	June
20	Housing starts and permits	June

The Monthly Release Schedule (*Continued*)

Schedule for July 1993

Date	Indicator	For Month/Quarter
28	Advance report on durable goods	June
29	Gross domestic product	Second quarter
30	Personal income, outlays, and saving	June
August		
3	Commerce composite indicators	June

BASICS IN ANALYZING THE INDICATORS EACH MONTH: THE LONG-TERM VERSUS THE LATEST RELEASE

There are many approaches to analyzing economic indicators—from highly judgmental to very sophisticated statistical techniques. However, for investors, market analysts, and policymakers, some basic facets of interpreting the data are common to all methods. First, there are two basic time perspectives: (1) the perceived phase of the business cycle and (2) the latest economic news release. Financial markets "move" when the latest economic news indicates that earlier perceptions about the current strength of the economy (the phase of the business cycle) are not quite correct. Since financial instruments are priced based on market perceptions of the strength of the economy, changes in perceptions lead to a repricing of bonds, stocks, and other securities.

The next key point is that market analysis of economic indicators therefore revolves around determining the strength of the economy and whether the latest economic news corroborates earlier perceptions or whether it changes market views on the strength of the economy. Certainly, the latest news is incorporated into how the markets view the strength of the economy, but importantly, analysts often discount news releases if the data are aberrant for special considerations. Basically, the latest economic news for any given month may not be a good indicator of the current state of the economy, and sophisticated analysts are aware of this. It is important to be able to differentiate between movements in data that are substantive and those that are merely technical noise. Monthly data are erratic at times, and financial markets must be able to have some sort of benchmark against which to judge whether the latest news provides useful information.

The basic steps in analysis are (1) to determine benchmark expectations for various indicators for different stages of the business cycle, (2) to determine what makes this business cycle different from the past and how these factors alter one's views on reasonable expectations for economic activity, and (3) to evaluate the latest economic release in terms of whether earlier expectations were correct. Step three can be quite complex, but some of the key features should be evaluating (a) the key components for each indicator, (b) components that are frequently erratic for technical reasons unrelated to underlying economic strength, and (c) whether the discounted data are close to expectations for the perceived phase of the business cycle. If recent news does not meet expectations, step four should be to apply the change in an indicator's strength to analysis of related sectors of the economy.

Benchmark Expectations: Learning from Past Business Cycles

Ongoing analysis of the economy requires some basis of determining what reasonable expectations are for an indicator for the current and upcoming phases of the business cycle. History is always a good starting point. Some reasonable questions among many are these: What is the typical growth rate for personal income during recovery? How much do auto sales rise in recovery? How much do housing starts typically rebound during recovery? To begin to answer these types of questions, one should compare and average previous business cycle movement for individual economic indicators.

Post World War II Business Cycle Peaks and Troughs

Monthly		Quarterly	
Peak	Trough	Peak	Trough
November 1948	October 1949	1948 Q4	1949 Q4
July 1953	May 1954	1953 Q2	1954 Q2
August 1957	April 1958	1957 Q3	1958 Q1
April 1960	February 1961	1960 Q1	1960 Q4
December 1969	November 1970	1969 Q3	1970 Q4
November 1973	March 1975	1973 Q4	1975 Q1
January 1980	July 1980	1980 Q1	1980 Q2
July 1981	November 1982	1981 Q3	1982 Q3
July 1990	March 1991	1990 Q2	1991 Q1

Note: Monthly peaks and troughs are official monthly dates set by the National Bureau of Economic Research (NBER). Quarterly peaks and troughs are unofficial and are based on real GDP levels with the lowest level closest to the quarter inclusive of the monthly peaks and troughs being defined as the peak and trough quarters. Because real GDP represents average activity for a given quarter, quarterly peaks and troughs do not always include the monthly peak and trough dates.

For example, one could obtain seasonally adjusted housing starts data over the last four recoveries/expansions and create one series for each economic rebound such that the trough of the previous recession is the base period for that series. If data are put into quarterly form (to cut down on the number of observations and also to make comparable with quarterly GDP figures), then the trough of the 1982 recession was the third quarter of that year (based on real GDP levels). To compare relative growth across business cycles, each recovery must be rebased so that the trough value is 1 (or 100 depending on one's preferences).

Since the quarterly average for housing starts in the third quarter of 1982 was 1.12 million units annualized, subsequent values for the post-1982 series all must be divided by this value to rebase the entire series (see the following table).

For this realigned and rebased series, levels subsequent to the base period—the trough—indicate cumulative growth in activity since the trough. Similarly, the quarterly trough of the 1974–75 recession was the first quarter of 1975, with the value of housing starts at .98 million units annualized. This is the divisor for the post-1975 recovery series for cyclical comparisons. With starts realigned to troughs and rebased to 1, comparisons can be readily made for relative growth since troughs. For example, the post-1975 and post-1982 recoveries had starts in the sixth quarter of growth that were 59 percent and 73 percent, respectively, higher than their trough levels of starts. In contrast, the post-1991 period had starts only 31 percent higher six quarters after the recession bottom.

Housing Starts in Millions of Units, Annualized

	Quarters Past Trough					
Trough	*1*	*2*	*3*	*4*	*5*	*6*
1991Q1 0.90	1991Q2 1.01	1991Q3 1.04	1991Q4 1.09	1992Q1 1.26	1992Q2 1.14	1992Q3 1.18
1982Q3 1.12	1982Q4 1.28	1983Q1 1.63	1983Q2 1.66	1983Q3 1.80	1983Q4 1.73	1984Q1 1.94
1975Q1 0.98	1975Q2 1.07	1975Q3 1.25	1975Q4 1.34	1976Q1 1.44	1976Q2 1.45	1976Q3 1.56

Housing Starts Data Rebased, Trough = 1.00

	Quarters Past Trough					
Trough	*1*	*2*	*3*	*4*	*5*	*6*
1991Q1 1.00	1991Q2 1.12	1991Q3 1.16	1991Q4 1.21	1992Q1 1.39	1992Q2 1.27	1992Q3 1.31
1982Q3 1.00	1982Q4 1.15	1983Q1 1.46	1983Q2 1.48	1983Q3 1.61	1983Q4 1.55	1984Q1 1.73
1975Q1 1.00	1975Q2 1.10	1975Q3 1.28	1975Q4 1.37	1976Q1 1.48	1976Q2 1.48	1976Q3 1.59

With data realigned, growth rates can be compared over different phases of the business cycle. For example, the residential investment component of real GDP can be compared with realigned and rebased series for each recovery. For housing starts, comparing levels over the business cycle is a standard type of analysis. However, for components of real GDP, growth rates often are more interesting. Once real residential investment series have been created and realigned for each recovery, quarterly annualized growth rates can be calculated and averaged for whatever time period is of interest. One might like to calculate the average quarterly annualized percent change for the first six quarters of recovery/expansion, or one might be interested in average growth rates for the second year of economic growth.

Such calculations provide guides for what are reasonable growth rates for a given indicator. Upper and lower growth rates over several business cycles would tend to set boundaries for reasonable projections unless one had very significant reasons for exceeding outlier growth rates. Similar tables can be constructed for postpeak economic activity. These types of cyclical comparisons are useful for heavily judgmental analysis as well as for a "reality check" for econometric projections.

For example, due to demographic factors (the aging of baby boomers and movement of the smaller baby-bust generation into home-buying years) and an overbuilt multifamily sector, many economists expected housing to have a below-average recovery in 1991. Based on the following table, housing investment averaged 29.8 percent annualized growth in the first four quarters of recovery in the previous four major recoveries. A reasonable forecast would have projected post-trough growth in 1991 to be below 29.8 percent for the first year. Indeed, actual growth of 13.9 percent was close to the lowest pace that occurred during the post-1969 recovery.

Previous business cycles are a good starting point for analyzing the current business cycle. But what is the next step?

Recovery and Expansion in Real GDP

	Average Annualized Growth Rates Following Recession Troughs of:					
GDP	1960Q4	1970Q4	1975Q1	1982Q3	Ave.*	1991Q1
1st 4 quarters	5.9	3.7	6.4	5.1	5.3	1.7
2nd 4 quarters	3.1	6.7	3.3	5.7	4.7	3.2
3rd 4 quarters	5.4	3.7	3.7	3.4	4.0	—
4th 4 quarters	4.9	—	5.4	2.4	4.2	—
Personal Consumption Expenditures (PCEs), Total	1960Q4	1970Q4	1975Q1	1982Q3	Ave.*	1991Q1
1st 4 quarters	3.9	4.6	6.2	5.5	5.0	1.8
2nd 4 quarters	4.2	6.7	4.2	4.4	4.9	3.1
3rd 4 quarters	3.6	1.8	3.3	5.0	3.5	—
4th 4 quarters	5.6	—	3.9	3.5	4.3	—
PCEs, Durables	1960Q4	1970Q4	1975Q1	1982Q3	Ave.*	1991Q1
1st 4 quarters	2.2	22.4	18.7	17.1	15.1	6.4
2nd 4 quarters	9.4	12.9	7.4	11.7	10.3	5.8
3rd 4 quarters	6.4	1.4	2.8	14.7	6.3	—
4th 4 quarters	5.5	—	6.5	11.2	7.7	—
PCEs, Nondurables	1960Q4	1970Q4	1975Q1	1982Q3	Ave.*	1991Q1
1st 4 quarters	3.0	1.0	5.0	4.0	3.2	0.4
2nd 4 quarters	2.6	6.1	3.6	3.5	4.0	2.3
3rd 4 quarters	1.4	0.4	2.0	2.4	1.6	—
4th 4 quarters	5.4	—	3.2	3.2	4.0	—

Recovery and Expansion in Real GDP (*Continued*)

	Average Annualized Growth Rates Following Recession Troughs of:					
PCEs, Services	*1960Q4*	*1970Q4*	*1975Q1*	*1982Q3*	*Ave.**	*1991Q1*
1st 4 quarters	5.2	4.2	4.7	4.3	4.6	1.7
2nd 4 quarters	4.7	5.8	4.0	3.5	4.5	2.9
3rd 4 quarters	5.1	3.1	4.5	4.5	4.3	—
4th 4 quarters	5.9	—	4.0	2.1	4.0	—
Business Fixed Investment	*1960Q4*	*1970Q4*	*1975Q1*	*1982Q3*	*Ave.**	*1991Q1*
1st 4 quarters	3.3	1.9	1.1	0.2	1.6	−2.1
2nd 4 quarters	5.1	13.6	8.9	18.5	11.5	10.2
3rd 4 quarters	8.5	11.0	9.0	3.5	8.0	—
4th 4 quarters	11.0	—	16.3	−4.6	7.6	—
Producers' Durable Equipment	*1960Q4*	*1970Q4*	*1975Q1*	*1982Q3*	*Ave.**	*1991Q1*
1st 4 quarters	9.3	4.1	1.9	6.7	5.5	1.5
2nd 4 quarters	4.1	20.0	13.4	19.4	14.2	15.9
3rd 4 quarters	12.7	12.8	10.2	3.5	9.8	—
4th 4 quarters	11.3	—	14.6	0.2	8.7	—

(Table continues next page)

*Average of growth rates for recoveries from 1960 up to 1991 (not inclusive of 1991). For the fourth four quarters, the average does not include the recovery/expansion that followed the 1970Q4 trough, since recession set in during those four quarters.

What's Different about This Business Cycle?

Every business cycle is different. An analyst must always ask what's different about the current recovery, expansion, or recession compared to the past. Importantly, how will these changes affect what one should expect for strength in various sectors?

The recovery/expansion following the 1990–91 recession provides excellent examples of how business cycles differ from each other by sector. Demographic factors play key roles in consumer spending and in housing. Baby boomers have aged past being in prime home-buying years and the smaller baby-bust generation is the major force in this market. Baby boomers are more inclined to save now than during the 1980s—both for retirement and for children's college expenses. Personal consumption is thereby dampened. In contrast to the post-1982 recovery/expansion, multifamily housing is constrained by excess supply. Employment levels and manufacturing output are being hurt by long-term defense cutbacks. Inventory investment decisions have been radically changed by computer inventory and tracking systems. Additionally, expanded world wide trade and competition have affected almost every facet of the economy—from consumer prices, to employment, labor/management relations, inventory control, and investment decisions.

Recovery and Expansion in Real GDP

Nonresidential Structures	1960Q4	1970Q4	1975Q1	1982Q3	Ave.*	1991Q1
1st 4 quarters	−2.4	−0.9	−0.1	−8.6	−3.0	−9.1
2nd 4 quarters	6.4	4.8	1.4	17.9	7.6	−2.9
3rd 4 quarters	4.2	8.2	7.0	3.9	5.8	—
4th 4 quarters	10.7	—	19.9	−11.7	6.3	—

Residential Investment	1960Q4	1970Q4	1975Q1	1982Q3	Ave.*	1991Q1
1st 4 quarters	10.3	26.9	26.0	56.0	29.8	13.9
2nd 4 quarters	4.9	13.3	20.1	7.8	11.5	14.3
3rd 4 quarters	17.1	−9.6	12.4	1.6	5.4	—
4th 4 quarters	−2.0	—	3.8	14.4	5.4	—

Government Purchases, Total	1960Q4	1970Q4	1975Q1	1982Q3	Ave.*	1991Q1
1st 4 quarters	5.8	−2.2	0.9	3.7	2.1	−0.6
2nd 4 quarters	2.0	0.0	−0.9	2.0	0.8	−1.2
3rd 4 quarters	3.0	−1.1	1.1	7.8	2.7	—
4th 4 quarters	1.5	—	2.3	5.6	3.1	—

Government Purchases, Federal	1960Q4	1970Q4	1975Q1	1982Q3	Ave.*	1991Q1
1st 4 quarters	5.6	−7.7	−1.2	6.4	0.8	−5.3
2nd 4 quarters	2.5	−2.4	0.3	0.8	0.3	−3.5
3rd 4 quarters	−0.4	−6.2	1.6	10.8	1.4	—
4th 4 quarters	−2.5	—	2.7	6.4	2.2	—

Government Purchases, State and Local	1960Q4	1970Q4	1975Q1	1982Q3	Ave.*	1991Q1
1st 4 quarters	6.3	2.6	2.4	1.9	3.3	2.9
2nd 4 quarters	1.6	2.1	−1.6	2.8	1.2	0.5
3rd 4 quarters	7.1	2.8	0.7	5.7	4.1	—
4th 4 quarters	5.9	—	2.1	5.2	4.4	—

Exports	1960Q4	1970Q4	1975Q1	1982Q3	Ave.*	1991Q1
1st 4 quarters	2.2	−4.4	2.7	−2.2	−0.4	10.1
2nd 4 quarters	4.2	24.3	2.3	7.7	9.6	3.1
3rd 4 quarters	14.7	19.0	2.4	−1.2	8.7	—
4th 4 quarters	11.2	—	16.3	8.7	12.0	—

Imports	1960Q4	1970Q4	1975Q1	1982Q3	Ave.*	1991Q1
1st 4 quarters	9.5	4.9	15.2	14.9	11.1	8.4
2nd 4 quarters	7.9	19.2	15.1	23.7	16.5	10.6
3rd 4 quarters	1.6	2.4	9.4	4.8	4.5	—
4th 4 quarters	7.2	—	2.8	9.3	6.4	—

Note: Inventory investment is not included in this table because analysis generally is in changes (first differences) in dollar values, not in percent changes.

In analyzing what reasonable expectations would be for a given component of the economy, one must ask what long-term fundamentals have changed. A few key questions are:

- How are sectors, such as housing and personal consumption, affected by demographic changes such as the aging of the large baby-boom population segment?
- Have key regulatory changes affected businesses, resulting in additional costs or in liberalized rules?
- Have the markets abroad for US products changed—for example, a greater share of US exports going to Latin America and Asia, thereby lessening dependence on the strength of European economies?
- Is the dollar weaker or stronger compared to this phase in the previous business cycle?
- Are foreign economies stronger or weaker than in previous US business cycles? Which countries are different?
- Has fiscal policy changed, and what sectors are affected?
- While interest rates are an obvious factor to be considered, have financial regulations or supervision changed such that credit conditions are different?
- Are energy costs higher or lower relative to other cost factors?

The Latest Monthly Release

Financial markets, immediately upon the release of new monthly data for an indicator, use the information to corroborate earlier perceptions about the current strength of the economy and to formulate any changes in market views of future strength of the economy. Prior to the release of a key economic indicator, market participants form opinions on what is expected for the change in the indicator's value. Analysts base their projections on many differing methodologies. When possible, if an indicator is based on earlier released information, analysts look at the earlier data to form projections. Such is usually the case for industrial production, personal income, the Commerce Department's index of leading indicators, and portions of real GDP.

Another method is to examine the statistical relationships between earlier released data and an indicator. One earlier released series may have an economically meaningful relationship even though one is not an input into the other. For example, changes in the producer price index are used to project changes in the consumer price index. Also, the purchasing managers' index (NAPM) is used to provide insight into movement in industrial production.

More complex econometric and flow of expenditure models are used to project merchandise trade balances and inventory changes as production and consumption flows are tracked. Finally, there are even various types of trend analysis (time series) in which past values of a series are examined using numerous methods of technical analysis.

Basically, many methodologies go into the formation of the market consensus for expectations for the pending release of new economic data. It is on the basis of these prior expectations that financial instruments are priced. These expectations are very important and a number of electronic vendors of real-time trading data (bid and ask prices for bonds, foreign currencies, futures prices, etc.) conduct their own surveys of projections by market participants. Some of these electronic vendors include Telerate, Money Market Services, and Knight-Ridder, among others.

Each vendor maintains running calendars of recent and pending releases, showing recent performance of economic indicators, the median expectations of the survey panel, as well as the range of the forecasts for upcoming economic indicators. These surveys are usually taken roughly 5 to 10 days prior to a news release. Survey results are posted on vendors' calendar pages for use by their clients. Similarly, bond houses, major banks, economic consultants, and others publish weekly calendars that include their own projections. These various published forecasts form the standard against which actual data are compared for evaluating earlier perceptions of the strength of the economy. One caveat is that expectations change daily, and by the date of an indicator's actual release, the consensus expectation may have changed due to new information and may differ from earlier published survey data.

At the time of the economic release, markets are interested in whether the data provide new information about the economy. If the actual release meets expectations (assuming there are no quirks in the figures), then there is no new information relative to expectations. If actual data differ from expectations, then the question is whether the divergence is substantive or merely statistical noise. Therefore, financial analysts find it prudent to learn what indicators and components of indicators are more reliable than others. A good analyst must learn what components of a series are critical for measuring the true strength of an indicator and which ones are minor. Many series also have specific components that are notoriously volatile, reflecting merely random rather than meaningful changes in the economy for a given month.

Within the series for personal income, the wages and salaries component is quite large and is generally indicative of changes in consumer purchasing power. In contrast, personal farm income is very volatile due to farm subsidy payments that vary significantly over the course of a year. For any given month, an experienced analyst therefore would focus more on wages and salaries than on overall personal income, which is pushed around by volatile farm income. Similarly, aircraft orders typically are large and irregular and cause overall new factory orders to seesaw. The impact of aircraft orders in a particular month is usually discounted by financial markets, but over many months they certainly must be tracked and evaluated for the impact on the economy.

Finally, when actual release data differ from expectations, the impact on other data series and the economy must be evaluated. Such an evaluation can be complex and is made by analysts using experience in following the data over the years as well as with formal economic models. This manuscript limits discussion on this topic to elaborating on the sectors affected and to typical cyclical behavior of series. Each chapter contains a summary section describing an indicator's key roles, listing the key long-term factors affecting the economic indicators, and encapsulating earlier discussions on key factors to watch with each month's release of economic news. These include the key components and key sources of volatility for each indicator.

As an overall summary, in order to determine the impact of an economic news release on financial markets, economic and financial analysts need to be aware of various types of information prior to an indicator's release and information extracted from the release. These include the following:

Prior to release, learn:

- What each series' key components are.
- What some of the regular irregularities are.
- What typical growth rates (or levels for some series) are for each major indicator over various phases of the business cycle.
- What market expectations are for an indicator.
- How you would expect financial markets to react to unexpectedly strong or unexpectedly weak data.

Following the news release:

- If a release differs from expectations, are the reasons significant or mere technicalities? What happened with the major components?
- Does the latest news release corroborate your view of the current phase of the business cycle? Are demands on financial markets as expected?
- Does the latest news indicate unexpected imbalances within the economy? Which sectors are affected?
- Is good news really "good news" or is it "bad news" in that monetary authorities react with a policy change? Similarly, is a weak economic indicator actually good news for financial markets?

CHAPTER 1

THE EMPLOYMENT REPORT

The first major economic release each month is the employment report prepared by the Bureau of Labor Statistics (BLS) of the US Department of Labor. This report generally is released on the first Friday of the month following the reference month. It contains the closely watched unemployment rate and the even more important nonfarm payroll job data. From these latter figures come key inputs in estimates for industrial production and personal income, one component in the Commerce Department's composite index of leading indicators as well as one in the coincident index; it even has inputs for some minor series in gross domestic product (GDP). Because of the early release date, its use in estimating other indicators, and its broad coverage of the many sectors in the economy, financial markets see this release as setting the tone for how subsequent economic releases for the month are likely to portray the health of the economy and, in turn, impact various financial markets. The employment data are noted as particularly important indicators of the health of consumer spending, since job creation is a key source of growth in personal income.

The employment report actually contains data from two separate, independent surveys. The establishment survey—also referred to as the payroll survey—is conducted as a mail-in survey by the BLS and is basically a job count based on employers' records. This survey also includes questions on earnings and hours worked. From another perspective, the Bureau of the Census conducts the *Current Population Survey* (CPS) as a survey of households, and the employment data are provided to the BLS under contract. This survey, which is often referred to as the household survey, measures job statistics from the workers' perspective and provides data on the work status of individuals in interviewed households.

The employment report first appears in the news release, "The Employment Situation." It is also published in the US Labor Department's *Employment and Earnings* and is found in secondary sources such as the Commerce Department's *Survey of Current Business* and the Federal Reserve Board's *Federal Reserve Bulletin.*

THE HOUSEHOLD SURVEY

The Current Population Survey provides the BLS's key statistics on the labor force, employment, unemployment, and on persons not in the labor force. Data are derived from a scientifically selected sample of about 60,000 households that are representative of the civilian noninstitutional population of the United States.[1]

Stratification of the sample takes into account urban and rural population distributions as well as different types of industry representation. The survey excludes persons under 16 years of age as well as the institutional population (inmates of penal and mental institutions, sanitariums, and homes for the aged, infirm, and needy).

In order to reduce the burden of reporting, a selected household is interviewed on a rotating basis rather than every month. For the initial interview, a household visit is made; follow-up interviews are by telephone. A household is interviewed for the first four months after being selected to be in the sample, is omitted from being interviewed for the next eight months, and is then interviewed for four consecutive months before being dropped from the sample. The 4–8–4 rotation scheme is used for reasons in addition to reducing the reporting burden. The most important is reduced discontinuities in the data as a result of month-to-month and year-to-year overlap. While specific panels rotate every four months, there is significant overlap in the survey sample each month. Only part of the sample is changed each month. On a month-to-month basis, 75 percent of the sample is common to both months, and on a year-ago basis, 50 percent of the sample overlaps.

The survey reflects employment status for the calendar week including the 12th day of the month and the actual survey is conducted during the following week. Once the survey is completed, the data are weighted in order to reflect the overall population intended.

The key concepts used to classify persons by the labor force activity are employment, unemployment, labor force, and not in labor force. Of course, the unemployment rate is derived from some of the above series.

Before going into how various series are defined, it is important to note that the household data underwent a major redesign of the survey questions that went into effect with January 1994 data. Broad classifications remained constant in definition, but questions that determined which classifications respondents fell into changed significantly for some series. These differences are discussed when appropriate for individual concepts. Also, the overall survey redesign is discussed below in a separate section. Importantly, data before and after the redesign are not directly comparable despite an apparent constancy in most broad definitions.

> Employed persons comprise (1) all those who, during the survey week, did any work at all as paid employees, or in their own business, profession, or on their own farm, or who worked 15 hours or more as unpaid workers in a family-operated enterprise; and (2) all those who did not work but had jobs or businesses which they were temporarily absent due to illness, bad weather, vacation, labor-management dispute, or various personal reasons—whether or not they were paid by their employers for the time off and whether or not they were seeking other jobs.[2]

For the level of employed, each person who holds a job is counted only once regardless of how many jobs are held. However, starting in 1994, employed persons are asked how many jobs are held, making possible comparisons with establishment data on payroll positions.

> Unemployed persons include those who did not work at all during the survey week, were looking for work, and were available for work during the reference period (except for temporary illness). Those who had made specific efforts to find work

within the preceding four-week period—such as by registering at a public or private employment agency, writing letters of application, canvassing for work, etc.—are considered to be looking for work. Persons who were waiting to be recalled to a job from which they had been laid off or were waiting to report to a new job within 30 days need not be looking for work to be classified as unemployed.[3]

The civilian labor force is defined as the sum of employed civilians and persons classified as unemployed. The total labor force includes members of the Armed Forces stationed in the United States. All persons who are 16 years of age and older and meet neither the criteria for employed nor unemployed are defined as "not in the labor force." Both the level of unemployed and the labor force appear to have been significantly affected by the 1994 household survey redesign as discussed further below.

The civilian unemployment rate is the number of civilian unemployed as a percentage of the civilian labor force. Of course, the overall unemployment rate uses the overall labor force figure as the denominator. The numerator is the same, since by definition if one is in the Armed Forces, then one is employed. For this reason, the overall unemployment rate is marginally lower—about one-tenth of a percentage point on average—than the civilian unemployment rate.

There is an additional useful classification for a portion of the working age population—discouraged workers. These are individuals who want a job but for various reasons have been discouraged from continuing to actively seek employment. Because discouraged workers are not actively seeking employment, they are not considered to be part of the labor force. While they are not employed, they also are not counted as unemployed.

However, the BLS's definition of discouraged workers changed with the January 1994 redesign of the methodology of the Current Population Survey (the 1994 redesigned survey is discussed below). Prior to 1994, to be classified as discouraged, an individual had only to tell the interviewer that he or she (1) wanted a job and (2) provide only discouraged reasons for not looking. Beginning with the 1994 redefinition, there are added qualifications.

> To be classified as discouraged, an individual has to want a job, provide a discouraged reason for not looking, have looked in the last year (or since last working), and be available to work (where one's own temporary illness does not disqualify an individual from being available.)[4]

The new definition of discouraged worker lowers the estimate of discouraged workers significantly because the measurement is more objective with the inclusion of specific requirements that an individual had to have looked for a job in the last year and also had to be available for work. These new requirements rule out respondents who merely say they want a job merely because they feel it is socially desirable and those who say they want a job but really are not available to work for such reasons as keeping house or tending ill relatives.

Household data—including the unemployment rate—are available by sex, age, race, Hispanic ethnicity, industry, occupation, and so forth, and for some combinations of these characteristics. Unemployment rates are available by reason of unemployment. These are job losers, job leavers, reentrants to the labor force, and new entrants to the labor force.

The household data for employment also are broken down between full-time and part-time status. Those indicating they work a schedule of 35 hours or more per week are full time, and those working 1 to 34 hours per week are considered part time. Part-time workers are generally divided into those working part time for economic reasons and those working part time for noneconomic reasons. The questions in the survey determining economic and noneconomic reasons changed significantly with the 1994 redesigned survey.

Prior to 1994, for those who were part-time workers, a question in the survey asked why they usually worked part time. These reasons varied according to whether they were for economic or noneconomic reasons. Economic reasons included slack work, material shortage, plant or machine repair, new job started during week, job terminated during week, and could find only part-time work. Noneconomic reasons were legal or religious holiday, labor dispute, bad weather, personal illness, vacation, busy with housework or other personal business, and did not want full-time work. Respondents were merely told possible answers, and economic or noneconomic status was deduced from the answer given.

Beginning in 1994, the requirements for being classified as working part time for economic reasons became more stringent. Individuals who usually work part time are explicitly asked if they want to work full time and whether they are available to work full time if offered the hours. In the earlier survey, this information was inferred from the answers provided for not working full time. With the redesigned survey, the reasons differ from the earlier survey. Economic reasons for working part time are limited to "slack work/business conditions" and "could only find part-time work." Noneconomic reasons are seasonal work, child-care problems, other family/personal obligations, health/medical limitations, school/training, retired/Social Security limit on earnings, and full-time workweek is less than 35 hours.

ANNUAL REVISIONS TO HOUSEHOLD SURVEY DATA

For all household series, each month's data are final in that there are no revisions in following months' releases except for annual revisions that update seasonal factors. Unadjusted data generally are not revised in the annual revisions. Each month, BLS uses independent population controls from the Census Bureau to weight individual responses from the household surveys. Weights by various social strata are based on population estimates produced by the Census Bureau. Generally, these population estimates have been very close to decennial Census figures and there has been no reestimation of household survey data. There have been recent exceptions.

In early 1982, population counts and other household survey statistics were matched to the 1980 Census, and data were refitted back to 1970. This was done because the yearly estimate differed significantly from the census count. More recently, household data starting in 1994 were matched to population controls from the 1990 census, but with an upward adjustment due to the undercount. In early 1994, the BLS announced the intent to wedge the data prior to 1994, but had not yet determined the extent or timing of likely revisions. The adjustment for the undercount was introduced at the same time as the 1994 redesign of the Current Population Survey, but was a separate technical issue.

THE 1994 REDESIGN OF THE CURRENT POPULATION SURVEY

Beginning with the release of January 1994 data, the household employment data reflected a redesigned Current Population Survey. Data using the new survey are not completely comparable to earlier data, since the 1994 redesign did not revise earlier data. The redesigned survey is based on the same definitions of key series—such as employed, unemployed, and labor force—but the questions designed to classify the respondents have changed. While earlier data were not revised, as usually occurs with the release of January household survey data, seasonal factors were revised several years back. The prior survey had been in use since 1967 when the last significant changes were made. The BLS redesigned the survey for several reasons: to incorporate more precise measurement methods (particularly for discouraged workers), to implement more efficient and less error-prone data collection procedures, and to modify survey questions to reflect societal changes. These societal changes include the more prominent role of women in the labor force, the growing importance of part-time workers, and the greater importance of the service sector.

Prior to 1994, most data collection was based on paper questionnaires with interviewers following written instructions on the form in order to determine which questions to ask each respondent. For example, a person not working during the reference week was given a different set of follow-up questions compared to those for a respondent who was working. Subsequent answers continued to affect the set of questions asked. Due to somewhat complex sequencing of alternative questions, an interviewer would occasionally ask improper follow-up questions. With the current computer-assisted telephone interviewing and the computer-assisted personal interviewing (CATI/CAPI), the computer program assures that the proper sequence of questions is asked—especially since follow-up questions are based on earlier, keyed-in answers.

The new procedures were tested in what BLS called the Parallel Survey and compared with the then in-use techniques over the July 1992 through December 1993 period. The parallel survey has also been referred to as the CATI/CAPI Overlap (CCO). The following are key differences between the new and old survey designs based on statistical inferences from the Parallel Survey and the old CPS design. The old CPS had a sample size of 58,900 households while the Parallel Survey had a sample size of 12,000.

Based on one year of data (September 1992 through August 1993), preliminary analysis of the two designs indicated that compared to the earlier survey, implementation of the new design would lead to an increase in the labor force due to wording that was not biased toward excluding women. The elimination of this bias is one of the biggest factors affecting differences in various series before and after the redesign.

As noted in the following table, the pre-1994 survey focused on what one did *most* of the week (working, housework, or something else) to determine labor force and employment status. The current survey asks if the respondent did *any* work for either pay or profit.

The early study also indicated that the new design would lead to:

* The overall civilian unemployment rate being about 0.5 percentage points higher.

* The labor force participation rate also being about 0.5 percentage points higher.

* The employment-to-population ratio being about 0.2 percentage points higher.

* Persons employed part time for economic reasons as a percentage of total employed being lower by roughly 1.2 percentage points overall.

* The distribution of unemployed by reason shifting significantly with job losers having a 13 percentage point drop in share of unemployed while reentrants' share rises about 7.8 percentage points.

* The level of estimated discouraged workers being about 691,000 lower.

The key factor to remember about these differences is that they are all essentially due to differences in the survey designs—for the most part, how various questions are reworded. These differences should be a crude baseline for comparing new and old CPS data. Also, a New Parallel Survey began in 1994. A small sample was given the old CPS questions to see how more recent economic conditions would have shown up in the data for comparison with the new CPS.

Employment and Unemployment Questions

Current CPS	Pre-1994 CPS
1. Does anyone in this household have a business or a farm?	
2. LAST WEEK, did you do ANY work for (either) pay (or profit)?	1. What were you doing most of LAST WEEK— (working or something else?) (keeping house or something else?) (going to school or something else?)
Parenthetical filled in if there is a business or farm in the household.	
If 1 is "yes" and 2 is "no," ask 3.	**If answer indicates "with a job, but not at work" (either temporarily or on layoff), ask 4. If answer indicates "working," skip 2. All others, ask 2.**
3. LAST WEEK, did you do any unpaid work in the family business or farm?	
If 2 and 3 are both "no," ask 4.	2. Did you do any work at all LAST WEEK, not counting work around the house?
4. LAST WEEK, (in addition to the business) did you have a job, either full or part time? Include any job from which you were temporarily absent.	Note: if farm or business operator in household, ask about unpaid work.)
	Questions continue.

Employment and Unemployment Questions (*continued*)

Current CPS	Pre-1994 CPS
Parenthetical filled in if there is a business or farm in the household.	3. Did you have a job or business from which you were temporarily absent or on layoff LAST WEEK?
If 4 is "no," ask 5. 5. LAST WEEK, were you on layoff from a job? **If 5 is "yes," ask 6. If 5 is "no," ask 8.** 6. Has your employer given you a date to return to work? **If "no," ask 7.** 7. Have you been given any indication that you will be recalled to work within the next 6 months? **If "no," ask 8.**	**If "no," ask 5. If "yes," ask 4.** 4. Why were you absent from work LAST WEEK?
8. Have you been doing anything to find work during the last 4 weeks? **If "yes," ask 9.** 9. What are all of the things you have done to find work during the last 4 weeks?	5. Have you been looking for work during the past 4 weeks? **If "yes," ask 6.** 6. What have you been doing in the last 4 weeks to find work?
Individuals are classified as employed if they say "yes" to questions 2, 3, or 4. Individuals are classified as unemployed if they say "yes" to 5 and either 6 or 7, or if they say "yes" to 8 and provide a job search method that could have brought them into contact with a potential employer in 9.	Individuals can be classified as "at work" at question 1 or 2. Individuals can be classified "employed, temporarily absent" with the combination of 1 and 4. Individuals can be classified as unemployed with combinations of 1 and 4, 3 and 4, 1 and 6, or 5 and 6.

Note that bold text lines are instructions to interviewer.

THE ESTABLISHMENT SURVEY

The establishment survey is based on a cooperative effort between the BLS and state employment security agencies. Data are collected each month from a sample of about 380 thousand nonagricultural establishments (including civilian government).[5] Formally, this data program is known as the Current Employment Statistics (CES) program and provides information on employment, hours, and earnings at the national, state, and local area levels. The primary focus of the data is by industries and economic sectors aggregated from industry data.

Employment in the establishment survey represents the number of persons on the payrolls on a full-time or part-time basis in nonagricultural establishments dur-

TABLE 1–1
A Comparison between Household and Establishment Employment Data

Household Survey	Establishment Survey
Door-to-door and telephone interviews conducted by census for BLS.	Mail-in, CATI, and Touch-Tone data entry (TDE) survey by BLS.[7]
Survey is for week including the 12th day of the month.	Survey is for pay period that includes the 12th day of the month.
Sample of 60,000 households.	Sample of about 380,000 business establishments.
Includes farm sector and some unpaid workers.	Nonfarm only and only paid workers.
Includes self-employed, proprietors, and some unpaid family workers.	Excludes self-employed, proprietors, and any unpaid workers.
Civilian and noncivilian employment counts.	Civilian employment only.
Covers ages 16 and older.	Counts jobs regardless of age.
Measures work/labor force status of individuals.	Acts as a job count from the employer perspective.
Data oriented toward socio-economic characteristics.	Data generally organized by industry.
Used to derive unemployment rates.	No unemployment measures.
Individual counted only once for level of employed.[8]	Multiple jobs are counted separately.
Data are not affected by work stoppages.	Strikes show up as job losses until strikers return to work.
Tallies part-time and full-time employed separately.	No differentiation between part-time and full-time jobs.

ing the pay period that includes the 12th of the month. The data include temporary workers. For federal government workers, employment represents the number of persons employed during the last full pay period of the calendar month. Importantly, since workers can hold jobs in more than one establishment, persons who appear on multiple payrolls are counted more than once. Workers are counted only once within an establishment even if they hold two jobs.

Workers on leave are counted as being on the payroll if the leave is paid leave (such as sick leave, paid holiday, or paid vacation). Also, one is counted as being on the payroll even if the worker is paid for only part of the specified pay period. However, if a worker receives no pay during the specified pay period, he or she is not considered employed. The key to the establishment definition of being employed is whether the person was a paid employee during the survey period. Since proprietors, the self-employed, and unpaid family workers are not paid employees, they are not included in the payroll employment figures. Salaried officers of corporations are part of the employment data while household domestic workers are not. The government sector includes only civilian workers, although employees of the Central Intelligence Agency and National Security Agency are explicitly excluded from the survey.[6]

The establishment data are revised in the two monthly releases immediately following the initial estimate. The first two estimates are referred to as preliminary, and the third as final. Revisions are due to late received reports. New seasonal factors are usually introduced in the employment report for the month of May as part of annual revisions and updated in November (see later section).

ORGANIZATION OF ESTABLISHMENT DATA

For the establishment survey, data are primarily organized and analyzed by industry and aggregated sectors of production. By sectors, overall nonfarm payroll employment is broken down into goods-producing and service-producing sectors. The goods-producing sector covers manufacturing, construction, and mining. In 1993, the goods-producing sector accounted for 20.9 percent of establishment survey jobs on average while service-producing had the lion's share at 79.1 percent.

For the goods-producing sector, the most closely watched detail is for manufacturing, which is readily divided into durables and nondurables and also two-digit Standard Industrial Classification (SIC) industries.[9] Durables industries include lumber and wood, furniture; stone, clay, and glass; primary metals; fabricated metals; industrial machinery and equipment (commonly referred to as "nonelectrical machinery"); electronic and other electrical equipment (generally called "electrical machinery"); transportation equipment; instruments; and miscellaneous durables. Nondurables industries are food, tobacco products, textiles, apparel, paper and allied products, printing and publishing, chemicals, petroleum and coal products, rubber and plastics, and leather and leather products. Of course, BLS has manufacturing (and nonmanufacturing as well) employment available at detail greater than the two-digit SIC level.

For mining, the only subcomponent of general interest is oil and gas extraction employment. Within construction, only the subcomponent for general building contractors is published in the press release, but other components such as highway construction and special trades also are available.

Service-producing industries encompass what goods-producing industries do not. Total payroll employment less goods-producing employment equals service-producing employment. More specifically, this sector includes transportation and public utilities; wholesale trade, retail trade; finance, insurance, and real estate (FIRE); (a narrowly defined) services; and government.

There are some interesting details about some of the service-producing subcomponents. Retail trade employment—like retail sales data—is *not* dominated by department store or general merchandise store employment. The largest component series is for eating and drinking establishments, which is about one-third of retail trade. The next largest is food store—for example, grocery stores—employment (about one-sixth of retail trade), followed by miscellaneous retail and then by general merchandise.

The narrowly defined services component is often confused with the broader category of service-producing employment. The narrow services component is led in size by health services and business services but also includes hotel and other lodging, (private) educational services, auto repair, amusement, and others.

As mentioned earlier, the government component is for only civilian employment. At the state and local level, education workers (e.g., teachers) make up the vast majority of government employment.

CHART 1–1
Establishment Survey Employment (Percent Shares in 1993)

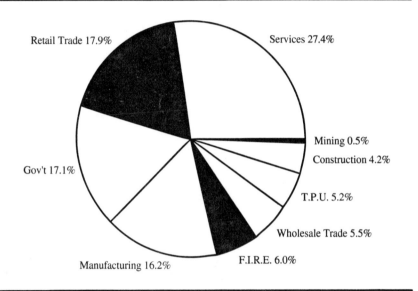

Retail Trade 17.9%

Services 27.4%

Mining 0.5%

Construction 4.2%

Gov't 17.1%

T.P.U. 5.2%

Wholesale Trade 5.5%

Manufacturing 16.2%

F.I.R.E. 6.0%

Source: US Department of Labor.

Average Workweek and Average Hourly Earnings

Data on average weekly hours, average hourly earnings, and average weekly earnings are series that are a part of the establishment survey. These three series are all actually based on other payroll data. The hours and earnings series are derived from reported gross payrolls and corresponding paid hours specifically for production workers, construction workers, and nonsupervisory workers. These series cover only what are broadly defined as nonsupervisory workers. As will be discussed later, the data for nonsupervisory workers are important for projecting various monthly indicators.

First, what do these series cover? For manufacturing, the production workers definition includes employees up through the level of working supervisors, who are directly involved in the manufacture of the establishment's product. Executive, professional workers, and routine office workers are excluded. Production workers in mining are defined similarly. In the construction industry, production workers cover employees up through the level of working supervisors, who work directly on the construction project at the work site or in shops or yards in activity normally performed by one in a construction trade. Executives, professionals, and office workers are excluded. For the service-producing industries, similar data are compiled for nonsupervisory workers and are basically defined as all workers except for top executive and managerial positions.

Average weekly hours is a published series derived from the number of production or nonsupervisory workers and unpublished data on total hours. Total hours are paid hours and reflect not just hours worked but also paid standby time and paid time for vacation, sick leave, and holidays. Premium pay periods (such as overtime or holidays) are included but are not converted to straight-time equivalent.

The concept of average hourly earnings differs from an average wage rate, since premium pay is included in aggregate payrolls as well as pay for holidays, vacations, and sick leave paid directly by the employer to employees for the pay period reported. Also by definition, these earnings exclude irregular bonuses, various fringe benefits, and the employers' share of payroll taxes. In addition, average hourly earnings for specific details industries are impacted by occupational shifts between high and low wage skills. Average hourly earnings at the aggregate level are also impacted by shifts in employment distribution among the component industries.

Annual Revisions to Payroll Data

Once a year—typically with a June release date—the Labor Department calibrates its initial establishment survey data on employment to more complete benchmarks. The initial three monthly estimates for national payroll employment figures are based on a large survey of about 380 thousand business establishments. This survey is a sample from the statistical "universe" for payroll data—administrative records from the unemployment insurance (UI) tax files. The insurance records filed by nearly all employers with state employment security agencies provide an almost full population count for payroll employment. However, the UI data come out with a long lag—about six or seven months—so these are not used in the initial monthly establishment reports.

Once these data are available, they are used to benchmark the month of March of the previous year. For example, in June of 1993, the establishment employment level was adjusted to the UI level for the month of March 1992. Adjustments are made for a few industries not covered by the UI program—such as railroads. BLS benchmarks only the March level for each year and interpolates the employment levels between March benchmarks with the pattern of monthly changes from the (CES) establishment survey data.

A new trend is created when the difference between the original CES estimate for March employment and the UI-based figure is spread gradually over the entire March-to-March period. BLS refers to the March-to-March period as the wedge period when month-to-month numbers are interpolated. The benchmarks, of course, create a new trend for the employment numbers only up to the latest benchmark month. Levels subsequent to the latest benchmark March are still based on the monthly percent changes in the establishment survey. Since only *lev-*

els in the postbenchmark period are affected and not percent changes in general, the postbenchmark *trend* remains the same as prior to the benchmark.

The annual revisions also incorporate the reestimation of new seasonal factors going back through the previous five calendar years. After employment revisions have been completed, other series are recomputed that have employment series as inputs. These include average hourly earnings, average weekly hours, and diffusion indexes.

Annual revisions incorporate data from a broader stratification of establishments, since this data comes from essentially the "universe" of establishments. However, the BLS, as discussed later, attempts to adjust for these differences prior to the revisions. The CES sample survey consists mainly of large firms. This increases coverage of the universe at a smaller cost and reduces sampling error. Smaller firms are included in the monthly sample but not to the degree as in the UI pool of firms. However, at the national level, payroll data are stratified by firm size, and data are weighted to compensate for low representation of small firms in the CES sample. A problem arises due to the need for the BLS to estimate a portion of payroll employment attributable to net growth in firms and due to changes in growth rates for small firms over the business cycle. To get full estimates for total employment, data must be adjusted for growth in the number of firms and their employers, since new firms are not fully represented in the Current Employment Statistics (CES) sample.

Importantly, statistical analysis finds that the BLS sample is biased toward including mature, well-established firms. An adjustment for changes in business start-up and failure rates is needed over the business cycle, since universe information on new business start-ups is not timely. Just as private sector economists have difficulty predicting the magnitude of recovery and recession, the BLS has had trouble estimating growth in employment for new firms entering and leaving the economy. Newer firms tend to gain employment more rapidly over expansion but also tend to go out of business more readily during recession. BLS attempts to correct for this problem with a regression-based "bias adjustment" (sometimes referred to as birth bias adjustment) for small firm entry and exit. This problem tends to be compounded during recession as firms fail more quickly than on average.

KEYS TO ANALYZING THE MONTHLY REPORTS

Overview and Key Components

The primary use of the employment report is to gauge the current strength of the economy. First, analysts usually try to get an overall impression from the unemployment rate and the total payroll job gains or losses. Second, more specific information is gleaned for projecting industrial production and personal income. Analysts even try to determine business expectations based on hiring in specific industries such as retail trade or construction.

For the household survey, analysts focus on the civilian unemployment rate simply because it is an apparently straightforward measure of the health of the economy. It is an indicator of strength in the real sector as well as an indicator of labor cost pressure affecting inflation. Low unemployment is generally associated with a strong economy and rising inflation potential.

Some caution is appropriate when comparing unemployment rates over various historical periods. This rate is affected as much by labor force growth as by employment growth, and this fact is often overlooked. Over the 1970s, labor force growth surged as more women and minorities entered the labor force and as baby boomers reached working age. Since the late 1980s, labor force growth has slowed due to the maturation of the baby boomers, the baby-bust generation reaching working age, and participation rates for the labor force peaking.

CHART 1–2
Household Employment and the Unemployment Rate

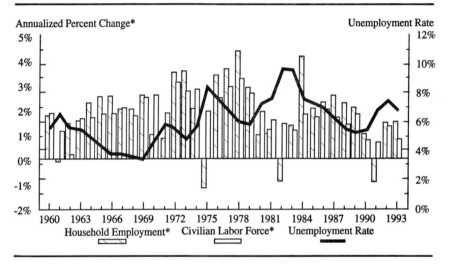

Source: US Department of Labor.

The change in overall payroll jobs gives an equally important view of the strength of the economy. It is the number of jobs—not just the number of unemployed—that plays a key role in the health of the consumer sector. Financial analysts actually pay more attention to changes in payroll employment than to the unemployment rate because of the establishment series' greater reliability. On a monthly basis, the payroll data are viewed as somewhat more dependable than the household employment figures because the significantly larger establishment survey and monthly changes in payroll employment are less volatile than household employment. The payroll data also give important information on subsequent economic indicators.

In analyzing either the unemployment rate (including household employment) or the payroll figures, one should try to discount any special factors that may be causing unusual monthly changes in the data. The types of special factors are varied but are usually recurrent throughout a business cycle. Two of the more common special factors include strike activity and seasonal adjustment problems.

What are some of the special factors that can mask the true strength or weakness in the employment data? As already mentioned, strike activity can affect the payroll data. The level of strike activity has declined sharply over the 1980s and into the 1990s, but this can still affect the data if a large firm such as an auto producer or major communications company is experiencing a work stoppage. Changes in payroll data are affected in the first month with the week of the 12th following the start of the strike and the first such month following the end of the strike. In addition, for the payroll data to be impacted, the affected firm's pay period must occur within the reporting period. In other words, payroll data may not reflect strike activity if a strike begins after the reporting period and ends before the next reporting period. Strike activity can be followed by subscription to the weekly publication *Current Work Stoppages,* which is compiled by the Bureau of Labor Statistics, US Department of Labor. Household data are not affected by strike activity.

Seasonal adjustment procedures can also create temporary distortions in the data since cyclical changes necessarily create divergences from assumed seasonal patterns. This phenomenon is hardly limited to employment data but is also seen in any series with large seasonal patterns such as construction or manufacturing data.

With the payroll employment data, two components that are more frequently affected are retail trade and construction. Strong seasonal movements occur at the beginning and end of the Christmas season and also at the start and end of summer. If the economy is particularly weak going into the holiday season, the hiring of temporary sales people might be below the levels assumed by seasonal factors and November retail trade employment could be weak on a seasonally adjusted basis. For the following January, the seasonal factor would assume that normal hiring increases had occurred in November and December and a typical number of layoffs would be incorporated into the seasonally adjusted data. Following weak unadjusted increases before Christmas, below average layoffs would occur in January. On a seasonally adjusted basis, January might see an increase in retail trade employment but not by the same magnitude as the November decline if employment is cyclically declining over this period. The January rise in this series during a cyclical downturn makes sense only as an effect of seasonal factors that do not "work" very well when the business cycle is not following the trend path that the seasonal factors are based on.

For construction, the winter months have large seasonal factors to adjust the unadjusted payroll employment levels upward. If weather is particularly favorable in a given February, for example, unadjusted employment might edge up and the seasonal factors would lead to an increase in adjusted data. Similarly, seasonal factors for construction employment over spring and early summer assume that strong seasonal hiring and a weak economy over these months would show sluggishness in adjusted construction data. Difficult to interpret months occur subsequent to such movement as seasons end. For the construction example, if hiring is strong early in the season but returns to a trend level at the end of the season, then the magnitude of layoffs would be greater than assumed by seasonal factors. In turn, the seasonally adjusted data would look weak.

For the household data, probably the most recurring seasonal adjustment problem involves the student population in the 16- to 19-year-old age bracket and the 20- to 24-year-old age group, to a lesser degree. Summer hiring does typically rise on an unadjusted basis in June, but the labor force rises dramatically as high school and college students seek summer employment. The seasonally adjusted labor force data assume a large jump in June and a similar decline in September. Given these very large factors, it does not take much deviation in either month to cause volatility in the seasonally adjusted labor force data for these age cohorts and, in turn, the respective unemployment rates.

The Five-Week Effect
Normal seasonal flows can be magnified when the number of weeks between surveys deviates from what is "expected" by seasonal factors. The number of weeks between surveys varies between four and five weeks depending on whether the survey in the "previous" month is "early" in the calendar month and whether the "current" month is "late." Because five-week months depend only on how the 12th falls each month, there is no constancy for which months have five weeks between survey periods. In effect, there is some randomness for which months seasonal factors "expect" a five-week intersurvey period. Each month's seasonal factors (for both surveys) are based on that month's data over the previous three years, and any given month could have anywhere from none to three instances with five-week intersurvey periods.

Whether the seasonally adjusted data are dampened or boosted depends on the type of seasonal activity. For example, during a layoff period, a four week intersurvey period when seasonals assume five would boost seasonally adjusted data. During a buildup period, a four week intersurvey period would lower seasonally adjusted levels since firms have less time to hire. These effects are magnified when seasonal flows are strong, such as before and after Christmas and before and after summer.

Use in Projecting Other Monthly Indicators
For making concurrent projections, industrial production and personal income are the primary economic indicators forecast with data from the employment report. Employment data also enter into estimates for the Commerce Department's indexes of leading and coincident indicators. For a given month, specific employment data released by the BLS during the first week of the month are used by other statistical agencies in the estimates for specific indicators released later in the month.

First, the Federal Reserve Board uses aggregate weekly hours of production workers in manufacturing for primary input in initial estimates of the manufacturing portion of industrial production (IP).[10] This estimation is done at the industry level and for industries that do not yet have information on actual output. About three-fourths of the manufacturing index is projected with production hours data for the initial release.

Output is essentially modeled as a function of aggregate production hours and productivity growth. Aggregate production worker hours is defined as the product of production workers and the average workweek for manufacturing. The BLS produces a specific table in the employment report for "indexes of aggregate weekly hours of production or nonsupervisory workers on private nonfarm payrolls by industry." Private forecasters who roughly duplicate the Federal Reserve's procedure can do so with the product of the published production worker and average weekly hours series, but percent changes in this derived series do vary slightly from those produced by the published indexes of aggregate production hours. The difference is primarily attributable to the fact that the index data are calculated from employment and hours figures that are kept to greater decimal precision than the one decimal place for published numbers.

Regressions for these types of models are usually just percentage changes in manufacturing output (or sometimes overall IP) regressed against percent changes in aggregate production worker hours and a constant term:

$$\%(IPmfg) = f[\%(\text{aggregate production hours}), \text{constant}].$$

Sometimes a productivity variable is added to the model and may be as simple as the percent change in lagged values of the ratio of manufacturing output to production hours. Otherwise, the productivity effect is often assumed to show up in the constant term.

For the BEA's estimates of personal income, the earnings data play a key role. For the private wages and salaries components of personal income, the average weekly earnings numbers are the primary inputs. These data are published in a separate table in the employment report and are the product of average weekly hours, average hourly earnings, and production workers. However, these earnings figures are just for production workers, and the salaries portion of wages and salaries is derived separately (though not publicly available separately). Hence, this is one source of error in the simple models used to mimic the BEA process. Private forecasts are usually based on the percent change in personal income (or more appropriately wages and salaries or even private wages and salaries) being regressed against the percent change in aggregate weekly earnings:

$$\%(\text{Wages and salaries}) = f[\%(\text{aggregate weekly earnings, constant})].$$

The last major indicators that employment report data are used for as inputs are for various components in the Commerce Department's indexes of leading, coincident, and lagging indicators.[11] These three composite indicators track changes in the business cycle. In the financial markets, the index of leading indicators is the most closely followed of the three. This index currently is derived from 11 data series, of which average weekly hours for manufacturing is one component. Manufacturing output and the number of labor hours used as input— that is, the average workweek—generally lead the business cycle. For the leading index, there is another employment component—average weekly initial claims for unemployment insurance—but this data series is not part of either the establishment or household surveys. It is produced through a separate state cooperative program.

For the index of current indicators, the nonagricultural payroll total employment series is one of four components. Also, two of the other three components of the coincident index are heavily impacted by the payroll survey—industrial production and real personal income less transfer payments. The indicator for average duration of unemployment in weeks is one of seven components in the lagging index and comes from the household survey.

Finally, some employment report data are used in estimates of some GDP components. For example, the BEA uses industry earnings data for early estimates for personal consumption of some health care services. Also, employment in various financial industries is used to derive estimates for real changes in personal consumption for certain financial services related to interest on checking accounts.

SUMMARY KEYS FOR ANALYSIS

Key Roles in the Economy and Underlying Fundamentals

Employment is a fundamental force behind the consumer sector. Consumer willingness to spend is heavily dependent on the level of employment as well as on perceptions of job stability. The nonfinancial media generally focuses on the civilian unemployment rate. Over the business cycle, the unemployment rate typically leads the economy going into recession but usually lags during recovery. Nonfarm payroll employment is a coincident indicator and reflects the current strength of the economy. Financial markets pay attention to payroll employment because of that indicator's inherent reflection of consumer purchasing power. Related to this issue, it is important to watch the distribution of job gains and losses in low-wage versus high-wage industries. In addition to being an important indicator of the current strength of manufacturing, manufacturing employment is watched because it is in a high-wage sector.

Underlying Fundamentals

Employment is affected by basic demand factors for the economy. Employment tracks the economy on a coincident basis but with less cyclical movement. Certainly, employment is affected by overall demand, but cyclical movement is tempered by average weekly hours being more responsive to changes in output. During recession, hours are cut back before employees are laid off. Hours rise more rapidly than jobs during recovery because a work schedule is easier and quicker to change by managers than is the size of the workforce. Additionally, there are fixed costs to hiring and laying off workers.

Other factors affecting employment trends are worker productivity, the relative cost of capital, and the overall cost of labor. While worker productivity is affected by available capital equipment per worker, the quality of the worker also is a consideration. Low wages are not the only consideration for hiring but also the educational facet of worker quality. As the US faces greater import competition and US output shifts toward higher value goods and services (requiring higher levels of technology), the education of the workforce is becoming more critical to maintaining a comparative advantage to other countries.

If labor costs are rising, an employer has the option of considering capital substitution for labor. This is encouraged if the cost of capital equipment is declining (i.e., interest rates as well as the price of the equipment). Finally, employers consider all costs when hiring labor. Total costs include not just wages but a wide variety of benefits. These include vacation, retirement, life and disability insurance, and health care coverage. Business decisions to hire are affected not just by current employment costs but also by anticipated changes (or fears of changes) in government-mandated benefits for employees.

Key Sources of Monthly Volatility

For the household data, the smaller sample is the basic source of monthly volatility in seasonally adjusted data for both primary series—employed and unemployed. Seasonal movement of students into and out of the labor force also creates seasonal adjustment problems because the timing of entry and exit is erratic relative to the survey week during critical months. For the overall unemployment rate, only changes greater than 0.1 percentage point are statistically significant.

For seasonally adjusted nonfarm payroll employment, unseasonal weather can affect a number of components—particularly construction and retail trade. Strike activity also may affect employment levels the month a work stoppage begins and ends, depending on timing relative to the survey period. The number of weeks between surveys each month does vary between four and five weeks, and this variance creates some volatility in seasonally adjusted data. While this effect is predictable to an analyst who is extremely attentive to detail (looking over calendars for the past few years), it is random in that different months are affected from year to year.

TABLE 1–2
Analyzing the News Release: Key Questions

Establishment Survey

- How strong was the change in overall nonfarm payroll employment?
- Were there significant revisions to the previous two months of data for the change in nonfarm payroll employment?
- Was there adequate growth in the goods-producing sectors, especially manufacturing and construction, or was growth in lower-wage services jobs—retail trade in particular?
- For projecting the month's industrial production figure, for manufacturing in particular, how strong were production worker jobs and the average workweek in manufacturing?
- To estimate growth in current month's personal income—the private wages and salaries component in particular—how strong were establishment employment, the average workweek, and average hourly earnings for the private sector?
- For projecting upcoming industrial production and personal income, is the survey period representative of the entire month for employment, hours worked, and earnings? Were these data series affected by adverse weather, holidays, or strikes?
- Was construction employment affected by atypical weather—for example, unusually wet during the normal construction season or perhaps unseasonably warm in late winter?
- For retail trade employment, how much of the change was in the large components for eating and drinking establishments and for grocery stores versus department stores?
- At the end of the Christmas selling season, does unusually strong (weak) retail trade employment reflect weaker-than-normal (stronger) hiring at the start of the season?

Household Survey

- Did the unemployment rate fall (rise) due to a rise (decline) in household employment or because of a drop (increase) in the labor force?
- Was there unusual seasonal movement before or after Christmas or before or after summer?
- For students entering the work force, did the survey period occur unusually early or late in May or in June?
- For part-time workers, was the change within the normal range of high volatility, or was there an obvious continuation of an uptrend or downtrend?

TABLE 1–3a
Household Survey Employment

			Annual Data, Millions			
	Civilian Employment	Number Unemployed	Civilian Labor Force	Civilian Unemployment Rate	Not in Labor Force	Noninstitutional Population, 16+
1960	65.778	3.852	69.628	5.5	47.617	117.245
1961	65.746	4.714	70.459	6.7	48.312	118.771
1962	66.702	3.911	70.614	5.5	49.539	120.153
1963	67.762	4.070	71.833	5.7	50.583	122.416
1964	69.305	3.786	73.091	5.2	51.394	124.485
1965	71.088	3.366	74.455	4.5	52.089	126.513
1966	72.895	2.875	75.770	3.8	52.288	128.058
1967	74.372	2.975	77.347	3.8	52.527	129.874
1968	75.920	2.817	78.737	3.6	53.291	132.028
1969	77.902	2.832	80.734	3.5	53.602	134.335
1970	78.678	4.093	82.771	4.9	54.315	137.085
1971	79.367	5.016	84.382	5.9	55.834	140.216
1972	82.153	4.882	87.034	5.6	57.091	144.126
1973	85.064	4.365	89.429	4.9	57.667	147.096
1974	86.794	5.165	91.949	5.6	58.171	150.120
1975	85.846	7.929	93.775	8.5	59.377	153.153
1976	88.752	7.406	96.158	7.7	59.991	156.150
1977	92.017	6.991	99.009	7.1	60.025	159.033
1978	96.048	6.202	102.251	6.1	59.659	161.910
1979	98.824	6.137	104.962	5.8	59.900	164.863
1980	99.303	7.637	106.940	7.1	60.806	167.745
1981	100.397	8.273	108.670	7.6	61.460	170.130
1982	99.526	10.678	110.204	9.7	62.067	172.271
1983	100.834	10.717	111.550	9.6	62.665	174.215
1984	105.005	8.539	113.544	7.5	62.839	176.383
1985	107.150	8.312	115.461	7.2	62.744	178.206
1986	109.597	8.237	117.834	7.0	62.752	180.587
1987	112.440	7.425	119.865	6.2	62.888	182.753
1988	114.968	6.701	121.669	5.5	62.944	184.613
1989	117.342	6.528	123.869	5.3	62.523	186.393
1990	117.914	6.874	124.787	5.5	63.262	188.049
1991	116.877	8.426	125.303	6.7	64.462	189.765
1992	117.598	9.384	126.982	7.4	64.593	191.576
1993	119.306	8.734	128.040	6.8	65.509	193.550

Source: US Department of Labor, Bureau of Labor Statistics, Employment and Earnings, March 1994.

TABLE 1–3b
Household Survey Employment

			Annual Percent Changes			
	Civilian Employment	Number Unemployed	Civilian Labor Force	Civilian Unemployment Rate	Not in Labor Force	Noninstitutional Population, 16+
1960	1.8	3.0	1.8	5.5	1.4	1.7
1961	0.0	22.4	1.2	6.7	1.5	1.3
1962	1.5	−17.0	0.2	5.5	2.5	1.2
1963	1.6	4.1	1.7	5.7	2.1	1.9
1964	2.3	−7.0	1.8	5.2	1.6	1.7
1965	2.6	−11.1	1.9	4.5	1.4	1.6
1966	2.5	−14.6	1.8	3.8	0.4	1.2
1967	2.0	3.5	2.1	3.8	0.5	1.4
1968	2.1	−5.3	1.8	3.6	1.5	1.7
1969	2.6	0.5	2.5	3.5	0.6	1.7
1970	1.0	44.5	2.5	4.9	1.3	2.0
1971	0.9	22.6	1.9	5.9	2.8	2.3
1972	3.5	−2.7	3.1	5.6	2.3	2.8
1973	3.5	−10.6	2.8	4.9	1.0	2.1
1974	2.0	18.3	2.8	5.6	0.9	2.1
1975	−1.1	53.5	2.0	8.5	2.1	2.0
1976	3.4	−6.6	2.5	7.7	1.0	2.0
1977	3.7	−5.6	3.0	7.1	0.1	1.8
1978	4.4	−11.3	3.3	6.1	−0.6	1.8
1979	2.9	−1.0	2.7	5.8	0.4	1.8
1980	0.5	24.4	1.9	7.1	1.5	1.7
1981	1.1	8.3	1.6	7.6	1.1	1.4
1982	−0.9	29.1	1.4	9.7	1.0	1.3
1983	1.3	−0.4	1.2	9.6	1.0	1.1
1984	4.1	−20.3	1.8	7.5	0.3	1.2
1985	2.0	−2.7	1.7	7.2	−0.2	1.0
1986	2.3	−0.9	2.1	7.0	0.0	1.3
1987	2.6	−9.9	1.7	6.2	0.2	1.2
1988	2.2	−9.8	1.5	5.5	0.1	1.0
1989	2.1	−2.6	1.8	5.3	−0.7	1.0
1990	0.5	5.3	0.7	5.5	1.2	0.9
1991	−0.9	22.6	0.4	6.7	1.9	0.9
1992	0.6	11.4	1.3	7.4	0.2	1.0
1993	1.5	−6.9	0.8	6.8	1.4	1.0

Source: US Department of Labor, Bureau of Labor Statistics.

TABLE 1–4a
Establishment Survey Employment

Annual Data, Millions

	Total Employment	Goods-Producing	Manufacturing	Construction	Mining	Service-Producing
1960	54.189	20.434	16.796	2.926	0.712	33.755
1961	53.999	19.857	16.326	2.859	0.672	34.142
1962	55.549	20.451	16.853	2.948	0.650	35.098
1963	56.653	20.640	16.995	3.010	0.635	36.013
1964	58.283	21.005	17.274	3.097	0.634	37.278
1965	60.765	21.926	18.062	3.232	0.632	38.829
1966	63.901	23.158	19.214	3.317	0.627	40.743
1967	65.803	23.308	19.447	3.248	0.613	42.495
1968	67.897	23.737	19.781	3.350	0.606	44.160
1969	70.384	24.361	20.167	3.575	0.619	46.023
1970	70.880	23.578	19.367	3.588	0.623	47.302
1971	71.214	22.935	18.623	3.704	0.609	48.278
1972	73.675	23.668	19.151	3.889	0.628	50.007
1973	76.790	24.893	20.154	4.097	0.642	51.897
1974	78.265	24.794	20.077	4.020	0.697	53.471
1975	76.945	22.600	18.323	3.525	0.752	54.345
1976	79.382	23.352	18.997	3.576	0.779	56.030
1977	82.471	24.346	19.682	3.851	0.813	58.125
1978	86.697	25.585	20.505	4.229	0.851	61.113
1979	89.823	26.461	21.040	4.463	0.958	63.363
1980	90.406	25.658	20.285	4.346	1.027	64.748
1981	91.152	25.497	20.170	4.188	1.139	65.655
1982	89.554	23.812	18.780	3.904	1.128	65.732
1983	90.152	23.330	18.432	3.946	0.952	66.821
1984	94.408	24.718	19.372	4.380	0.966	69.690
1985	97.387	24.842	19.248	4.668	0.927	72.544
1986	99.344	24.533	18.947	4.810	0.777	74.811
1987	101.958	24.674	18.999	4.958	0.717	77.284
1988	105.210	25.125	19.314	5.098	0.713	80.086
1989	107.895	25.254	19.391	5.171	0.692	82.642
1990	109.419	24.905	19.076	5.120	0.709	84.514
1991	108.256	23.745	18.406	4.650	0.689	84.511
1992	108.519	23.142	18.040	4.471	0.631	85.377
1993	110.178	22.975	17.802	4.574	0.599	87.203

Source: US Department of Labor, Bureau of Labor Statistics.

TABLE 1–4b
Establishment Survey Employment

			Annual Data, Millions			
	Transportation and Public Utilities	Wholesale Trade	Retail Trade	Finance, Insurance, and Real Estate	Services	Government
1960	4.004	3.153	8.238	2.628	7.378	8.353
1961	3.903	3.142	8.195	2.688	7.619	8.594
1962	3.906	3.207	8.359	2.754	7.982	8.889
1963	3.903	3.258	8.520	2.830	8.277	9.226
1964	3.951	3.347	8.812	2.911	8.660	9.596
1965	4.036	3.477	9.239	2.977	9.036	10.074
1966	4.158	3.608	9.637	3.058	9.498	10.785
1967	4.268	3.700	9.906	3.185	10.045	11.392
1968	4.318	3.791	10.308	3.337	10.567	11.839
1969	4.442	3.919	10.785	3.512	11.169	12.195
1970	4.515	4.006	11.034	3.645	11.548	12.553
1971	4.476	4.014	11.338	3.772	11.797	12.880
1972	4.541	‹ 4.127	11.822	3.908	12.276	13.333
1973	4.656	4.291	12.315	4.046	12.857	13.732
1974	4.725	4.447	12.539	4.148	13.441	14.170
1975	4.542	4.430	12.630	4.165	13.892	14.685
1976	4.582	4.562	13.193	4.271	14.551	14.871
1977	4.713	4.723	13.792	4.467	15.302	15.127
1978	4.923	4.985	14.556	4.724	16.252	15.673
1979	5.136	5.221	14.972	4.975	17.112	15.947
1980	5.146	5.292	15.018	5.160	17.890	16.241
1981	5.165	5.375	15.171	5.298	18.615	16.031
1982	5.081	5.295	15.158	5.340	19.021	15.837
1983	4.952	5.283	15.587	5.466	19.664	15.870
1984	5.156	5.568	16.512	5.684	20.746	16.023
1985	5.233	5.727	17.315	5.948	21.927	16.394
1986	5.247	5.761	17.880	6.273	22.957	16.693
1987	5.362	5.848	18.422	6.533	24.110	17.010
1988	5.514	6.030	19.023	6.630	25.504	17.386
1989	5.625	6.187	19.475	6.668	26.907	17.779
1990	5.793	6.173	19.601	6.709	27.934	18.304
1991	5.762	6.081	19.284	6.646	28.336	18.402
1992	5.709	6.045	19.346	6.571	29.053	18.653
1993	5.708	6.113	19.743	6.604	30.192	18.841

Source: US Department of Labor, Bureau of Labor Statistics.

TABLE 1–4c
Establishment Survey Employment

			Annual Percent Changes			
	Total Employment	Goods-Producing	Manufacturing	Construction	Mining	Service-Producing
1960	1.7	0.1	0.7	−2.6	−2.7	2.7
1961	−0.4	−2.8	−2.8	−2.3	−5.6	1.1
1962	2.9	3.0	3.2	3.1	−3.3	2.8
1963	2.0	0.9	0.8	2.1	−2.3	2.6
1964	2.9	1.8	1.6	2.9	−0.2	3.5
1965	4.3	4.4	4.6	4.4	−0.3	4.2
1966	5.2	5.6	6.4	2.6	−0.8	4.9
1967	3.0	0.6	1.2	−2.1	−2.2	4.3
1968	3.2	1.8	1.7	3.1	−1.1	3.9
1969	3.7	2.6	2.0	6.7	2.1	4.2
1970	0.7	−3.2	−4.0	0.4	0.6	2.8
1971	0.5	−2.7	−3.8	3.2	−2.2	2.1
1972	3.5	3.2	2.8	5.0	3.1	3.6
1973	4.2	5.2	5.2	5.3	2.2	3.8
1974	1.9	−0.4	−0.4	−1.9	8.6	3.0
1975	−1.7	−8.8	−8.7	−12.3	7.9	1.6
1976	3.2	3.3	3.7	1.4	3.6	3.1
1977	3.9	4.3	3.6	7.7	4.4	3.7
1978	5.1	5.1	4.2	9.8	4.7	5.1
1979	3.6	3.4	2.6	5.5	12.6	3.7
1980	0.6	−3.0	−3.6	−2.6	7.2	2.2
1981	0.8	−0.6	−0.6	−3.6	10.9	1.4
1982	−1.8	−6.6	−6.9	−6.8	−1.0	0.1
1983	0.7	−2.0	−1.9	1.1	−15.6	1.7
1984	4.7	5.9	5.1	11.0	1.5	4.3
1985	3.2	0.5	−0.6	6.6	−4.0	4.1
1986	2.0	−1.2	−1.6	3.0	−16.2	3.1
1987	2.6	0.6	0.3	3.1	−7.7	3.3
1988	3.2	1.8	1.7	2.8	−0.6	3.6
1989	2.6	0.5	0.4	1.4	−2.9	3.2
1990	1.4	−1.4	−1.6	−1.0	2.5	2.3
1991	−1.1	−4.7	−3.5	−9.2	−2.8	0.0
1992	0.2	−2.5	−2.0	−3.8	−8.4	1.0
1993	1.5	−0.7	−1.3	2.3	−5.1	2.1

Source: US Department of Labor, Bureau of Labor Statistics.

TABLE 1–4d
Establishment Survey Employment

	Annual Percent Changes					
	Transportation and Public Utilities	Wholesale Trade	Retail Trade	Finance, Insurance, and Real Estate	Services	Government
1960	−0.2	2.0	2.5	3.1	4.1	3.3
1961	−2.5	−0.3	−0.5	2.3	3.3	2.9
1962	0.1	2.1	2.0	2.5	4.8	3.4
1963	−0.1	1.6	1.9	2.8	3.7	3.8
1964	1.2	2.7	3.4	2.9	4.6	4.0
1965	2.2	3.9	4.8	2.3	4.3	5.0
1966	3.0	3.8	4.3	2.7	5.1	7.1
1967	2.6	2.5	2.8	4.2	5.8	5.6
1968	1.2	2.5	4.1	4.8	5.2	3.9
1969	2.9	3.4	4.6	5.2	5.7	3.0
1970	1.6	2.2	2.3	3.8	3.4	2.9
1971	−0.9	0.2	2.8	3.5	2.2	2.6
1972	1.5	2.8	4.3	3.6	4.1	3.5
1973	2.5	4.0	4.2	3.5	4.7	3.0
1974	1.5	3.6	1.8	2.5	4.5	3.2
1975	−3.9	−0.4	0.7	0.4	3.4	3.6
1976	0.9	3.0	4.5	2.5	4.7	1.3
1977	2.9	3.5	4.5	4.6	5.2	1.7
1978	4.5	5.5	5.5	5.8	6.2	3.6
1979	4.3	4.7	2.9	5.3	5.3	1.7
1980	0.2	1.4	0.3	3.7	4.5	1.8
1981	0.4	1.6	1.0	2.7	4.1	−1.3
1982	−1.6	−1.5	−0.1	0.8	2.2	−1.2
1983	−2.5	−0.2	2.8	2.4	3.4	0.2
1984	4.1	5.4	5.9	4.0	5.5	1.0
1985	1.5	2.9	4.9	4.6	5.7	2.3
1986	0.3	0.6	3.3	5.5	4.7	1.8
1987	2.2	1.5	3.0	4.1	5.0	1.9
1988	2.8	3.1	3.3	1.5	5.8	2.2
1989	2.0	2.6	2.4	0.6	5.5	2.3
1990	3.0	−0.2	0.6	0.6	3.8	3.0
1991	−0.5	−1.5	−1.6	−0.9	1.4	0.5
1992	−0.9	−0.6	0.3	−1.1	2.5	1.4
1993	0.0	1.1	2.1	0.5	3.9	1.0

Source: US Department of Labor, Bureau of Labor Statistics.

NOTES FOR CHAPTER 1

1. This is the sample size as of June 1993.
2. US Department of Labor, Bureau of Labor Statistics, "Chapter 1. Labor Force, Employment, and Unemployment from the Current Population Survey," *BLS Handbook of Methods,* September 1992, Bulletin 2414, p.4.
3. Ibid.
4. US Department of Labor, Bureau of Labor Statistics, *Briefing Materials on the Redesigned Current Population Survey,* November 16–17, 1993, p. 13.
5. This is the survey size as of August 1993.
6. Roy H Webb and William Whelpley, "Labor Market Data," *Macroeconomic Data: A User's Guide,* 1990, Federal Reserve Bank of Richmond, p. 18.
7. CATI is computer-assisted telephone interview and TDE is Touch-Tone data entry.
8. For the level of employed, jobholders are counted only once, but in 1994 the CPS began tracking how many jobs individuals hold.
9. Industrial classification refers to the grouping of reporting establishments into industries on the basis of their major product or activity as determined by the establishments' percent of total sales or receipts. Data are currently classified in accordance with the *Standard Industrial Classification Manual,* Office of Management and Budget, 1987. The two-digit reference is in regard to the level of aggregation of data. Industries can be narrowly defined or broadly defined as at the two digit level as listed in main text.
10. The other sectoral components in industrial production are mining and public utilities.
11. These composite indexes were revised to their current form with the March 3, 1989, release for January 1989 estimates.

BIBLIOGRAPHY

Bowie, Chester E; Lawrence S Cahoon; and Elizabeth A Martin. "Overhauling the Current Population Survey: Evaluating Changes in the Estimates." *Monthly Labor Review.* US Department of Labor. September 1993, pp. 29–33.

Bregger, John E, and Cathryn S Dippo. "Overhauling the Current Population Survey: Why Is It Necessary to Change?" *Monthly Labor Review.* US Department of Labor. September 1993, pp. 29–33.

Green, Gloria. "Comparing Employment Estimates from Household and Payroll Surveys." *Monthly Labor Review.* US Department of Labor. December 1969, pp. 9–20.

Polivka, Anne E, and Jennifer M Roghgeb. "Overhauling the Current Population Survey: Redesigning the CPS Questionnaire." *Monthly Labor Review.* US Department of Labor. September 1993, pp. 10–28.

US Department of Labor. Bureau of Labor Statistics. *BLS Handbook of Methods.* Bulletin 2285. "Chapter 2. Employment, Hours, and Earnings from the Establishment Survey." April 1988, pp. 13–27.

———. *BLS Handbook of Methods.* Bulletin 2285. "Chapter 1. Labor Force, Employment, and Unemployment from the Current Population Survey." April 1988, pp. 3–12.

———. *Briefing Materials on the Redesigned Current Population Survey.* November 16–17, 1993.

———. *Employment and Earnings.* "Explanatory Notes. November 1992, pp. 130–158.

————. Press Release. "Revision of Payroll Survey Employment Estimates to March 1991 Benchmarks." June 3, 1992.

Webb, Roy H, and William Whelpley. "Labor Market Data." *Macroeconomic Data: A User's Guide.* Federal Reserve Bank of Richmond. 1990, pp. 17–24.

CHAPTER 2

THE PERSONAL
INCOME REPORT

The personal income report, which also includes personal outlays and savings, is produced by the Bureau of Economic Analysis (BEA) in tandem with the gross domestic product (GDP) release. Personal income and its components are part of the quarterly GDP series (the national income and product accounts—NIPA) but are released as a separate set of monthly indicators the next business day after the GDP report. This is generally during the fourth week of the month following the reference month.

Personal income is a broad measure of household income. It is important because it is one of the primary measures of the health of the economy—that of the ability of consumers to make purchases. Over the long run or business cycle in particular, personal income is considered to be the primary determinant of household spending, and this behavioral consideration is one of the main reasons that data on personal income are closely tracked. Also, personal consumption accounts for about two-thirds of final demand in the economy and is part of the personal income report. The importance of personal income is demonstrated by the fact that it is one of the four components of the index generally used to define turning points in the business cycle—the Commerce Department's index of coincident indicators.[1]

Since the personal income report is an integral part of the effort to produce data for the national income and product accounts, data are derived for both the income and product (or expenditure) sides of the NIPA accounting ledger. On the expenditure side, the personal income report details the disposition of personal income. Disposition of personal income gives us data series for personal outlays (mainly personal consumption), personal taxes, and personal saving. Through the accounting process, disposable personal income also is derived.

The monthly report is known as *Personal Income and Outlays,* but these data are also published in the Commerce Department's *Survey of Current Business* and in the *Federal Reserve Bulletin,* a secondary source. Data for personal income, outlays, taxes, and saving are available in both monthly and quarterly form, not seasonally adjusted and seasonally adjusted, and in both current- and constant-dollar series. As in the case for most NIPA series, personal income and disposition data are expressed in annualized rates—that is, the income level, should that income flow continue at the same rate for an entire year.

Monthly personal income and disposition of income series are subject to revision until the quarter inclusive of the reference month is closed out for GDP revisions. This means that monthly data can be revised for two to four months after the initial release depending on whether the reference month is late in a given quarter or early. Annual revisions are usually released in July, along with GDP revisions, and typically cover the previous three calendar years and earlier monthly releases of the current year.

OVERVIEW OF INCOME AND DISPOSITION COMPONENTS

Personal income is derived by the BEA from a number of sources. Early estimates—for both the income and expenditure sides—are often based on separate sources than later estimates in annual or benchmark revisions.

As mentioned above, personal income is part of the NIPA system. Specifically, the BEA has created a Personal Income and Outlay Account in which the total disposition of personal income by definition equals personal income; that is, the dollar value of sum of the personal income components equals all of the uses of personal income. This is seen on the two sides of the ledger (see Table 2–1). As shown, the three basic uses or ways to dispose of personal income are paying taxes, making outlays, and saving.

TABLE 2–1
Personal Income and Its Disposition[2]

	Billions of Current Dollars		
	1991	1992	1993
Personal income	4,850.9	5,144.9	5,388.3
Wage and salary disbursements	2,815.0	2,973.1	3,080.5
Other labor income	296.9	322.7	350.7
Proprietors' income with inventory valuation and capital consumption adjustments (CCA)	376.4	414.3	443.1
Rental income of persons with CCA	−12.8	−8.9	12.6
Personal dividend income	127.9	140.4	158.3
Personal interest income	715.6	694.3	695.2
Transfer payments to persons	769.9	858.4	912.1
Less: Personal contributions for social insurance	237.8	249.3	264.3
Less: personal tax and nontax payments	620.4	644.8	681.6
Equals: disposable personal income	4,230.5	4,500.2	4,706.7
Less: personal outlays	4,029.0	4,261.5	4,516.8
Personal consumption expenditures	3,906.4	4,139.9	4,391.8
Durables	457.8	497.3	537.9
Nondurables	1,257.9	1,300.9	1,350.0
Services	2,190.7	2,341.6	2,503.9
Interest paid by persons	112.2	111.1	114.0
Personal transfer payments to rest of world (net)	10.5	10.4	11.0
Equals: personal saving	201.5	238.7	189.9
Addenda: personal saving as percentage of disposable personal income	4.8	5.3	4.0

Personal Income, Components, and Sources

The first key series in this report is, of course, total personal income.

> Personal income is the income received by persons from all sources, that is from participation in production, from transfer payments from government and business, and from government interest, which is treated like a transfer payment.[3]

Going into personal income are wage and salary disbursements, other labor income, proprietors' income (farm and nonfarm) after inventory valuation and capital consumption adjustments, rental income of persons (with capital consumption adjustment), dividends, personal interest income, and transfer payments to persons from both business and government. After these income estimates are summed, personal contributions for social insurance are subtracted to define total personal income.

Wage and Salary Disbursements
By far, the largest component of personal income is wage and salary disbursements. For example, this component was a little over 57 percent of nominal personal income in 1993. It broadly covers monetary earnings of employees.

> Wage and salary disbursements consists of the monetary remuneration of employees, including the compensation of corporate officers; commissions, tips, and bonuses; and receipts in kind that represent income to the recipients.[4]

Wage and salary data are derived at the industry level and then aggregated. Data are generally analyzed at a moderate level of aggregation such as for commodity-producing industries (including manufacturing), distributive industries, and service industries. These are for the private sector, and there is also a separate wage and salary component for government and government enterprises.

Sources for data vary by components. For most private-sector wage and salary disbursements, annual estimates are based on wage data from reports filled with state employment security agencies by employers. For industries not subject to state unemployment insurance taxes, a variety of other sources are used. These other sources are largely for farms, railroads, private households, and nonprofit membership organizations. For manufacturing, earnings are divided between wages and salaries according to the ratio of production worker earnings to total earnings based on information from the Census Bureau's Annual Survey of Manufactures and to a less degree from Bureau of Labor Statistics (BLS) monthly production worker data. Annual wages and salaries data for federal civilian employees are obtained primarily from the office of Personnel Management, while military wages and salary figures come from the Department of Defense.

Monthly estimates for most private industries are derived by extrapolation using changes in the product of BLS data on employment, hours, and earnings from wages. This information is part of BLS's monthly employment report. For manufacturing, salaries are estimated separately. Other monthly wage and salary component estimates, such as for government, are largely simple extrapolations primarily based on recent employment and earnings trends.

Other Components of Personal Income
"Other labor income" is basically employer contributions to private pensions and to private welfare funds. Group health insurance is over half of this component with pensions and workers' compensation also being large subcomponents. It also includes supplemental unemployment and directors' fees. However, this personal income component does not include contributions to publicly administered funds, such as Social Security, nor does it include civilian government employees retirement. Annual data for other labor income series primarily come from the Internal Revenue Service (IRS) and the US Department of Health and Human Services. Monthly estimates for other labor income are extrapolations based on BLS employment figures.

Proprietors' income with inventory valuation and capital consumption adjustments is the monetary and in-kind incomes of proprietorships and partnerships after taking into account two special factors. Proprietors' income is originally available in a form including inventory changes and depreciation charges—to more accurately measure profits—but these allowances do not necessarily reflect appropriate economic accounting to measure current income. Instead, these figures usually have been distorted by inflation and tax laws. Therefore, the inventory valuation adjustment is the difference between changes in inventories valued in current period prices and the value reported on a historical basis. The capital consumption adjustment is the difference between depreciation based on tax returns versus those based on economic service lives, straight-line depreciation, and replacement cost. This personal income component excludes interest and dividend income received by proprietors as well as most rental income. If the primary business of the person receiving rental income is real estate, then the rental income is included.

Annual estimates for proprietors' income come from several sources including the IRS and the US Department of Agriculture (USDA). Monthly estimates of farm income are based on annual projections for farm income published by the USDA with monthly interpolations taking into account natural disasters and any unusual changes in prices, crop yields, or subsidy payments. Monthly estimates for the nonfarm component are extrapolations and interpolations by industry and are estimated using a variety of data for projections, including Census retail sales and Census value of new single-family housing put-in-place.

Rental income of persons with capital consumption adjustment contains both monetary and imputed components. First, it is monetary personal income from the rental of real property except that, as noted above, the income of persons primarily earning their income in the real estate business is allocated to proprietors' income. Rental income also includes an imputed component for net rental income of owner-occupants of nonfarm dwellings. These owner-occupants are treated in a strict economic sense as renting their houses to themselves and deriving imputed income and an equal amount of personal consumption of housing services (after taking into account intermediate goods and services used in maintaining the houses). Finally, this personal income component includes royalties paid to persons from patents, copyrights, and rights to natural resources.

Annual estimates for the monetary net rental income components are primarily based on data from the Census Bureau's Annual Housing Survey (AHS) for income from residential properties and from the IRS for income from nonresidential properties. The census data provide information on the number of housing units and average rent per unit, but the BEA must make its own estimates for various expenses netted against rent from residential properties. Some rental income from farm realty to nonfarm landlords comes from the Department of Agriculture, and royalty income is derived from IRS data. For the imputed net rental income of owner-occupied nonfarm residential properties, estimates are based on housing units from the AHS and on BEA estimates for the imputed rents and expenses. However, the imputed rent figures are derived from actual rents for tenant-occupied units with comparable housing characteristics. Monthly estimates for rent components are interpolations of annual estimates for past years and are extrapolations of past years for months of the current year, with adjustments for natural disasters and changes in property tax rates.

> Dividends is payments in cash or other assets, excluding stock, by corporations organized for profit to stockholders who are US persons.[5]

Annual estimates for dividends are from IRS data for corporate income tax returns with various adjustments by the BEA. These adjustments are to include Federal Reserve banks, other federal banks, and to add in dividends to US persons from the rest of the world. Exclusions are made for capital gains and return of capital distribution, dividends paid to other US corporations (these profits remain in the business sector), and for dividends paid to non-US residents and to pension plans. Following the most recent IRS tabulation, annual data are derived from data from the Federal Trade Commission for manufacturing, mining, and trade industries; from various regulatory agencies for transportation and utilities industries; and from a BEA sample of publicly reporting companies for other industries.[6] Monthly estimates are interpolations for historical years and extrapolations from recent months based on the BEA's sample of publicly reporting corporations.

Personal interest income is monetary and in-kind (imputed) interest income of persons from all sources. Monetary personal interest income is derived as a net flow of interest paid and received by consumers with the government and business sectors. Mortgage payments by consumers are excluded from these calculations, since, for home purchases, consumers are treated as business entities.

The imputed component is for (1) earnings from life insurance carriers and private noninsured pension plans and (2) from "services furnished without payment by financial intermediaries except life insurance carriers and private noninsured pension plans."[7] For personal interest income, about 45 percent is imputed interest income. Roughly 60 percent of this is accrued interest income on insurance policies and pension funds. For these funds, interest is counted the year it is earned rather than the year it is withdrawn or paid out, and an imputation is required. The rest of the imputed interest income is interest returns made by financial institutions on personal accounts above the monetary interest actually paid to individuals. Basically, this is the imputed income paying for various financial services such as checking accounts, no-fee travelers checks, and so on. Combined with monetary interest received by individuals, this is basically the opportunity cost of holding the funds in these accounts. The BEA assumes that individuals implicitly earn the market rate even though not all of it is received in actual monies. On the expenditure side of the NIPA ledger, the BEA also creates imputed personal consumption for these financial services, which equals the income component.

The methodology for estimating annual interest income is somewhat complex but is based on data from the IRS, the Treasury Department, Federal Trade Commission, the Federal Deposit Insurance Corporation, the Census Bureau, and the Federal Reserve. Recent monthly estimates are extrapolations based on debt outstanding from regulatory agencies and on recent interest rates.

Transfer payments to persons generally are monetary payments for which current services are not rendered. These transfer payments are from both government and business. For businesses, transfers are for gifts to nonprofit institutions and for bad debt from the consumer sector. Government transfer payments are made under a number of programs including federal old-age, survivors, disability, and hospital insurance; supplementary medical insurance; unemployment insurance for federal and state employees and for railroad employees; government retirement and railroad retirement; workers' compensation; veterans' benefits and veterans' life insurance; food stamps; black lung; supplemental security income; direct relief; and earned income credit. Government payments to nonprofit institutions also are included. These are to nonprofit institutions serving households, such as the Red Cross or universities offering scholarships funded by government.

Corporate transfers are estimated with data from the IRS; preliminary annual and monthly figures are extrapolations. Federal government transfers are based primarily on the *Budget of the United States,* Treasury Department data, and various agency data for specific programs. For state and local government transfer payment series, estimates are dependent upon Census Bureau surveys and reports from federal agencies funding specific nonfederal programs. Recent monthly figures are extrapolations.

Personal contributions for social insurance are the payments made by employees, the self-employed, and other persons participating in the applicable programs (for example, the food stamp program does not involve personal contributions) listed under transfer payments. Annual estimates for contributions to federal programs are based on data from the Social Security Administration and the Treasury Department, among others. Yearly data for contributions to state and local programs are derived from figures from the Census Bureau and from the Department of Labor. Monthly estimates for contribution subcomponents are based on monthly wages and salaries estimates and applicable tax rates.

Personal Taxes and Nontax Payments, Components, and Sources

Personal tax and nontax payments is tax payments (net of refunds) by persons (except personal contributions for social insurance) that are not chargeable to business expense, and contain other personal payments to general government that it is convenient to treat like taxes.[8]

At the federal level, the subcomponents are for income taxes, estate and gift taxes, and "other." Personal income taxes have been about 97 to 98 percent of the federal tax and nontax payment totals. At the state level, income taxes also provide the bulk of personal taxes and nontax payments, running at roughly 75 percent of the total. The rest is a variety of nontaxes and "other." Sales taxes and property taxes are considered to be indirect business taxes and are not part of the disposition of personal income. Since homeowners are treated as businesses, property taxes are treated as taxes on business and are moved from the household sector to the business sector.

As just indicated, personal taxes and nontax payments do not cover all sources of receipts for government. The concept of overall receipts differs significantly from that of personal taxes and nontax payments. Government receipts also come from sources such as direct corporate taxes, indirect taxes on businesses and consumers, contributions for social insurance, grants-in-aid, and others.

Annual data for federal personal income tax withholdings are derived from Treasury Department figures while state and local taxes data are based on the Census Bureau's *Quarterly Summary of State and Local Taxes*. Monthly data are interpolations for past years and extrapolations for recent months. For income taxes (at all levels), extrapolations are based on wage and salary estimates and changes in tax rates.

Disposable Personal Income

Next in the accounting hierarchy, personal income less personal tax and nontax payments equals disposable personal income. Disposable personal income is the concept that most economists use as a measure of consumer spending capacity. It is from this measure of income that consumers can choose either to spend or to save, and it is used as a base for the calculation of the personal saving rate.

Personal Outlays, Components, and Sources

There are three definitional ways in which consumers can spend or make outlays. Personal outlays consist of personal consumption expenditures (PCEs), interest paid by consumers to business, and personal transfer payments to foreigners (net). PCEs usually make up over 95 percent of personal outlays (current dollars) and with interest paid to business added, typically account for over 99 percent of personal outlays.

Personal consumption expenditures generally are viewed as purchases of goods and services made by consumers for their own use. However, housing purchases by individuals are classified as fixed investment in the NIPA accounts—in this activity, consumers are treated as businesses. A more detailed definition of PCEs is that they are:

> Goods and services purchased by individuals; operating expenses of nonprofit institutions serving individuals; and the value of food, fuel, clothing, housing, and financial services received in kind by individuals. Net purchases of used goods are also included.[9]

Personal consumption expenditures are broken down by major type of product. The three broad categories are durables, nondurables, and services. Consumer durables are defined as those goods with expected lifetimes of three years or longer. Durables include motor vehicles and parts, furniture and household equipment, and "other durables." Durables purchases tend to be very cyclical because these purchases can be postponed during difficult times and because of the interest rate sensitivity caused by the need to finance most big-ticket items.

Under nondurables are food, clothing and shoes, gasoline and oil, fuel oil and coal, and "other nondurables." Nondurables are not very cyclical because they are necessities for the most part. These purchases generally track population growth.

Finally, the services category covers housing services, household operation (including electricity and gas), transportation, medical care, and "other services." The housing services component is basically use of dwellings—including owner-occupied nonfarm, tenant nonfarm, farm, and lodging such as hotels and motels. Transportation services' largest subcomponent is mainly for repair, rental, and leasing with other significant subcomponents for public transportation and for insurance. The Other services series is largely personal business services (including brokerage, banking, insurance, and legal services), but it also has services subcomponents for personal care, recreation, education, and religion. By dollar volume, most services are necessities, are not very cyclical, and trend along population growth.

Also, services includes sizable components that are imputed rather than components for which monetary payment is made. Imputed items are basically series reflecting opportunity costs, and a corresponding income series is derived for each expenditure series. The largest imputed components in services personal consumption expenditures (PCEs) are space rent for owner-occupied housing (nonfarm and farm), employer-paid health and life insurance premiums, and services furnished without payment by financial intermediaries except life insurance carriers and private noninsured pension plans. There also are a few imputed PCE series for nondurables, but they are very minor—such as employer-provided food, clothing, and lodging. There are no imputed components in durables PCEs.

There are a variety of sources for PCE data. For durables and nondurables, preliminary estimates for most components are based on data from the Census' monthly survey of retail trade using the retail-control method (as discussed in the chapter on retail sales). Estimates for purchases of autos and trucks are largely based on estimates from trade sources such as *Ward's Automotive Reports* and the American Automobile Manufacturers' Association. Estimates of consumption of gasoline and oil come from figures from the Energy Information Administration and the Bureau of Labor Statistics. The remaining minor durables and nondurables series come from various miscellaneous sources. Consumption of food furnished to employees is derived from employment data from the BLS and from federal outlays data from the Office of Management and Budget. Various federal agencies report data for expenditures by US residents abroad (net).

Annual data for these durable and nondurable series often come from the same preliminary sources. Other sources for annual data are the Census Bureau's quinquennial census and the Census Bureau's merchandise trade report, among others.

Services expenditures are based on dozens of government and private-sector sources for preliminary and annual estimates. A few examples for preliminary estimates are wage and salary data from BLS for estimating physician, dentists, and other medical professional services; brokerage services based on transactions data from trade sources; and hospital services and electricity being based on separate data from private organizations.

However, a noticeable number of services subcomponents have preliminary estimates that are derived as extrapolations or judgmental series due to the lack of timely data. Some examples are farm housing rent; numerous medical services; financial services furnished without payment by banks, credit agencies, and investment companies; domestic services; some entertainment services; and some educational services. Annual estimates for services PCEs are generally based on trade reports and reports from numerous government agencies.

Although it is less followed by the financial community's media, PCEs also are organized by "type of expenditure" (durables, nondurables, and services are categorized by "major type of product"). The major expenditure type categories are (1) food and tobacco; (2) clothing, accessories, and jewelry; (3) personal care; (4) housing; (5) household operation; (6) medical care; (7) personal business; (8) transportation; (9) recreation; (10) education and research; (11) religious and welfare activities; and (12) foreign travel and other, net.

Interest Paid by Consumers to Business

This component is basically installment credit payments. It covers payments on revolving credit, auto finance payments, personal bank loans, finance companies, and even insurance policy loans among others. However, interest paid by consumers to business does not include mortgage payments or payments on home improvement loans because homeowners are treated as businesses in the national income and product accounts.

Personal Transfer Payments to Foreigners (Net)

Personal transfer payments to foreigners (net) is the final component of personal outlays. These are a variety of payments between US residents and foreign residents and include goods, services, and financial claims. Included are cash and goods distributed abroad by various US nonprofit organizations, some foreign government pensions forwarded to the United States, and numerous financial transfers between private residents—including through banks, communications companies, and the US Postal Service. Quarterly and annual data are based on reports to the BEA by US banks, nonprofit organizations, and US and foreign government agencies and publications.

Personal Saving and Definitional Constraints

Personal saving is a residual series. It is simply disposable personal income less personal outlays (not just PCEs). While personal income, taxes, and outlays are all derived from many independent sources, there are no sources used specifically for the purpose of estimating personal saving. Personal saving is derived through an accounting identity after personal income, taxes, and outlays are estimated.

The personal saving rate is the ratio of personal saving to disposable personal income. Because personal saving is an accounting derivative of several large components, the personal saving rate is quite volatile. Small movements in personal income, taxes, and outlays can lead to relatively large movements in the much smaller personal saving series and, in turn, the personal saving rate.

SPECIAL TOPICS

Farm Subsidies

As mentioned above, farm income in the personal sector is included under proprietors' farms income. Federal subsidies are the primary source of volatility in this component. There are two basic types of farm subsidies in the United States: (1) price subsidies and (2) payments from the Conservation Reserve Program. Price subsidies are deficiency payments to farmers and are the difference between a target price (set by Congress) for a given crop and the market price. The Conservation Reserve Program is used to reduce acreage planted for various crops, and the federal government makes a "rental payment" for not planting.

Farm subsidy payments are not seasonally adjusted since there is some variation in the timing of payments. Farm program legislation typically is written for five-year periods, and the timing of subsidy payments has varied with different five-year plans. Currently, Conservation Reserve Program payments are usually made in October, while deficiency payments are crop dependent for the timing. The Agriculture Department now makes an estimate for a given year's deficiency, and an advance payment is made at the time farmers sign up for the program. The advance is one-half of the expected deficiency, and the remainder is paid after the end of the crop season. February through May is usually heavy in final payments for the previous year and for advances for the coming year.

Natural Disasters

Natural disasters can have a major impact on personal income and some impact on personal consumption. The biggest impact on personal income is in terms of depreciation expenses, that is, capital consumption. Damage to assets directly lowers personal income components for rental income and proprietors' income. For initial estimates the BEA makes an upward adjustment for its estimate of depreciation expenses that would be included on an accounting basis in IRS data (upon which the BEA extrapolates initial figures). The BEA also raises its estimates for the adjustments to capital consumption allowances for rental income and proprietors' income. These adjustments transform the accounting-based depreciation to an economic basis. These higher depreciation expenses and capital consumption adjustments are made on an incurred basis and affect the month in which a natural disaster occurs. For example, Hurricane Andrew, which hit south Florida and

Louisiana in late August 1992, caused a large decline in personal income for August 1992 primarily due to dramatic falls in proprietors' income (farm and non-farm) and rental income. A modest part of the decline was due to the loss of revenues, but the vast majority was a result of accelerated depreciation and adjustments to capital consumption allowances.

For the farm sector, the impact of natural disasters on proprietors' income is heavily dependent on the type of natural disaster. (The farm sector is represented in personal income only in the farm proprietors' income subcomponent, that is, farm income of personal income.) Disasters affect farm income through higher capital consumption due to damage to structures and equipment and through lost revenues due to damage to crops and livestock. Not all natural disasters affect farm facilities, however. Hurricanes would damage property, whereas a drought would not.

When there is asset damage, farm income is adjusted by two factors: (1) there is higher consumption of fixed capital, which is raised by the market value of structures and equipment destroyed or damaged; and (2) property insurance expenditures are lowered by insurance indemnities earned (incurred as opposed to received). Basically, farm income is reduced by the amount of uninsured property losses. There is a one-time adjustment for farm residential and service structures.

The third and final adjustment to farm income is for crop (and livestock, if applicable) losses. Crops represent current income and are not considered assets. In contrast to asset damage, crop losses frequently are not recognized all at once. Crop revenues usually are heavily seasonal and the BEA distributes estimated revenues (based on projections from the US Department of Agriculture) over the entire year. Once crop damages have occurred, revenues for the rest of the year are usually lowered. This is a general rule; allocation of crop losses is very dependent upon the type of disaster (hurricane versus an extended drought) as well as the types of crops affected.

Wage and salary figures are usually adjusted to a small degree to take into account the impact of natural disasters. Taxes and contributions to social insurance—which initially are estimated using wage and salary estimates and appropriate tax rates—also are affected by disasters due to this methodological tie to wages and salaries. Adjustments to wages and salaries are made regardless of whether the relevant month's payroll employment and earnings data from the BLS capture the impact (whether the disaster is before or after the survey week for that month's employment reports).

The only major effect on personal consumption typically occurs for services consumption for property insurance. However, the impact is only the current dollar component, which is on a net basis—premiums paid less benefits received. A jump in benefits received causes a decline in this services component; benefits are estimated on an incurred basis. In contrast, the constant-dollar subcomponent for this insurance is based on gross payments that are then deflated. Hence, benefits paid do not affect the constant-dollar services series. Monthly real figures continue to be based on trend, while the nominal data are significantly affected by natural disasters.

For rental income, natural disasters typically cause some accelerated depreciation for the imputed series for owner-occupied housing as well as for the other types of rental income. However, there usually is no impact on housing services consumption for owner-occupied housing. Normally, the impact of natural disasters on the local housing stock is negligible relative to the US stock, and no adjustment is made to this imputed consumption component. For Hurricane Andrew, a minor adjustment was made to the imputed housing services component in services personal consumption. This was the first natural disaster to be large enough to cause such an adjustment in this outlays component.

Generally, no other special adjustments are made for estimates of personal consumption expenditures at times of natural disasters. Data from standard sources—such as retail sales and industry reports on motor vehicle sales—are used "as is" in deriving other PCE subcomponents. If a natural disaster affects retail sales data, then that impact will carry through to PCE figures. There are no special adjustments. However, the impact on national data is rarely discernable due to the size of the US economy relative to the area affected by a natural disaster.

In sum, natural disasters can dramatically affect personal income at the national level due to the effect of accelerated depreciation (and due to loss of farm income when applicable). Generally, there is no noticeable impact on *real* PCEs, but nominal PCEs can be negatively affected through insurance benefits received (on an incurred basis) being lowered by a drop in net insurance premiums.

KEYS TO ANALYZING THE MONTHLY REPORT

Overview and Key Components

Because consumer spending is so critical to the health of the economy, the monthly personal income report is closely watched by financial markets. Analysts look for clues on changes in the underlying ability of consumers to be able to spend through changes in income growth and whether consumers' support (or lack of support) of the economy is in the process of changing as reflected in personal consumption. Over the business cycle, personal income is a coincident indicator, tracking peaks and troughs and providing the fuel for consumer spending—a major force in the economy. Within personal consumption, nondurables and services growth is relatively stable, being largely dependent on population growth. Nondurables such as for clothing also appear to be very price sensitive and affected by the cost of imports. Durables are interest-rate sensitive and dependent on demographics to the extent that housing (and, in turn, household durables) and automobile markets are affected.

For measuring the current strength of consumer spending power, the broadest measure of personal income is not always the best indicator of monthly changes in consumers' ability to spend. Total personal income can be affected by temporary factors that do not really affect the typical consumer. The most frequent distortion is probably caused by gyrations in farm proprietors' income as government subsidy payments are large and irregular and are not seasonally adjusted. This problem of farm subsidy payments can be avoided by watching changes in nonfarm personal income, which is less volatile than total personal income. By definition, nonfarm personal income equals total personal income less farm proprietors' income as well as farm wages, farm other labor income, and agricultural net interest.

However, nonfarm personal income also includes a number of components that do not quickly translate into consumer purchasing power. For example, dividend income is usually not a major factor in affecting near-term spending. Monthly gyrations are of minor importance (although longer changes in the trend can affect consumers' willingness to spend). Natural disasters also impact personal income significantly due to depreciation expenses (see section below) but have less impact on spending patterns. The wages and salaries component of personal income avoids most of these problems and is a good measure of consumer ability to spend, since it is directly tied to the health of the labor sector. The wages and salaries series is methodologically tied to payroll employment, hours worked, and hourly earnings. Its importance in personal income is underscored by the fact that it was a little over 57 percent of personal income in 1993.

The argument is often made that disposable personal income is the best measure to track because it takes into account changes in taxes as well as changes in gross earnings. It is what consumers can spend. By definition, disposable personal income is the measure from which consumers can choose to spend or save. However, for an analyst tracking recent monthly data, disposable personal income has the same volatility problems as total personal income. Therefore, unless there are noticeable changes in tax rates or withholdings[10] over the time period under study, the wages and salaries component is probably the best indicator of the near-term health of the consumer.

For personal consumption expenditures, the durables and nondurables series largely reflect the appropriate retail sales series[11] and unit new auto and light truck sales. The services series are derived from a wide array of industry sources although early estimates are largely extrapolations.

Most of the volatility in durables PCEs is attributable to changes in sales of autos and light trucks and to how the BEA includes the sales in PCEs. Even though motor vehicles have long lives and in actuality depreciate slowly over time, the BEA assumes that motor vehicles are fully depreciated at the time of purchase. In fact, the BEA counts basically the entire purchase price as the amount entering into the personal consumption data.[12] Neither the amount of down payment nor the monthly payment is a factor.

The primary consideration by the BEA for choosing to fully depreciate a vehicle at time of sale is that this accounting method does not change the BEA's overall measure of GDP, since a fully depreciated vehicle is shifted from one GDP account (perhaps inventories) to another (durables PCEs) without incorrectly measuring overall production. The BEA agrees that using some type of depreciation schedule technically would be more correct but would complicate the accounting procedures without improving the overall measure of GDP. However, in a true economic sense, some distortions remain in the monthly personal consumption figures and in personal saving.

Because personal saving is a residual of disposable personal income and personal outlays, the method of calculating personal consumption affects personal saving and the personal saving rate. For months when motor vehicle sales rise over previous rates, the personal saving rate declines significantly (assuming no change in recent trends in disposable personal income) because motor vehicle sales are fully depreciated at the time of purchase. Similarly, a relative decline in auto and light truck sales leads to an upswing in the personal saving rate. Studies indicate that the BEA method of treating durables as fully depreciated at the time of sale does raise the volatility of the personal saving rate.[13]

The personal saving rate is quite volatile on a monthly basis, since it is a small residual of several much larger components. Small movements in personal income, outlays, or even taxes lead to larger relative movement in the level of personal saving. It is primarily for this reason that the BEA only reports a three-month average for the personal saving rate even though the data are available for calculating the most recent month.

Despite popular opinion to the contrary, monthly movements in the personal saving rate do not directly reflect changes in consumers' monetary saving at financial institutions. The BEA measure of personal saving is not a measure of saving at financial institutions and should not be construed as such. The earlier-mentioned effect of auto purchases on personal saving is a clear example of a divergence between popular concepts of financial flows versus those measured in the BEA data. The practical interpretation of the impact of a surge in durables consumption is not necessarily that consumers "dipped into their savings" but that consumers assumed further debt. A decline in the level of personal saving in the personal income accounts does not directly reflect activity in personal savings accounts. To get a measure of saving at financial institutions, the "flow of funds" data published by the Federal Reserve Board are more appropriate.

SUMMARY KEYS FOR ANALYSIS

Key Roles in the Economy and Underlying Fundamentals

Personal income is primarily a coincident indicator (once transfer payments are excluded). It cyclically tracks employment but with larger cyclical movement due to greater adjustments to changes in output with hours worked—which in turn affects aggregate earnings. However, for its impact on consumer spending, disposable income is less cyclical because of the stabilizing impact of progressive income taxes. Over the business cycle, durables PCEs are seen as a leading indicator since durables, particularly motor vehicles, are interest rate sensitive.

Over the long run, personal consumption is affected by both growth and shifting preferences in saving. For individuals, preferences in saving are generally influenced by what stage in life one is in—as stated in the life-cycle hypothesis. The basic life-cycle hypothesis states that a consumer is more inclined to spend income (and less toward saving) during youth and during old age. Before income-producing years, a consumer dis-saves (consumes more than earns) and during youth, a typical consumer simply does not worry about saving. In retirement, a consumer consumes by drawing down wealth. It is during middle age—when income earning capabilities are at their peak—that consumers have the greater propensity to save for retirement and other long-term needs.

From the overall economy's perspective, the impact of the life-cycle hypothesis is seen if there is an uneven distribution of the population in terms of age. For example, as the baby-boom generation ages, its life-cycle phase dominates consumer spending habits. Currently, most baby boomers are in the midlife phase, saving for kids' college education and for their own retirement. However, business-cycle movement usually dominates long-term factors. Nonetheless, long-term factors affect the magnitude of business cycle peaks and troughs as well as long-term trends.

Key Sources of Monthly Volatility

Personal Income.   Wages and salary disbursements closely reflect changes in employment, the average workweek, and average hourly earnings (that is, these are aggregate earnings from the BLS establishment survey). However, wage and salary disbursements can diverge from earnings due to BEA adjustments if the employment report's survey period does not appear to be representative of the entire month. Strikes or significant differences in weather during the months are factors that can cause BEA to make adjustments. Wage and salary data also are affected by irregular bonus payments (generally other than regular commissions) that are often made in certain industries such as automobile and finance. Also, while government wages and salaries trend relatively smoothly, pay raises for federal workers or Postal Service employees often lead to spikes in the data.

While it is important to understand sources of volatility in the large wages and salaries component, the largest overall source of volatility in total personal income probably is from the farm proprietors' income component, which includes farm subsidy payments. Farm subsidy payments are not seasonally adjusted even when entered as a component of seasonally adjusted personal income. Natural disasters also cause significant changes in personal rent income and in proprietors' income due to depreciation effects more so than due to temporary loss of revenues. These two factors are discussed in more detail in special topics above.

Personal Consumption.   Personal consumption changes on a monthly basis for many very practical reasons in addition to various technical factors. Retailers frequently have off and on again incentives (sales). For any given month or two, consumers may binge, get bills in the mail a month later, and cut back accordingly for a few months. Spending responds to the latest news in the economy about layoffs as well as favorable developments on interest rates. These types of volatility are very real, but obtaining this type of information from the data requires tracking the data over years and corroborating with other series such as consumer installment credit. That is, a logical question to ask when PCEs are rising quickly is, Are sales being funded by credit?

The number of technical factors behind monthly volatility that can be somewhat verified are few. First, some industries are relatively obvious when special incentives are given. For durables, one must track not only changes in prices (rebates) for autos, but also whether dealers are pushing leases more so than on average. Leases go under producers' durable equipment for the purchase amount rather than durables PCEs. For nondurables, price changes affect apparel purchases significantly. Price changes also are a factor in nondurables PCEs due to oil prices that can move sharply at times.

Finally, the two most volatile components for services PCEs are for utilities and for brokerage services. These can be tracked prior to release date reasonably well by following weekly or monthly utility production and stock market volume for the month. Unseasonable weather generally causes the largest deviations in services PCEs from trend.

TABLE 2–2
Analyzing the News Release: Key Questions

- How strong was the wages and salaries component?
- Were wages and salaries affected by special bonus pay in the current month or in the previous month (as in the auto industry)?
- Were January data affected by government pay increases in the wages and salaries component or by cost-of-living adjustments (COLAs) for transfer payments?
- Were overall personal income figures affected by large changes in farm subsidy payments (which are not seasonally adjusted)?
- How strong was nonfarm personal income?
- If disposable income is weak, was it due to softness in personal income growth or was it due to a rise in tax payments?
- Were any significant changes in tax payments due to temporary changes in withholdings or due to atypical patterns in tax returns?
- For sharp swings in personal consumption, how were the changes allocated between durables, nondurables, and services?
- Were durables gains/losses due to special incentives or rebates for motor vehicles being promoted/discontinued?
- Were nondurables changes due to price changes (either higher prices or discounting)— especially for apparel or for gasoline?
- Were services temporarily affected by atypical weather (utilities usage) or by swings in the stock market (brokerage fees)?
- For the personal saving rate, were changes due to changes in outlays or to changes in disposable personal income?
- Did a swing in durables personal consumption (especially autos) affect the personal saving rate (since durables are considered fully consumed at the time of purchase)?

TABLE 2–3a
Personal Income and Components

	Billions of Current Dollars				
Year	Personal Income, Total	Wage and Salary Disbursements	Other Labor Income	Proprietors' Income, Total with Capital Consumption Allowances	Farm Proprietors' Income with Capital Consumption Allowances
1970	831.0	551.5	32.5	79.9	14.6
1971	893.5	583.9	36.7	86.2	15.2
1972	980.5	638.7	43.0	97.4	19.1
1973	1,098.7	708.7	49.2	116.5	32.2
1974	1,205.7	772.6	56.5	115.3	25.5
1975	1,307.3	814.6	65.9	121.2	23.7
1976	1,446.3	899.5	79.7	132.9	18.3
1977	1,601.3	993.9	94.7	146.4	17.1
1978	1,807.9	1,120.7	110.1	167.7	21.5
1979	2,033.1	1,255.4	124.3	181.8	24.7
1980	2,265.4	1,376.6	139.8	171.8	11.5
1981	2,534.7	1,515.6	153.0	180.8	21.2
1982	2,690.9	1,593.3	165.4	170.7	13.5
1983	2,862.5	1,684.7	174.6	186.7	2.4
1984	3,154.6	1,849.8	184.7	236.0	21.3
1985	3,379.8	1,986.5	191.8	259.9	21.5
1986	3,590.4	2,105.4	200.7	283.7	22.3
1987	3,802.0	2,261.2	210.4	310.2	31.3
1988	4,075.9	2,443.0	230.5	324.3	30.9
1989	4,380.3	2,586.4	251.9	347.3	40.2
1990	4,673.8	2,745.0	274.3	363.3	41.9
1991	4,850.9	2,815.0	296.9	376.4	36.8
1992	5,144.9	2,973.1	322.7	414.3	43.7
1993	5,388.3	3,080.5	350.7	443.2	46.0

Source: US Department of Commerce, Bureau of Economic Analysis.

TABLE 2–3b
Personal Income and Components

	Billions of Current Dollars				
Year	Rental Income, Personal	Dividend Income, Personal	Interest Income, Personal	Transfer Payments to Persons	Personal Contributions for Social Insurance
1970	17.8	23.5	69.2	84.6	27.9
1971	18.2	23.5	75.7	100.1	30.7
1972	16.8	25.5	81.8	111.8	34.5
1973	17.3	27.7	94.1	127.9	42.6
1974	15.8	29.6	112.4	151.3	47.9
1975	13.5	29.2	123.0	190.2	50.4
1976	12.1	34.7	134.6	208.3	55.5
1977	9.0	39.4	155.7	223.3	61.2
1978	8.9	44.2	184.5	241.6	69.8
1979	8.4	50.4	223.2	270.7	81.0
1980	13.2	57.1	274.0	321.5	88.6
1981	20.8	66.9	336.1	365.9	104.5
1982	21.9	67.1	376.8	408.1	112.3
1983	22.1	77.8	397.5	438.9	119.7
1984	23.3	78.8	461.9	452.9	132.8
1985	18.7	87.9	498.1	485.9	149.1
1986	8.7	104.7	531.7	517.8	162.1
1987	3.2	100.4	548.1	542.2	173.6
1988	4.3	108.4	583.2	576.7	194.5
1989	−13.5	126.5	668.2	625.0	211.4
1990	−14.2	144.4	698.2	687.6	224.9
1991	−12.8	127.9	715.6	769.9	237.8
1992	−8.9	140.4	694.3	858.4	249.3
1993	12.6	158.3	695.2	912.1	264.3

TABLE 2–3c
Personal Income and Disposition

			Billions of Current Dollars[14]			
Year	Personal Income, Total	Personal Tax and Nontax Payments	Disposable Personal Income	Personal Outlays	Personal Saving	Personal Saving Rate
1970	831.0	109.0	722.0	664.5	57.5	8.0
1971	893.5	108.7	784.9	719.4	65.4	8.3
1972	980.5	132.0	848.5	788.7	59.7	7.0
1973	1,098.7	140.6	958.1	872.0	86.1	9.0
1974	1,205.7	159.1	1,046.5	953.1	93.4	8.9
1975	1,307.3	156.4	1,150.9	1,050.6	100.3	8.7
1976	1,446.3	182.3	1,264.0	1,171.0	93.0	7.4
1977	1,601.3	210.0	1,391.3	1,303.4	87.9	6.3
1978	1,807.9	240.1	1,567.8	1,460.0	107.8	6.9
1979	2,033.1	280.2	1,753.0	1,629.6	123.3	7.0
1980	2,265.4	312.4	1,952.9	1,799.1	153.8	7.9
1981	2,534.7	360.2	2,174.5	1,982.6	191.8	8.8
1982	2,690.9	371.4	2,319.6	2,120.1	199.5	8.6
1983	2,862.5	368.8	2,493.7	2,325.1	168.7	6.8
1984	3,154.6	395.1	2,759.5	2,537.5	222.0	8.0
1985	3,379.8	436.8	2,943.0	2,753.7	189.3	6.4
1986	3,590.4	459.0	3,131.5	2,944.0	187.5	6.0
1987	3,802.0	512.5	3,289.5	3,147.5	142.0	4.3
1988	4,075.9	527.7	3,548.2	3,392.5	155.7	4.4
1989	4,380.3	593.3	3,787.0	3,634.9	152.1	4.0
1990	4,673.8	623.3	4,050.5	3,880.6	170.0	4.2
1991	4,850.9	620.4	4,230.5	4,029.0	201.5	4.8
1992	5,144.9	644.8	4,500.2	4,261.5	238.7	5.3
1993	5,388.3	681.6	4,706.7	4,516.8	189.9	4.0

TABLE 2-3d
Personal Income: Outlays and Subcomponents

Billions of Current Dollars

Year	Outlays	Total Personal Consumption Expenditures	Durables Personal Consumption Expenditures	Nondurables Personal Consumption Expenditures	Services Personal Consumption Expenditures	Interest Paid	Transfers (Net)
1970	664.5	646.5	85.3	270.4	290.8	16.8	1.2
1971	719.4	700.3	97.2	283.3	319.8	17.8	1.3
1972	788.7	767.8	110.7	305.2	351.9	19.6	1.3
1973	872.0	848.1	124.1	339.6	384.5	22.4	1.4
1974	953.1	927.7	123.0	380.8	423.9	24.2	1.2
1975	1,050.6	1,024.9	134.3	416.0	474.5	24.5	1.2
1976	1,171.0	1,143.1	160.0	451.8	531.2	26.7	1.2
1977	1,303.4	1,271.5	182.6	490.4	598.4	30.7	1.2
1978	1,460.0	1,421.2	202.3	541.5	677.4	37.5	1.3
1979	1,629.6	1,583.7	214.2	613.3	756.2	44.5	1.4
1980	1,799.1	1,748.1	212.5	682.9	852.7	49.4	1.6
1981	1,982.6	1,926.2	228.5	744.2	953.5	54.6	1.8
1982	2,120.1	2,059.2	236.5	772.3	1,050.4	58.8	2.1
1983	2,325.1	2,257.5	275.0	817.8	1,164.7	65.7	1.8
1984	2,537.5	2,460.3	317.9	873.0	1,269.4	75.0	2.3
1985	2,753.7	2,667.4	352.9	919.4	1,395.1	83.6	2.7
1986	2,944.0	2,850.6	389.6	952.2	1,508.8	90.9	2.5
1987	3,147.5	3,052.2	403.7	1,011.1	1,637.4	92.3	3.0
1988	3,392.5	3,296.1	437.1	1,073.8	1,785.3	93.7	2.7
1989	3,634.9	3,523.1	459.4	1,149.5	1,914.2	103.0	8.9
1990	3,880.6	3,761.2	468.2	1,229.2	2,063.8	109.3	10.1
1991	4,029.0	3,906.4	457.8	1,257.9	2,190.7	112.2	10.5
1992	4,261.5	4,139.9	497.3	1,300.9	2,341.6	111.1	10.4
1993	4,516.8	4,391.8	537.9	1,350.0	2,503.9	114.0	11.0

NOTES FOR CHAPTER 2

1. More specifically, the relevant component is personal income excluding the transfer payments subcomponent, and it is in 1987 dollars.
2. US Department of Commerce, *Personal Income and Outlays: February 1994.*
3. James C Byrnes et al., "Monthly Estimates of Personal Income, Taxes, and Outlays," *Survey of Current Business,* US Department of Commerce, November 1979, p. 19.
4. Ibid.
5. Ibid., p. 22.
6. Ibid.
7. See any July *Survey of Current Business,* US Department of Commerce, for the table, "Imputations in the National Income and Product Accounts."
8. Byrnes et al., "Monthly Estimates," p. 23.
9. Carol S Carson, "GNP: An Overview of Source Data and Estimating Methods," *Survey of Current Business,* US Department of Commerce, July 1987, p. 105.
10. For initial estimates, the tax and nontax payments component is based on estimates of actual withholdings rather than on estimates of taxes owed. Changes in the withholding schedules for federal personal income taxes lowered personal taxes (and raised disposable personal income) in the second quarter of 1992 even though the tax rates were unchanged.
11. See the section on the retail sales control series in the chapter on retail sales.
12. The BEA fully depreciates all durables at the time of purchase but motor vehicle sales are probably the most prominent for economy watchers.
13. See R Mark Rogers, "Measuring the Personal Savings Rate: Some Technical Perspectives," *Economic Review,* Federal Reserve Bank of Atlanta, July/August 1990, p. 47.
14. Except for the personal saving rate that is expressed as a percentage, personal saving relative to disposable personal income.

BIBLIOGRAPHY

Byrnes, James C, et al. "Monthly Estimates of Personal Income, Taxes, and Outlays." *Survey of Current Business.* US Department of Commerce. November 1979, pp. 18–38.

Carson, Carol S. "GNP: An Overview of Source Data and Estimating Methods." *Survey of Current Business.* US Department of Commerce. July 1987, pp. 103–126.

Rogers, R Mark. "Measuring the Personal Savings Rate: Some Technical Perspectives." *Economic Review.* Federal Reserve Bank of Atlanta. July/August 1990, pp. 38–49.

US Department of Commerce. "Annual Revisions of the US National Income and Product Accounts." *Survey of Current Business.* July 1992, pp. 6–43.

CHAPTER 3

RETAIL SALES

The retail sales series is probably the most closely followed indicator used for judging the strength of the consumer sector. In popular analysis, it also tends to be used as a broad yardstick for the health of the economy. While this series is followed closely by economists and financial markets, it is not a direct component of gross domestic product (GDP). However, the data do figure prominently in the derivation of personal consumption expenditures within GDP even though there are substantial differences between the series. Importantly, the retail sales series does cover a broader portion of consumer spending than just department store sales as is often portrayed by the media.

The monthly retail sales series is released by the Commerce Department around the middle of the month following the reference month. These data are published as part of the Census Bureau's Current Business Reports. Retail sales data are actually released each month with the initial release entitled *Advance Monthly Retail Sales*. This is the midmonth release and contains only sales data. Generally the next working day, retail inventories are made available—but for the prior reference month. About two weeks later, retail sales data for the month prior to the advance sales data are released as part of the publication *Monthly Retail Trade: Sales and Inventories*. These numbers do differ somewhat from the earlier released data due to differences in the samples. The advance figures are based on about 3,250 establishments, while the later data are derived from the full monthly panel of about 12,500 sampling units. Sampling units can be multiestablishment companies, parts of companies, or single-establishments.

KEY CONCEPTS

Retail sales reflect sales of merchandise for cash or credit by establishments that sell primarily to the public.[1] Some wholesale and service transactions enter the data, since some establishments that are primarily engaged in retail trade also have some wholesale and service customers. Payments made on layaway and rentals also are part of the sales figures. Manufacturers rebates are not included while retailer rebates are.[2] Sales and excise taxes collected directly from customers and paid directly to a local, state, or federal tax agency are excluded. While the sales figures include wholesale and service transactions made by retailers, retail transactions made by manufacturers, wholesalers, or service establishments are not.

To be classified as a retail establishment, a store generally must have a fixed place of business and operate to sell to the general public. Firms may also buy or receive merchandise as well as act as a retailer, but must be considered a retailer by the industry. Some processing of products may occur as long as it is not the primary function. These characteristics are general; there are some exceptions.

Retail sales data are organized by kind-of-business or establishments rather than specifically by types of goods sold. Of course, many businesses, such as apparel stores, do sell a narrow range of goods, while others—such as department stores or drug stores—sell a wide variety of items. In effect, kind-of-business classifications are not the same as commodity classifications. An establishment is classified according to its primary source of receipts.

SURVEY METHODOLOGY AND REVISIONS

The Census Bureau asks approximately 28,000 retail businesses to report in the Current Retail Sales Survey. Of this number, about 10,000 are also asked to participate in the Current Retail Inventory Survey. About 2,700 large retail firms are asked to report their sales each month. The remaining 25,300 businesses, selected by Employer Identification (EI) number, are asked to report sales four times a year (about 8,400 in any given month). Of the 10,000 retailers selected to report sales and inventory values, about 700 large firms are asked to report each month, and 9,300 EI numbers are asked to report four times a year (3,100 per month). Each rotating panel reports data for the latest two months so that the reporting burden is lessened, but there also is overlap between panels. Each panel is representative of the overall survey sample with the entire sample stratified according to the most recent Census of Retail Trade, which occurs every five years. Updating of businesses in the survey—since some firms go out of business and new ones begin business—is based on information from the Internal Revenue Service and the Social Security Administration and from annual surveys.

The advance estimate for a given month is based primarily on a subsample of the initial panel's data. Because of time constraints in meeting the release deadline, data from only about 3,250 firms are used instead of the full sample of about 11,100 (8,400 rotating and 2,700 fixed). The advance retail sales estimate is derived by applying the ratio of current month sales-to-previous month sales from the advance subsample to the estimate of sales levels for the previous month based on the full sample. For example, if the advance subsample reports sales up 0.2 percent (reflecting a ratio of 1.002) and the preliminary estimate for June is $1,000 million, then the July advance estimate would be $1,002 million.

The use of a small subsample does play a role in the relatively large revisions that often occur following the initial estimate. However, the major contributing factor is likely the fact that the initial panel's figures for their own firms' sales data often are estimates, since they generally do not yet have access to the book value of sales when their reports to Census are due. When the book value data are not available, the respondent is asked to provide an estimate for the full month. Importantly, the retail firms with the largest impact on sales are included in both surveys, thereby reducing the effect of the smaller sample on revisions in data from the advance report to the preliminary report. The majority of reported sales for the advance report are based on records of the full month or the sum of four or five weeks.

Preliminary and final estimates (second and third estimates) incorporate full panel samples rather than the 3,250 reporting unity subsample. These figures are weighted averages of data reported for those months and estimates based on ratios to earlier reported months. A small portion of respondents also report estimated sales for the preliminary estimates. Nonetheless, given that a high percentage of reported sales are based on actual data for both the preliminary and final estimates, the responses from a second rotating panel of retailers likely contributes more to the revision from the preliminary estimate to the final estimate of monthly sales.

Major Retail Sales Groups

The major groups (kinds of business) in retail sales are based on classifications in the 1987 edition of the Standard Industrial Classification (SIC) manual. Table 3–3 shows the major categories generally followed by financial analysts. Brief descriptions follow below. Chart 3–1 also gives some perspective of the importance of each category.

Each kind of business category is defined by its primary activity; there often are many other types of sales incorporated in a given component. Some of the

CHART 3–1
Retail Sales (Percent Shares in 1993)

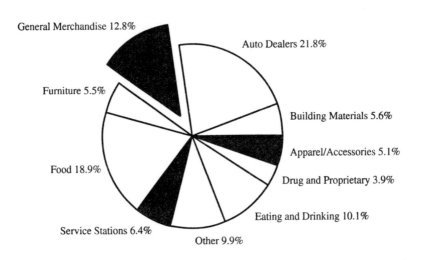

Source: US Department of Commerce.

more important examples of this are automotive dealers, service stations, and drug stores. This is elaborated more below.

The **building materials group** includes building materials (such as lumber, paint, glass, and wallpaper), hardware, nursery stock, lawn and garden supplies, and mobile homes. Some of these establishments also sell housewares, household appliances, and, to a small degree, electronics.

Automobile dealers primarily sell new motor vehicles, but a significant portion of receipts also come from sales of used cars, boats, recreational trailers, motorcycles, auto accessories, and tires. Some stores classified as auto accessory stores also sell a wide variety of goods such as household appliances, electronics, sporting goods, housewares, and hardware. In each case, however, the majority of the sales are automotive related.

Furniture group stores include stores primarily selling furniture (including sleep equipment), floor covering, household appliances, and radio and television, music, electronics, and computers to the general public.

The **miscellaneous durable goods stores group** includes all retail durable goods stores not classified in the building materials, automotive, or furniture groups. This includes used merchandise stores, sporting goods stores and bicycle shops, book stores, jewelry stores, hobby shops, camera and photographic supply stores, gift, novelty and souvenir shops, luggage and leather goods stores, optical goods stores, and "miscellaneous retail stores not classified elsewhere."

Under the nondurables umbrella, the closest followed series is department store sales, but this is part of the major group known as **general merchandise group** stores. These establishments sell a broad line of merchandise. Stores in this group include department stores, variety stores, and miscellaneous general merchandise stores. Department stores have been accounting for the vast majority of sales in this group. Mail-order houses, direct selling establishments, and a few other related kinds of businesses are no longer classified under general merchandise but are now under miscellaneous durable goods stores.

The Census Bureau officially defines department stores based on the following:

Establishments normally employing 50 people or more, having sales of apparel and soft goods combined amounting to 20 percent or more of total sales, and selling each of the following lines of merchandise:

1. Furniture, home furnishings, appliances, and radio, and TV sets.
2. A general line of apparel for the family.
3. Household linens and dry goods.

To qualify as a department store, sales of each of the lines listed above must be less than 80 percent of total store sales. An establishment with total sales of $10 million or more is classified as a department store even if sales of one of the merchandise lines listed above exceed the maximum percent of total sales, provided that the combined sales of the other two groups are $1 million or more.[3]

The **food stores group** includes retail stores that primarily sell food for home preparation and consumption. This definition excludes restaurants, which fall under the category "eating and drinking places." All but a very small percentage of food store sales are from grocery stores. Minor food store components are meat and fish (seafood) markets and retail bakeries. Very minor components include fruit stores and vegetable markets; candy, nut, and confectionery stores; dairy products stores; and "other miscellaneous" food stores.

The **apparel and accessory stores group** covers stores that primarily sell clothing and related accessories. The major components are men's and boys' clothing and furnishings stores, women's ready-to-wear stores, women's accessory and specialty stores, children's and infants' wear stores, family clothing stores, shoe stores, and miscellaneous apparel and accessory stores.

Eating and drinking places are establishments that primarily sell *prepared* foods and drinks. Naturally, the two broad components of this group are eating places and drinking places. Under eating places, further classification is based on establishments selling a full menu of items versus a limited line of refreshments and prepared foods. Restaurants have full menus, have waiter or waitress service, and have seating for at least 15 customers. Fast-food stores are not restaurants by technical definition but fall under the category "refreshment places." Drinking establishments are defined by the primary activity of selling alcoholic beverages for consumption on the premises.

The **drugstores and proprietary stores** group consists almost entirely of drug stores by sales volume. Drugstores sell prescription drugs as well as many other related goods. These stores are not defined by prescription drug sales being the primary source of receipts but rather by trade designation. Proprietary stores do not sell prescription drugs but sell items such as health and beauty aids.

Liquor stores mainly sell packaged alcoholic beverages.

ANALYZING THE MONTHLY REPORT: KEY INSIGHTS

Overview and Key Components

The nonfinancial media usually focus on department store sales, since this series typifies the concept of retail sales often held by the public. However, department store sales are only one of several major components. The retail sales series truly covers a wide array of consumer spending, and analysis of retail sales should examine all major components to ascertain the health of the consumer sector. Nonetheless, some components are more important than others. Of course, sales by auto dealers are important because of their volume and because of their cyclical nature. Additionally, department store sales, while not a majority, are still a sizable component. But a more appropriate series to follow for department store type sales is the (GAF) series, as discussed later. For projecting personal consumption components of durables and nondurables within real GDP, an analyst should become familiar with the concept of the retail control series. All of these issues and others are discussed as individual topics below.

In the overall economy, retail sales have much the same role as personal consumption expenditures, except for the definitional differences: for example, there is no basic services component in retail sales. However, retail sales, along with data for wholesale sales and manufacturers' shipments, are better suited for tracking inventory and sales flows than are personal consumption expenditures. Retail sales, along with the above-mentioned series, are collected by the Census Bureau on a similar statistical basis. Hence, retail sales data should be closely watched along with inventories (and even exports and imports) in order to project trends in production. Now, what are key components to watch?

The Auto Component

The auto sales component of retail sales is fairly sizable. Over the 1980s, auto sales averaged 20 percent of total retail sales. As such, analysts have paid close attention in trying to interpret trends in this component. As is often the case, economists have looked to another data source—unit new auto sales, in this case—to gain insight. However, the typical methodology used is not appropriate given the way these two data series are derived.

Typically, unit new auto sales and the auto component of retail sales move together on a monthly basis. When they do not, analysts often are quick to point out that the divergence is due to significant price changes. For example, if unit sales rise by perhaps 3 percent one month while the auto component of retail sales is unchanged, the presumption is that auto dealers cut prices sharply to get the increase in sales volume. This, in fact, may have occurred but cannot be proven with the two data series. These series are compiled by two completely different sources, and the coverage of each series is significantly different.

First, the unit new sales data come from the American Automobile Manufacturers Association (AAMA) (formerly the Motor Vehicle Manufacturers Association or MVMA) in Detroit, Michigan. The data are from an industry sample that is very close to being the full universe; that is, the data do not just represent all sales; they are all sales, at least for all practical purposes. There is almost no measurement error or sampling error.[4]

In contrast, the auto component of retail sales comes from survey data collected by the Census Bureau. As is the case with any data derived from small sample surveys, there is sampling error. For any given month, sampling error can cause the variations in sales that often are alleged to be caused by dealer changes in prices.

The second factor that precludes any reliable monthly comparison between the unit auto data and Census series is that the auto component of retail sales is actually sales *by* auto dealers and includes sales other than automobiles. The biggest difference is that auto dealer sales figures include parts and repair. In recent years, these have become an increasingly larger share of dealers' sales. Auto dealers' sales also include items such as used autos, recreational vehicles (RVs), recreational and utility trailers, motorcycles, and boats. Automobile repairs are included, but only if the shops are maintained by an establishment selling new cars. These other items are not individually broken down in the figures reported to Census by auto dealers.

For two very different reasons, rarely can any significant price inferences be made between the two series on a monthly basis. To do so risks attributing sales with a trend that does not exist. As an aside there are relatively easy methods of looking at price movement for autos.

Although the data usually come out a few days later, price trends for autos are best derived from consumer price data. Also, producer price data for motor vehicles come out at about the same time as retail sales and can be used to corroborate any suspicions about price trends associated with the two auto sales series.

There is one important inference that can be made by comparing these two auto sales series. As is discussed in the GDP chapter, the Commerce Department uses the unit new auto sales data in its personal consumption estimate for durables. Should the unit auto data be noticeably stronger (or weaker) than the auto component in retail sales, then the unit sales generally suggest that the durables personal consumption in constant dollars will be stronger (or weaker) for that month than implied by the Census auto sales data. This type of analysis is further elaborated in the retail control discussion that follows.

The Links between General Merchandise, Department Store, Chain Store, and GAF Sales

The common public perception of retail sales is often of department store sales. By now, one should realize that department store sales are only a small portion of retail sales. In 1993, this component's share of the total was only 9.7 percent. Of course, the general merchandise category is slightly broader than the department store definition, since variety stores and some miscellaneous general merchandise stores also are included. See Chart 3–1 for the relative importance of this sales group.

Even though general merchandise is a small component of retail sales, analysts often focus on this concept for forecasting purposes. Various national department stores (unofficial definition) release their monthly sales figures to the public about 10 days prior to the release of Census' retail sales data. These data come from firms such as Sears, Wal-Mart, Kmart, J. C. Penney, and others.

The difficulties in using these data to forecast retail sales are many: (1) the announced percent changes from these so-called chain stores are year-over-year, not month-to-month; (2) the levels are not seasonally adjusted; (3) some firms open new stores or close old ones, and "same store sales" are not always available; and, of course, (4) general merchandise sales are a small part of retail sales. Incidentally, the media usually refers to these figures as chain store sales. However, a number of these firms, such as Kmart and Wal-Mart, come under the "discount department stores" subcomponent rather than the Census definition of national chain department stores. Common usage and Census definitions differ.

Since the concept of department store sales is somewhat ingrained in the public's consciousness, there is a broader definition that covers this. This is the GAF category defined below. Simply put, GAF data represent sales from stores that specialize in department store types of merchandise. GAF includes *general merchandise stores, apparel and accessories, furniture group sales,* and miscellaneous shopping goods stores. Even with this definition, this popular concept of retail sales was still a little less than one-fourth of the total of officially defined retail sales in 1993.

TABLE 3–1
Differences between Retail Sales and PCEs[5]

Components in Retail Sales but Not in PCEs:

1. Survey estimates of new and used motor vehicles and parts sales, including imports, business sales, and government purchases.
2. Building materials, hardware, garden supplies, and mobile home dealer sales.

Components in PCEs but Not in Retail Sales:

1. Services.
2. Unit new motor vehicle sales from manufacturers data.
3. Dealers' margins on used car sales (which are implicitly part of used car sales in the retail sales series).
4. Gasoline and oil sales, based on Department of Transportation and Department of Labor data.
5. Food and fuel produced and consumed on farms.
6. Food and clothing received as compensation in kind.
7. Expenditures abroad by U.S. residents.
8. Personal remittances in kind to foreigners.

The Retail Control Series and PCEs

One of the primary objectives of many money market economists in analyzing the retail sales report is to derive an estimate for personal consumption expenditures (PCEs) for the same month as the latest retail sales data. The PCE data are released by the Commerce Department about two weeks later. Economists usually remove the auto component and substitute some version of unit new auto sales to "move" the forecast for monthly PCEs. However, the appropriate mover for PCEs is known as the retail control series.

The retail control series concept is based on two considerations. First, not all retail sales series conceptually apply to personal consumption expenditures. Secondly, some key PCE series are estimated with source data other than retail sales.

In terms of matching concepts, retail sales, of course, can only be used to estimate portions of goods PCEs. Also, retail sales data include some components that are less related to consumer expenditures and are more related to residential investment. The series for building materials and supply stores are excluded in the retail control concept because they reflect homeownership costs and are tied more to residential investment than to personal consumption. This group includes building materials stores, hardware stores, garden supply stores, and mobile home dealers.

In the early official definition of retail control, auto dealers and service station sales *also* were omitted, since they were estimated for their respective PCE components with source data separate from retail sales. However, the definition has changed somewhat in recent years. Over the 1980s, service station sales had a noticeable and rising share of nongasoline sales. Since service station sales are not broken down between gasoline and nongasoline sales, the overall service station sales figures have been used to move the nongasoline components of service station sales for PCEs. Currently, the retail control series does not exclude service station sales.

Further elaboration is useful for explaining how the auto dealers component is treated to obtain the control series. First, there is a broadly defined auto dealers series. The broad series is the sum of the narrow series plus two other subcomponents— "other auto dealers" and "auto and home supply stores." These last two subcomponents are part of the control series, while it is the narrowly defined auto dealers series that is excluded. Other auto dealers primarily are stores that sell motorcycles, boats, and RVs. For the advance release of retail sales data, the complicating factor is that only the broad auto dealers component and the subcomponent for auto and home supply stores are available. Therefore, the BEA must use a ratio method (from earlier data) to estimate the narrowly defined auto dealers component for exclusion until more detailed data become available. Table 3–1 details some of the differences between retail sales and PCEs.

KEY SOURCES OF MONTHLY VOLATILITY

Retail sales are affected by a number of factors any given month. These are variability in the significant auto dealer component, various price factors, and seasonal considerations. One of the problems with the auto dealer component is rather straightforward—the sample size is small. Some variability in this component is due to sampling difficulties rather than to other technical factors or changes in demand. Other factors affecting auto dealer sales are discussed in the next section.

Price Factors

In interpreting the "real" strength in each month's retail sales report, price is always a factor. An analyst must always be aware if an industry is having greater- or less-than-average discounting in price. The auto industry has long been known to have off-and-on rebates and other discounts. In turn, the practice of looking at nonauto sales has been adopted partly in order to "remove" the auto industry's volatile price behavior. However, some other retail sales components have very erratic and sharp price movements.

The two primary components that have this price behavior are apparel store and service station sales. Apparel sales have very strong seasonal price swings, and if inventories are out of line with desired levels, prices can change dramatically, thereby making estimates of real sales difficult to ascertain by forecasters. If sales are stronger than normal early in a clothing season, a normal amount of discounting may not take place late in the season. This will push clothing prices up on a seasonally adjusted basis. Also, the timing of the introduction of seasonal clothing can vary from year to year, and earlier (or later) introduction can also cause large monthly swings in prices and complicate making estimates for real sales.

The other key series is for service station sales, which are primarily gasoline sales. Its price volatility also is high and is due to relatively inelastic demand and supplies that can be quickly affected by political decisions within Organization of Petroleum Exporting Countries (OPEC), strikes, and temporary shutdowns at refineries for maintenance. These price considerations mask not only the real strength in gasoline sales but also in broader retail sales aggregates such as non-durables and nonauto sales. Coincidentally, apparel sales are also under non-durables, which means that price effects can play a large role in monthly movement in that broad category. In essence, price considerations for these two components—apparel and gasoline—mean that nonauto retail sales should not be taken as an accurate barometer of consumer spending without first examining and discounting price factors in at least these subcomponents.

Seasonal Considerations

Retail sales are very seasonal for many components. Deviations from average patterns can lead to sharp, month-to-month changes in the data once the data are put into seasonally adjusted form. Seasonal adjustment assumes stability in seasonal patterns, but this is not always the case. Abnormal weather during the Christmas selling season can dramatically affect seasonally adjusted data, since volume is relatively strong this time of year. For example, early snow-storms in November in the Northeast or rain storms in other regions can lead to weak sales that month and tremendous "catch-up" the next month. Warm weather in January can depress winter apparel sales or an early summer could really boost clothing sales in the spring. Finally, sales around Easter and Thanks-giving are difficult to seasonally adjust, since sales are typically relatively strong in many components, but the date of these holidays, particularly Easter, varies from year to year.

RETAIL INVENTORY DATA

The *Monthly Retail Trade* publication also includes data on inventories and inventory-to-sales ratios by kinds of business categories. Inventories are estimated on an end-of-month basis. An end-of-period basis is standard for inventory data rather than period averages. The inventory data come from a subsample of the monthly sales sample. However, inventories are valued at cost for both inventories on hand at retail stores and at warehouses that maintain merchandise primarily for distribution to retail stores within the same organization.[6]

REGIONAL DATA

Monthly Retail Trade also includes moderately detailed monthly sales figures by Census regions. For selected large states, monthly sales figures are published for totals, durables for the states where the sampling error is sufficiently low, nondurables, department store sales, and the GAF total. For specific metropolitan areas, department store sales and GAF totals are available. Some metropolitan areas also have data for nondurables. None of the regional data are published in seasonally adjusted form due to the relatively high level of imputation and sampling error. These regional and subregional series are first available in the publication that is released about eight weeks after the end of the reference month.

TABLE 3–2
Analyzing the News Release: Key Questions

- How were sales, excluding autos?
- How do unit new auto sales and light truck sales add to the picture?
- Did price changes affect apparel store and service station sales?
- Were previous months, especially for the control series, revised significantly?
- Did atypical weather affect sales—especially for apparel, department store, and hardware sales?
- Are changes in housing starts affecting sales of hardware and building materials as well as furniture and household furnishings?

TABLE 3–3
Retail Sales: Selected Major Sales Groups

Annual Data, Billions of Dollars

	1980	1981	1982	1983	1984
Total	957	1,038	1,069	1,170	1,287
Total excluding autos	793	856	876	940	1,014
Durable goods stores	299	324	336	391	454
Building materials, hardware, garden supply, and mobile home dealers	51	52	51	59	67
Automotive dealers	164	182	192	230	273
Furniture group stores	44	47	47	55	61
Nondurable goods stores	658	714	733	779	832
General merchandise	109	121	125	136	150
Food group	220	236	246	256	272
Gasoline service stations	94	103	97	103	108
Apparel and accessory stores	49	54	56	60	64
Eating and drinking places	90	98	105	113	121
Drug and proprietary stores	31	34	36	41	44
	1985	**1986**	**1987**	**1988**	**1989**
Total	1,375	1,450	1,541	1,657	1,761
Total excluding autos	1,072	1,123	1,198	1,285	1,376
Durable goods stores	498	541	576	630	659
Building materials, hardware, garden supply, and mobile home dealers	71	77	83	92	94
Automotive dealers	303	326	343	372	385
Furniture group stores	68	76	78	86	93
Nondurable goods stores	877	909	965	1,028	1,103
General merchandise	159	169	182	193	207
Food group	285	297	309	327	349
Gasoline service stations	113	102	105	110	121
Apparel and accessory stores	70	76	79	85	92
Eating and drinking places	128	139	153	168	177
Drug and proprietary stores	47	51	54	58	63

Annual Totals, Billions of Dollars

	1990	1991	1992	1993
Total	1,849	1,863	1,959	2,082
Total excluding autos	1,462	1,492	1,555	1,627
Durable goods stores	671	653	707	785
Building materials, hardware, garden supply, and mobile home dealers	97	95	106	116
Automotive dealers	386	371	404	454
Furniture group stores	95	96	103	114
Nondurable goods stores	1,177	1,209	1,252	1,297
General merchandise	217	228	249	267
Food group	372	379	382	392
Gasoline service stations	136	134	132	133
Apparel and accessory stores	96	97	104	106
Eating and drinking places	188	194	201	211
Drug and proprietary stores	71	76	78	81

Source: US Department of Commerce.

NOTES FOR CHAPTER 3

1. Definitions of terms are based primarily on information from the Appendix in *Monthly Retail Trade.*
2. Since the respondents are asked to report their operating receipts, they should include the amounts that they receive from their customers. If the customers get some of their costs back from the manufacturer because of a rebate, the retailer is not involved in that transaction. If the retailer offers a rebate, that in effect is a reduction in the amount of the operating receipts.
3. *Monthly Retail Trade: Sales and Inventories, December 1992*, Appendix E, p. E–3.
4. As discussed in the chapter on unit new auto sales, the 10-day sales do include estimates for Chrysler, although full-month data are actual counts from the manufacturer.
5. R Mark Rogers, "Retail Sales: A Primer," *Economic Review*, Federal Reserve Bank of Atlanta, April 1985, p. 29. This table differs from the earlier published version, since retail service station sales had been excluded previously from PCEs to allow substitution of another source. Service station sales from retail sales are now part of the PCE control series.
6. *Monthly Retail Trade*, Appendix A, p. A–4.

BIBLIOGRAPHY

Rogers, R Mark. "Retail Sales: A Primer." *Economic Review*. Federal Reserve Bank of Atlanta. April 1985, pp. 28–33.

U.S. Department of Commerce. *Monthly Retail Trade: Sales and Inventories, December 1992.*

CHAPTER 4

UNIT NEW AUTO SALES AND OTHER RELATED MOTOR VEHICLE DATA

The unit new auto sales series is the primary indicator of the strength of the auto sector. Autos are important in tracking the economy because over the business cycle, changes in auto demand can be quite dramatic. Sales are very interest-rate sensitive and also are affected by consumer confidence, which is a general barometer of the economy. Essentially, auto sales is a leading indicator of the economy because of these factors. Also, unit new auto sales are important as an economic indicator because of the series use in the auto component in personal consumption expenditures. It is less well known, but these data also end up in producers' durable equipment and in other GDP components. Auto sales also provide an indication of the sustainability of auto production levels.

In addition to being a leading indicator, auto production is still a sizable part of the US economy. In terms of real GDP, auto output's share peaked at 3.7 percent in 1969, but was still very significant with a 2.2 percent share in 1992. Combined auto and truck output reached 4.8 percent of real GDP in 1977 and is still sizable with a 3.6 percent share in 1992.[1] Swings in auto output can be sharp and cause noticeable changes in growth rates for real GDP for any given quarter. Understanding these effects on the economy is the primary reason for following auto sales. Other related data on the motor vehicle industry also are useful. Of secondary importance are data for auto production and inventories. As is discussed in the next section, these monthly series are not always consistently defined relative to each other. Finally, in recent years, sales of light trucks have increased and warrant much more attention than in the past.

UNIT NEW AUTO SALES DATA

For the automobile industry, the monthly data most closely followed by the general economics community are the series referred to as unit new auto sales. Data are released each month by the BEA around the third business day of the month for the previous month's sales figures. While the BEA unit new auto sales data are frequently quoted in the news media, the only published government source is the *Survey of Current Business* in the table for transportation equipment. Data for this series come primarily from the American Automobile Manufacturers Association or AAMA (formerly the Motor Vehicle Manufacturers Association or MVMA) and *Ward's Automotive Reports.* The BEA combines the various components and seasonally adjusts the data. The AAMA is a trade association for US domestic auto producers and is based in Detroit; *Ward's* is a commercial, for-profit publisher of automotive industry news and data. *Ward's* is also based in Detroit.

As an overview of BEA's unit new auto sales data, data for domestic sales come primarily from the AAMA, while information on import sales is reported by *Ward's. Ward's,* as an industry news source, also tracks domestic sales that are frequently seen in many of their statistics. With domestic sales, the AAMA is generally the original data source, while *Ward's* is the original collection point for import sales across the United States.

Data initially are released only for totals and a breakdown between domestics and imports. Sales of domestic units are closely watched to determine if manufacturers need to raise or lower production levels to keep up with sales and to keep inventories at desired quantities. Unit sales also are divided into components by sector: consumer, business, and government. However, these components are published with a lag of two months. This breakdown is based on estimates using the privately compiled Polk auto registration data.[2] However, early figures for the consumer, business, and government sectors are available at the end of the month of the initial release as a by-product of GDP component derivation. These numbers are available by subscription to unpublished computer tables produced by the BEA. Before Polk registration data become available, these sectoral expenditure components are derived from industry contacts, trends, and a variety of miscellaneous sources.

For the GDP accounts, new unit auto sales data are used in the motor vehicle components for (1) personal consumption of durables, (2) purchases of producers' durable equipment, and (3) government purchases. This is in contrast to the typical assumption by many economy watchers that these sales essentially are to consumers only. In fact, there is not perfect timing in the changes in overall unit auto sales and the relevant personal consumption component because the consumer sector's share in unit new sales does vary. In particular, business purchases for fleets can change sharply—especially since US auto producers have taken large ownership positions in major car rental firms.

Leased vehicles create special problems in allocating sales between consumer and business sectors. Sales are allocated according to *Polk* registration data, and leased sales are still registered to businesses even though the vehicles are for consumer use. Essentially, cars leased by consumers are counted as sales to the business sector and show up in producers' durable equipment in the GDP accounts. This also means that shifts in preferences by car buyers between leasing and purchasing affect the relative strength of autos in consumer durables expenditures compared to business investment in producers' durable equipment. However, the monthly value of motor vehicle leases to consumers is allocated to personal consumption of services.

BEA's domestic sales are for what the industry refers to as sales from North American production. For some time, General Motors, Ford, and Chrysler have had plants in Canada and Mexico for US makes sold in the United States. Currently, Honda and Toyota also have foreign name plates that have been transplanted to the United States and subsequently have had some production shifted to Canada. Sales of these are counted as "domestics" because auto producers primarily keep sales data in terms of North American operations.

Ten-Day Sales

Prior to the end of 1993, domestic motor vehicle manufacturers reported 10-day sales figures. In early December 1993, Ford and General Motors announced they would no longer report sales figures on a 10-day basis, ending nearly 40 years of economic tradition. Chrysler stopped reporting these intramonth data at the end of 1990 (although *Ward's* continued to estimate the 10-day sales of Chrysler). Major auto manufacturers cited volatility in the data as the reason for ending the 10-day reports.

For historical reference, as a precursor to the monthly sales figures, industry analysts watched the 10-day sales figures that were compiled by *Ward's* for domestics only. Domestic sales include "transplants"—foreign makes produced in the United States.[3] The 10-day figures were based on each month being divided into three sales periods with the first two having 10 days each and with the final period of the month consisting of the remaining days of the month. The last period can be as short as 8 days or as long as 11, but for a given month, they are always the same except for February during leap year.

Seasonal adjustment procedures removed most of the differences in sales rates caused by different lengths in the final sales period for specific months. However, differences often occurred in the number of business days per period due to changes in when weekends occur each month and due to changes in holidays such as Easter and Thanksgiving, which do not have a set month and/or day of month for observance. Despite the use of sophisticated seasonal adjustment programs, these factors made the sales data volatile. This was further compounded by the shortness of the 10-day period, which could be significantly affected by random events such as unseasonable weather. For example, over such a short time span, special promotions (rebates, subsidized interest rates, etc.) can cause significant differences.

Consequently, comparisons of sales with a 10-day period date were somewhat unreliable, especially in the short run. Typically, 10-day data were compared on a year-ago basis with year-ago comparisons often using unadjusted data. Even though year-ago percentages frequently appeared in headlines in the news media, they did not always indicate the latest direction in sales. For this, the more appropriate comparison was with period-to-period data in seasonally adjusted form. Given the volatility of the 10-day sales numbers, determination of current trends had to be based on several periods—perhaps three to four weeks of seasonally adjusted data.

The monthly averages of the 10-day sales for domestics did not quite match the BEA monthly domestics figures. First, Chrysler stopped reporting 10-day sales in 1991, and *Ward's* then estimated Chrysler's sales. Not all transplant producers reported 10-day sales either, and *Ward's* estimated their sales also. Second, beginning in 1989, *Ward's* shifted some vehicles from the light truck category that previously were considered passenger cars. The BEA did not make this change, and, consequently, BEA's figures for domestic passenger cars tended to run slightly higher.

Truck Sales

Over the 1980s, truck sales became more important to the consumer sector as pickup trucks became more popular; this was also the case for minivans. Truck's share of motor vehicle's contribution to GDP has risen from about 24 percent in 1970 to 39 percent in 1992. To properly follow the impact of the motor vehicle sector on the economy, one must watch sales of trucks as well as passenger cars.

Data for light-weight truck sales actually cover both trucks and buses weighing 10,000 pounds and under. The series officially published by the BEA is "trucks and buses, retail sales, 0–10,000 lbs GVW⁴, domestics" (and a matching series for imports). Figures are both seasonally adjusted as well as not seasonally adjusted and appear in the Commerce Department's *Survey of Current Business* in the transportation equipment section of the statistical tables. Sales of imported trucks were first published in the August 1990 issue of *Survey of Current Business*, although domestics had been published earlier.

In contrast to the passenger car data, seasonally adjusted truck data are not annualized and are in thousands of units rather than millions. Therefore, in order to compare the truck data with unit figures for new passenger car sales, the seasonally adjusted truck figures must be multiplied by 12 and then divided by 1,000. This gives sales in millions of units, seasonally adjusted, annualized.

As is the case for passenger car data, unit sales for light trucks and buses are used not just in national income and product accounts (NIPA) estimates for personal consumption, but also for investment in producers' durable equipment and to a lesser extent for government purchases and exports.

In the *Survey of Current Business*, the BEA also publishes retail unit sales figures for trucks weighing 10,001 pounds and over. Retail inventories for domestic trucks are available as well as factory sales (in contrast to the retail unit sales) from US plants.

PRODUCTION DATA

Monthly output figures for motor vehicles that are comparable to the unit sales data are most readily available from the Federal Reserve Board of Governors as part of the monthly industrial production releases. In addition to the standard indexes based for the year 1987 being set equal to 100, data are also available in terms of annualized production rates for units of vehicles. The most often cited terminology is assembly rate, which is in millions of units annualized and seasonally adjusted. Production rates for both passenger cars and trucks can be compared to seasonally adjusted annualized sales rates to see if unit production rates are sustainable. That is, one can see if production has been running above or below a sales pace that might be considered sustainable given the current economic conditions—including inventory levels and import penetration.

Federal Reserve assembly rates for passenger cars are released with the monthly industrial production report while truck data are unpublished but are generally available from electronic data vendors.

The Federal Reserve assembly rates average a little below the BEA sales rates because the Fed data are US production and exclude Canadian and Mexican output of domestic makes. *Ward's* also publishes weekly production figures for US and Canadian car and truck output. The BEA unit sales data cover North American operations.

The BEA also releases unpublished monthly data (in computer printout form) for unit production rates on a BEA basis. The BEA data differ from Federal Reserve data primarily in terms of the seasonal factors used. Both series are based on the same monthly reports from auto manufacturers. The unpublished data (which can be subscribed to) also contain the Federal Reserve production figures as well as additional BEA estimates for nominal and real-dollar values for output and unit and dollar values for sales.

For the current quarter and upcoming quarter, *Ward's* publishes production schedules that are announced by the manufacturers. While the production schedules frequently change during each quarter, they do provide good information on the near-term direction for motor vehicle production.

TABLE 4–1
Analyzing the News Release: Key Questions

- How do the latest auto sales figures compare to recent months?
- Are data being compared on the same statistical basis, that is, units sold on a seasonally adjusted basis?
- How strong were domestic sales compared to import sales?
- Are domestic sales in line with production rates?
- Were recent sales affected by special incentives either for the current month or previous month?
- How strong were light truck sales?
- Was there a shift from traditional auto to light trucks, which include vans and minivans?
- Has there been a shift between sales to businesses versus sales to consumers in recent months?
- Has a shift between sales to consumers or businesses been affected by changes in preferences for leasing by consumers, since leases remain counted as business purchases?
- Have motor vehicle sales been affected by fleet sales to car rental agencies?

TABLE 4–2
Unit New Auto Sales

			Millions, Annual Averages			
	Total	Domestic Origin	Import Origin	Consumer Purchases	Business Purchases	Government Purchases
1970	8.402	7.119	1.283	6.252	2.056	0.094
1971	10.228	8.662	1.566	7.611	2.510	0.107
1972	10.873	9.253	1.621	8.230	2.523	0.120
1973	11.350	9.589	1.762	8.423	2.811	0.116
1974	8.774	7.362	1.412	6.084	2.565	0.126
1975	8.538	6.951	1.587	5.907	2.508	0.123
1976	9.994	8.492	1.502	7.036	2.822	0.137
1977	11.046	8.971	2.075	7.657	3.253	0.136
1978	11.164	9.164	2.000	7.540	3.474	0.150
1979	10.559	8.230	2.329	7.172	3.246	0.141
1980	8.982	6.581	2.401	6.100	2.758	0.124
1981	8.534	6.209	2.326	5.639	2.781	0.114
1982	7.980	5.758	2.221	5.288	2.580	0.101
1983	9.179	6.793	2.386	6.047	3.024	0.108
1984	10.390	7.951	2.439	6.590	3.661	0.139
1985	11.038	8.205	2.833	7.130	3.773	0.135
1986	11.450	8.215	3.235	7.608	3.713	0.128
1987	10.246	7.066	3.180	6.674	3.437	0.135
1988	10.634	7.539	3.095	6.801	3.694	0.138
1989	9.911	7.084	2.827	6.374	3.410	0.127
1990	9.498	6.897	2.601	5.805	3.567	0.139
1991	8.387	6.137	2.250	4.550	3.738	0.098
1992	8.384	6.277	2.107	4.557	3.682	0.113
1993	8.713	6.743	1.970	4.676	3.931	0.107

Source: Bureau of Economic Analysis, US Department of Commerce. Data are averages of monthly seasonally adjusted annualized sales rates.

TABLE 4–3
Unit New Auto and Light Truck Sales

	Total Autos and Light Trucks	Total Domestic Autos and Light Trucks	Total Light Trucks	Domestic Light Trucks	Imported Light Trucks
1970	na	8.528	na	1.408	na
1971	na	10.362	na	1.700	na
1972	na	11.369	na	2.116	na
1973	na	12.102	na	2.513	na
1974	na	9.538	na	2.176	na
1975	na	9.006	na	2.055	na
1976	12.966	11.225	2.972	2.733	0.239
1977	14.486	12.087	3.440	3.116	0.323
1978	14.973	12.633	3.809	3.469	0.340
1979	13.768	10.970	3.209	2.740	0.469
1980	11.192	8.312	2.211	1.730	0.480
1981	10.564	7.794	2.030	1.585	0.444
1982	10.364	7.729	2.384	1.971	0.413
1983	12.120	9.273	2.941	2.480	0.461
1984	14.197	11.150	3.807	3.198	0.609
1985	15.441	11.838	4.403	3.634	0.769
1986	16.056	11.891	4.606	3.676	0.930
1987	14.842	10.843	4.596	3.777	0.819
1988	15.430	11.730	4.795	4.190	0.605
1989	14.532	11.201	4.621	4.117	0.504
1990	13.854	10.848	4.356	3.951	0.405
1991	12.304	9.736	3.917	3.599	0.318
1992	12.829	10.490	4.445	4.214	0.231
1993	13.886	11.733	5.173	4.990	0.183

Source: Bureau of Economic Analysis.

NOTES FOR CHAPTER 4

1. *Economic Indicators: The Motor Vehicle's Role in the US Economy, 4th Quarter 1992,* Motor Vehicle Manufacturers Association of the United States, Inc., Detroit, Michigan, p. 15. Data also sourced from the BEA.
2. R L Polk & Co., Statistical Services Division, Detroit, Michigan.
3. Monthly BEA data for domestics also include transplants.
4. Gross vehicle weight.

BIBLIOGRAPHY

Economic Indicators: The Motor Vehicle's Role in the US Economy. Motor Vehicle Manufacturers Association of the United States, Inc., Detroit, Michigan, 4th Quarter 1991 and 4th quarter 1992.

CHAPTER 5

THE CONSUMER PRICE INDEX

The consumer price index (CPI) is one of the more important economic indicators published by the government, since this series provides one of the broadest, most followed measures of inflation. It is used as a tool for analysis for both monetary and fiscal policy. Financial markets track this series and use it and expectations for its trend to help price financial securities. Importantly, businesses and labor unions use the CPI for contract escalation clauses, and the federal government uses it similarly for Social Security payments. Federal income tax brackets and standard deductions are also affected by the movement of the CPI.

Inflation as measured by the CPI is important from an analyst's perspective largely because expected inflation affects the prices of financial securities—notably bond prices. In particular, changes in bond prices are, in effect, changes in interest rates. If expected inflation rises, financial markets generally bid bond prices lower. For a given, promised dollar return in the future for a bond, a lower price is equivalent to a higher interest rate. Essentially, investors want to protect their real rates of return, and, when expected inflation rises, investors demand a higher rate of return for new issues of debt.

For holders of existing debt, CPI inflation data are important because changes in interest rates for new debt affect the market value of old debt. If old debt is sold on the market for cash, the interest rate on previously issued debt must be competitive with returns on new issues. This means that when interest rates rise on new debt, rates rise on existing debt when placed on the market; prices for existing debt fall. The importance of inflation data, particularly the closely watched CPI, is that rising inflation cuts into the market value of old debt, which is assets, if interest rates are rising at the same time. Typically, this is the case as investors seek to maintain real rates of return.

The CPI is a measure of the average change in the prices paid by urban consumers for a fixed market basket of goods and services. Currently, the CPI includes over 360 categories of items. As of 1993, data were collected from more than 21,000 retail establishments and 60,000 housing units in 85 urban geographic areas in the United States to develop the national index. Basic price data are collected monthly (and bimonthly from some cities) from individual retail and service establishments while housing rents are collected on a rotating basis (once every six months for rental units and once every two years for owner-occupied).

However, the index is not a cost-of-living index, since it is not defined in absolute dollars. Intercity or interregional cost-of-living comparisons are not possible with the CPI data. The CPI simply measures the cost of maintaining the same purchases over time for each geographic area. CPI data do not show base year figures for each geographic area in dollar terms.

The market basket defining the CPI generally is not altered to reflect changes in consumer spending patterns. However, about once every 10 years, the basket is redefined and is based on the Consumer Expenditure Survey (CES) (which is conducted by the Census Bureau for the BLS). This survey also determines the weight each component in the index is given. With the 1987 revision of the CPI market basket of goods and services, the base period was established as 1982 through 84, being set equal to 100 for the index. The market basket therefore reflected the spending habits of urban consumers over the 1982–84 period as shown in Consumer Expenditure Surveys for those years. For 1989, the CPI averaged 124.0 and indicates that its market basket cost 24 percent more in 1989 than in 1982 through 84 on average.[1]

Prices measured by the CPI include sales taxes and other indirect taxes (i.e., gasoline taxes). The major expenditure categories (formally called "product groups") covered by the CPI include food and beverages, housing, apparel and upkeep, transportation, medical care, entertainment, and "other goods and services."

The consumer price index is a measure of changes in prices for purchases made by urban consumers only. There are two basic versions: the original Urban Wage Earners and Clerical workers index (CPI-W) and the broader, more representative, All Urban Consumers index (CPI-U). The CPI was begun in World War I and was initially estimated to assist in calculating cost-of-living adjustments in wages in highly industrialized areas that were hard-hit by war-time inflation.[2] The all urban index was introduced in 1978 and as of the introduction of the 1987 revision covered about 80 percent of the noninstitutional population of the United States, compared to 42 percent for the CPI-W.

The all urban index is based on the expenditures of all urban consumer units (the official definition of household[3]). Income levels or employment status do not affect inclusion or not. Excluded from the index population are rural residents outside metropolitan areas, all farm residents, the military, and individuals in institutions. The consumer price index for wage earners and clerical workers is also based on urban households, but these consumer units must meet two additional employment-related requirements: (1) more than one-half of the consumer unit's income must be earned from clerical or wage occupations, and (2) at least one of the members has to have been employed for 37 or more weeks in an eligible occupation during the last 12 months.

While the coverage of the two indexes differs, the methodologies for the calculation of the indexes are identical and even use the same surveys. The two indexes differ only in terms of how the individual components are weighted according to expenditure patterns (as measured by the Consumer Expenditure Survey in the base year period) for urban wage and clerical workers versus those for all urban consumers. For example, wage earners spent an average of 40.0 percent of total expenditures on housing in the 1982–84 period compared to 42.6 percent by all urban consumers. For transportation, wage earners spent an average of 20.9 percent versus 18.7 percent by the broader group.[4] Today the all urban index is generally more closely followed by the media, although the wage earners index is still used to a noticeable degree in contract price escalation clauses and also in Social Security cost-of-living adjustments.

TIMING OF RELEASES AND REVISIONS

The CPI is released monthly by the Bureau of Labor Statistics in the US Department of Labor. The data are typically provided to the public during the second or third full week after the month to which they refer. Published data appear in the BLS's periodical, the *Monthly Labor Review*, the Bureau's *CPI Detailed Report* (which is quite voluminous) and in secondary sources such as the Commerce Department's *Survey of Current Business* and in the *Federal Reserve Bulletin*.

Annual revisions for seasonally adjusted data generally are released in February and cover the previous five calendar years. Unadjusted data are not revised after the initial month's release. When the data are rebased, previous percentage changes are maintained except for differences created by rounding error from index levels being rounded to one decimal place. Also, with rebasing, component weights are not changed in earlier years although the index levels are changed to be consistent with the new base year. The maintaining of earlier percentage changes is desirable primarily due to the need for consistency by users of the CPI for contract purposes. This also is the case for unadjusted data not being revised after the initial release, except in the rare occurrence of an error in reporting or processing that meets stated correction policy. Contracts with price-escalation clauses generally use the unadjusted data, since there are no seasonal factors to be revised each year as is the case for seasonally adjusted CPI series for the subsequent five calendar years after the initial release.

SURVEYS AND SCOPE OF THE CPI

Because it is not practical to measure prices in all consumer transactions, the CPI is based on a set of statistically designed samples. The result is a CPI that is representative of prices paid for all urban areas of the United States. The samples are:

- Urban areas selected from all US urban areas.
- Consumer units within each selected urban area.
- Outlets from which these consumer units purchased goods and services.
- Specific, unique items—goods and services—purchased by these consumer units.
- Housing units in each urban area for the shelter component of the CPI.[5]

For the CPI, price data for goods and services are collected in 85 urban geographic areas and from about 21,000 retail and service establishments. Rent data are collected from about 40,000 tenants and 20,000 owner-occupied units. Each month prices for food, fuels, and a few other items are obtained in all 85 urban geographic areas. For most other goods and services, prices are collected monthly in the five largest urban areas,[6] bimonthly in the remaining 80 areas.[7] A portion of the housing sample is collected each month.

The basic bundle of goods and services included in the CPI is determined by the BLS's Consumer Expenditure Survey. However, to choose the establishments that are surveyed, an annual Point-of-Purchase Survey (POPS)[8] is used. This household interview survey asks consumers to provide information about purchases made over a specific recall period or time span. The survey, taken over a four-to-six week period each spring, asks consumers by purchase category how much was spent at each outlet. From this information, outlets are then selected for BLS's monthly price surveys with the probability of being selected proportional to expenditures reported in the POPS for each outlet. Currently, one-fifth of the CPI pricing areas have their outlet samples reselected each year. Even though the basket of goods in the CPI is fixed in between major revisions, the places surveyed are updated on an ongoing basis to track consumer changes in outlet preferences.

Since the various surveys used in producing the CPI may be a little confusing, the surveys and their roles can be summarized as follows:

1. Consumer Expenditure Survey, conducted by the Census Bureau, is used to determine the weights for the components in the CPI.

2. The Point-of-Purchase Survey, also produced by the Census Bureau, is used to select outlets—stores and other retail establishments—to be priced.

3. The CPI survey, conducted by BLS, actually selects and prices the goods and services.

4. Housing units are selected from information provided by the 1980 Census, combined with ongoing new permit sample.

ORGANIZATION OF THE DATA

CPI data are primarily organized by expenditure category and reflect the organization of the Consumer Expenditure Survey. Although the categories are less familiar to the public, data are also broken down by commodities and services groups.

This section on the CPI first looks at the data by the more traditional expenditure groupings but then primarily focuses on data arranged by commodities and services. The reason for this change in focus is straightforward. Within the expenditure groups, there is considerable mixing of subcomponents by types of behavioral factors. In other words, the commodity and service groups are arranged such that they tend to have similar behavioral variables within a few major components. For forecasting purposes and interpreting behavior, this commonality is important. Also, producer prices—a key factor often used to explain consumer price behavior—are not cleanly organized by expenditure type. They are instead arranged by industry and commodity. Between consumer and producer prices, data are more easily compared by commodity.

As mentioned above, CPI data are organized by types of expenditures as arranged in the Consumer Expenditure Survey. Table 5–1 shows the relative

TABLE 5–1
Consumer Price Index: The Seven Major Expenditure Groups

Expenditure Category	Relative Importance Dec. 1993
All items	100.000
Food and beverages	17.398
Food	15.799
Food at home	9.853
Food away from home	5.946
Alcoholic beverages	1.600
Housing	41.394
Shelter	27.948
Renters' costs	7.984
Rent, residential	5.771
Other renters' costs	2.213
Homeowners' costs	19.768
Owners' equivalent rent	19.386
Household insurance	0.382
Maintenance and repairs	0.196
Fuel and other utilities	7.262
Fuels	3.983
Fuel oil and other household fuel commodities	0.369
Gas (piped) and electricity	3.614
Other utilities and public services	3.279
Household furnishings and operation	6.183
Apparel and upkeep	5.897
Transportation	16.954
Private transportation	15.295
New vehicles	5.025
New cars	4.031
Used cars	1.245
Motor fuel	3.010
Maintenance and repairs	1.533
Other private transportation	4.483
Public transportation	1.659
Medical care	7.108
Medical care commodities	1.287
Medical care services	5.821
Entertainment	4.351
Other goods and services	6.897

importance figures for the major expenditure categories. The CPI has four official levels of classification with the broadest aggregation consisting of seven major product groups: food and beverages, housing, apparel and upkeep, transportation, medical care, entertainment, and other goods and services. These groups are then broken down into 69 expenditure classes (ECs), which are further divided into 207 item strata. The final level of detail for the CPI is for the 364 entry level items (ELIs). Within the item strata, they form one or more levels of substrata. ELIs are the ultimate sampling units from which unique items are selected for actual pricing.

Within the food and beverage product group, two examples of expenditure classes are "cereals and cereal products" and "bakery products." Under the first, one item strata is "rice, pasta, and cornmeal," which includes the entry level item of "rice." While there is no official designation for the level of aggregation, expenditure classes are often put into common groups such as "meats," which is a combination of the expenditure classes of "beef and veal," "pork," "poultry," "fish and seafood," and "other meats." As such, meats is a grouping that falls in between product groups and expenditure classes.

Under the product group apparel and upkeep, two examples of expenditure classes are "women's apparel" and "girls' apparel." One item strata under the first is "women's underwear, nightwear, and accessories." An entry level item under this is "women's hosiery."[9]

INDEX WEIGHTS VERSUS RELATIVE IMPORTANCE

Understanding the size of the components in the CPI is important in comprehending long-term changes in the behavior of the index. However, users of the data often confuse the meaning of a component's index weight with that of its relative importance.

The consumer price index is based on spending patterns of consumers as represented by the data in the 1982–84 Consumer Expenditure Survey. In the base period, the average expenditure per component as a percentage of all items determines that component's weight in the CPI. Essentially, a component's index weight is equal to its share of expenditures in the Consumer Expenditure Survey for the 1982–84 period. However, away from the base period, components do not grow at the same rate. The value of each component weighted by the base period index weights *and* the component's change relative to other components is its relative importance in the CPI. This is essentially a component's index weight times its price change since the base period relative to the overall index. The relative importance figure measures an index's share of the CPI in any given year, whereas the index weight generally refers to the base period.

Why are these changes in relative importance significant? First, sources of inflation have changed dramatically. Services inflation not only remains above average, but its higher share in the CPI makes inflation-fighting more difficult. Services are much less interest rate sensitive and purchases of items such as medical care and housing are not discretionary as many goods that are bought.

Second, the shift in relative importance affects how one should forecast the CPI. A CPI figure for 1979 does not represent the same expenditure bundle as in 1993 in terms of dollars spent. While the weights in the CPI are fixed (in physical quantities), the relative importance figures change every year and even every month. The reason is that some components have different rates of growth over long periods of time. Components with rapid inflation rates have a growing share of relative importance. Rapid changes in shares for the various components make using a component approach for academic studies or business forecasting very desirable.

Over the years, relative importance figures have changed dramatically. In particular, the sustained, rapid inflation for nonenergy services has led to an increase in this component's relative importance from 37.5 percent in December 1979 to 52.8 percent in December 1993.[10] (See Table 5–2.) Official relative impor-

TABLE 5–2
Relative Importance Figures for Selected CPI Components

	Food	Energy	Commodities less Food and Energy	Services less Energy
1979	17.655	10.313	34.488	37.544
1980	17.322	10.834	33.739	38.104
1981	16.577	11.133	32.792	39.498
1982	18.963	12.405	26.201	42.431
1983	18.743	11.896	26.501	42.861
1984	18.711	11.466	26.276	44.544
1985	18.513	11.252	25.875	44.360
1986	16.246	7.360	26.052	50.342
1987	16.055	7.618	25.760	50.567
1988	16.171	7.330	25.650	50.849
1989	16.318	7.366	25.188	51.127
1990	16.188	8.191	24.528	51.093
1991	16.007	7.361	24.757	51.876
1992	15.777	7.294	24.656	52.273
1993	15.799	6.993	24.369	52.839

Source: *Relative Importance of Components in the Consumer Price Indexes, 1993,* and earlier years, Department of Labor, Bureau of Labor Statistics. Data shown from 1979 through 1985 are based on consumer expenditures in 1972 through 1973 while data from 1986 forward are based on 1982–84 expenditures.

tance figures are released only for December of each year by the Labor Department. In contrast, energy's share dropped from a high of 12.4 percent in 1982 to 7.0 percent in 1993, and the share for nonfood, nonenergy commodities fell a little over 10 percentage points over the 1979–93 time span to 24.4 percent.

These trends in relative shares would continue as long as relative inflation rates remain the same. However, when the CPI is rebased, component weights—starting in the new base period—are changed to reflect the latest information on consumer spending patterns. The typical result is that consumers purchase fewer goods that have strong price increases, and this would show up in Consumer Expenditure Surveys, which are used to determine base weights. For a new base period, the initial weights would reflect changes in quantities purchased relative to the old base as well as relative price changes. Therefore, after rebasing, goods or services with rapidly rising prices over long periods of time generally end up with lower weights relative to just before rebasing.

UNDERSTANDING THE COMPONENTS BY COMMODITY AND SERVICE GROUPS

Food

The product group of food is broken down into major groups, food at home and food away from home.[11] The respective relative importance figures for December 1993 are 9.853 percent and 5.946 percent. The food at home group reflects items primarily purchased at grocery stores and prepared at home. Almost all of these items are of the commodity type—that is, there may be numerous brand names (national and regional), but there also are readily available perfect substitutes. For example, there are brand names for eggs as well as brand names for carbonated beverages, but in both instances brand names are very close substitutes for each other for these types of food items.

Major categories for food at home include cereals and bakery products; meats, poultry, fish and eggs; dairy products (fresh and processed); fruits and vegetables (fresh and processed); and "other food at home." In this last category are sugar and sweets, fats and oils, nonalcoholic beverages (including carbonated drinks and coffee), canned foods, frozen prepared food, seasonings and related items, and miscellaneous prepared food (including baby food).

Food away from home is broken down into four categories: lunch, dinner, other meals and snacks, and unpriced items. There is no greater level of detail for data series for food away from home.

For those who like to follow data on supply of food from the producer perspective, *Agricultural Outlook,* a monthly publication of the US Department of Agriculture (USDA) provides a wide array of data and other information. Forecasts are occasionally published for the food component of the CPI and detailed subcomponents as projected by the Economic Research Service of the USDA.

Energy

First, energy is best understood by separating this component into energy commodities and energy services. For December 1993, the commodities subcomponent made up 3.380 percent of the total CPI while energy services were 3.614 percent.

Energy commodities include the items that first come to mind when discussing energy costs. The major items are motor fuel (including gasoline) and fuel oil (for heating) along with the minor component, "other household fuels." Motor fuel is about three-fourths of energy commodities. By expenditure group, motor fuel falls under transportation while fuel oil is a part of overall housing expenses. Energy services consists of two major subcomponents, electricity and utility (piped) gas. Both of these are in the expenditure category of housing.

In terms of behavior, energy commodities are much more volatile than services. Of course, these commodities are rapidly and significantly affected by the price of crude oil. Additionally, supply and demand shocks quickly lead to price changes. For example, refinery shutdowns, (caused by fire, strike, or even hurricane) can cut supply. Over- or underproduction by members of the Organization of Oil Exporting Countries (OPEC) relative to quotas can lead to sharp price swings. OPEC played key roles in price surges in 1974 and 1979 through 80, and OPEC overproduction (primarily Saudi Arabia) led to a dramatic decline in oil prices in 1986. More recently, supply problems created by the Persian Gulf War in 1991 and preceding invasion of Kuwait by Iraq in 1990 caused large swings in oil prices and energy commodities in the CPI.

For energy commodities, the key behavioral factor affecting the price level is oil prices. This in turn is affected by supply (OPEC and non-OPEC production), alternative energy commodities for the consumer and industry—such as natural

CHART 5–1
Consumer Price Indexes and Oil Prices

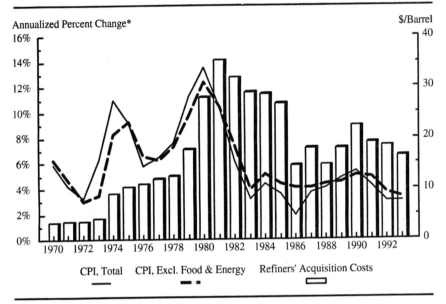

Annualized Percent Change* $/Barrel

CPI, Total   CPI, Excl. Food & Energy   Refiners' Acquisition Costs

Sources: US Department of Labor and US Department of Energy.

gas and coal and by energy demand worldwide. Demand generally is separated into trend growth based on strength in the economies of the industrial world and temporary demand factors such as unseasonable weather.

Within energy services, electricity made up 2.438 percent of the total CPI in December 1993, while utility gas was 1.175 percent. These subcomponent prices are less volatile than the energy commodities. Electricity and utility gas prices are regulated by government agencies with the result that changes in producer costs are smoothed and reach consumers with a lag. Also, for electricity, coal prices are an important cost factor and are relatively slow to change. The exception to this are many of the electric utilities in New England, which use oil to power the electricity-generating turbines. Additional influences on electricity rates include changes in regulations in the construction and operation of nuclear power plants and also changes in clean air emission standards.

Commodities Excluding Food and Energy

This broad commodity group contains many items that are both discretionary and/or subject to significant import competition. Therefore, many items are inordinately affected by the strength of consumer demand in the economy and/or by the value of the dollar in foreign exchange markets. Many consumer durables goods are particularly cyclically sensitive. These items would include furniture, appliances, and autos. Dollar sensitive goods cover a variety of examples such as video and audio products, apparel, and autos.

While the relative importance of this broad commodity group was 24.369 percent in 1993, over half occurs in a few subcomponents. The largest is apparel commodities (5.333) with numerous entry level items for men, women, and children. From the transportation product group, the subcomponent for new vehicles accounts for 5.025 percent and used cars, 1.245 percent. Under the product group of housing, there are a variety of relevant subcomponents with the major ones being house furnishings (3.601), which includes furniture, appliances, and other goods. Many of these detail items carry much less weight than might be expected. Examples are furniture and bedding (1.136) and televisions (0.166). Their small weight largely reflects the *average* expenditure per year rather than the much higher total cost.

Other major subcomponents are relatively small with the next largest groups being entertainment commodities (1.986), housekeeping supplies (1.109), and medical care commodities (1.287). For entertainment commodities, examples are newspapers, magazines, sporting equipment, toys, and photographic supplies and equipment.

Within commodities excluding food and energy, the really significant components are new vehicles and apparel commodities. This is particularly true since both series are very seasonal and are difficult to seasonally adjust. Additionally, pricing for these items tends to occur with very large changes. Early in the season, price increases may be very large, and then significant discounting may or may not occur depending on sales strength.

Services Excluding Energy

The services less energy component is the largest major component of the CPI by commodity and services categories. At the end of 1993, its relative importance in the all urban index was almost 53 percent. This component also is important because longer-run inflation rates for these services subcomponents are slow to change.[12] They basically set the trend around which other components, especially food and energy, oscillate.

The largest grouping of these services components is housing related and includes various types of rental components (combined, they account for over one-fourth of the CPI) and also other household services.

Rent of Shelter

Under the current BLS philosophy for measuring costs, it is important to understand that the CPI seeks to measure the cost of services currently being consumed rather than measuring the cost of obtaining an asset (buying a house). For shelter, the CPI measures the cost of housing services, that is, the use of shelter.

For rent of shelter, the two largest subcomponents are owners' equivalent rent (OER) and residential rent. These have relative importance figures of 19.386 percent and 5.771 percent, respectively, for December 1993. These two series are a lot more closely related than one would initially suspect since each measures a very different expenditure concept. OER is designed to measure the cost of renting the same type and quality housing as owner-occupied housing excluding utilities but including maintenance. Such housing is largely single-family houses but also condominiums and town homes. Residential rent measures the cost of housing in a broad rental market and includes rent for suburban apartment complexes, town-house rentals, central city flats and efficiencies, and of course single-family rental houses, among others.

While there is considerable variety and range in the types of housing represented in costs for owners' equivalent rent, the residential rent series covers a far broader spectrum of types of housing with owner-occupied housing by type making up only a small subset of housing units in the residential rent component. As is discussed in a later section, this overlap provides a key link between the estimation of residential rent and OER.

Data for both rent series come from the BLS's housing survey, which in its current form started in 1983.[13] The housing unit sample is stratified and consists of approximately 40,000 rental units and 20,000 owner units. Units are surveyed either in person or by telephone with individual rental units surveyed every six months and owner-occupied units contacted once every two years. The BLS actually tracks rents for individual units as separate time series. Of course, each month a portion of the sample is surveyed.

Field agents for the BLS gather from rental units information for the rent for the current month and the previous month and also for services provided. From owner-occupied units, they obtain an estimated or implicit initial rent. This implicit rent is the rent the owner says the unit would rent for on the market. However, because of the unreliability of owners' responses for implicit rent, field agents enter their own estimates. The field agents' figures are used by the BLS for actual computations for the OER index. Also, field agents collect information on the characteristics of the housing units including structure type, number of rooms, and the age of the home.

After the initial implicit rent is established for a given unit, subsequent values of implicit rent are moved by matching units from the rental sample to owners units. The rental units are matched to owners by location, structural type, and other characteristics. The BLS first tries to match owners with rental units that fit for all variables, but, if necessary, constraints are relaxed one at a time until a satisfactory set of renters is found for all owners.

After the initial interview, owners' responses on housing characteristics are more important than their implicit rent estimate, since it is the match of housing characteristics to corresponding rental units that determines the change in OER. This is especially true since field agents' figures are used for the initial implicit rent number. In essence, a small subset of the rental sample is used to estimate the owners' equivalent rent index, which is about 20 percent of the overall CPI. Following this matching process, OER is estimated in the same technical manner as residential rent. Even though owner-occupied units are contacted only once every two years to check for quality and tenure changes, the characteristics of these units are used in the matching process and index calculations every six months.

For residential rent, the housing survey data are directly used (after adjustments for changes in quality) to estimate changes in the residential rent index by calculating one-month-ago and six-month-ago percent changes for units surveyed in the latest month. The rental index numbers are moved by a weighted average of the one-month and six-month percent changes with the one-month change getting a weight of 65 percent. Of course, percentage changes are applied by stratified components. Also, rents are quality adjusted for each month's aging of units surveyed.

Rent figures collected in the housing survey are on a contract basis for residential rent and on a pure rent basis for owners' equivalent rent. The collected rents for residential rent include any labor provided as part of payment and also covers all services and facilities provided on a contract basis, such as furniture or utilities. Owners' equivalent rent excludes payment for these extra services. Both rental components are adjusted for changes in quality. These factors cover changes in services and facilities provided by the landlord. Examples include the elimination of the inclusion of utilities in the rent or might include the addition of a room to an apartment. Beginning in 1988, the BLS also began to adjust rent for aging, which is viewed as reducing the quality of housing units.

Other shelter services include lodging while out of town, lodging while at school, tenants' insurance, household insurance, and maintenance and repair services. These components are small, with'the largest being lodging while out of town, followed by household insurance, with 1993 relative importance of about two percent and four-tenths of one percent, respectively. However, with the 1987 revisions to the CPI, the lodging while out of town component had a significant change in the sample. Previously, hotels and motels in the sample were in urban areas covered by the CPI or were within a minimal distance from them. With the revision, the sampled hotels and motels could be anywhere that households from those urban areas went on vacation in the United States. Essentially, there was a switch from sampling hotels and motels in the central business district to sampling outlets primarily in tourist and vacation areas.

Other Services

Other nonenergy services are found in all of the other expenditure categories except for food. Relative importance figures for 1993 are in parentheses. Apparel services (0.564) are primarily laundry and dry cleaning. Within transportation services some of the components are automobile maintenance and repair (1.533), automobile insurance (2.554), automobile finance charges (0.531), airline fares (1.141), and intracity public transportation (0.360). Medical care services (5.821) include professional medical services (3.353) (for physicians' services, dental, eye care, and other), hospital and related services (2.154), and health insurance (0.313). Various medical tests, X rays, imaging, and the like are counted as services. Medical care commodities are by definition limited to prescription drugs, nonprescription drugs, and nonprescription medical equipment and supplies. Entertainment services (2.365) cover club memberships, fees for participant sports, admissions (movies, theater, etc.), fees for lesson or instructions, and "other entertainment services." Finally, under the expenditure group, "other goods and services," the services categories are for personal care (0.556) (e.g., haircuts) and for personal and educational services expenses (3.863). These include legal and personal financial services, funeral expenses, and college tuition.

KEY ROLES IN THE ECONOMY
AND UNDERLYING FUNDAMENTALS

The Long Term

The CPI's place in analyzing the economy is that it is the primary measure of inflation in the United States, and, to understand uses of the CPI, it is important to understand some basics about the causes or explanations of inflation, either from a theoretical or technical perspective.

There are numerous theories and explanations of inflation. Theories range from monetarist to Keynesian, among others. Monetarist economists prefer to explain inflation in terms of growth in the money supply exceeding growth in output of goods and services. When monetary growth is excessive, inflation rises, and when monetary growth slows relative to output, then inflation declines. Based on monetarist views of inflation, growth in monetary aggregates and growth in real output will largely determine inflation trends. Indeed, markets do compare these trends for long-term inflation projections.

However, there are two major limitations to the monetarist view of inflation. First, the demand for money is neither stable nor very predictable. Consumers and businesses do not always have the same desire to hold money as they may have in the past. Additionally, the definitions of money supply have not been constant from a practical perspective, since changes in financial regulations have affected money growth. Therefore, the relationship between money growth and inflation is not as tight as theorists would like. Nonetheless, tracking growth in money supply is useful for projecting long-term changes in inflation trends.

Keynesian theory generally explains inflation in terms of aggregate demand relative to aggregate supply. Shortages of goods caused by heavy demand drive up prices and inflation. For this type of analysis, attention usually focuses on the strength of consumer and business demand along with watching indicators of supply bottlenecks. A few examples of indicators of supply bottlenecks include the unemployment rate for labor markets, the capacity utilization rate for manufacturing as well as vendor performance, and sensitive raw materials prices for both manufacturing and construction.

Inflation can also be temporarily affected by supply shocks such as for crude oil. Hence, crude oil prices are an important indicator for tracking cost push inflation.

Price levels can be affected directly by government policy changes. For example, government price supports for farmers affect a number of food items, including peanuts, sugar, and milk. Changes in import tariffs and export subsidies by foreign countries can lead to significant shifts in US prices for various goods and services. Along this same line, international exchange rates clearly have an impact on inflation. A rise in the value of the dollar makes imports cheaper, thereby lowering the cost of imported goods plus constraining prices of similar domestically produced goods. Inflation rates are affected by changes in exchange rates until trade patterns fully adjust to the change in relative costs for domestically produced versus foreign produced goods.

Over the business cycle, inflation rates are affected by changes in supply and demand. Following a recession trough, demand rises, but resources are not strained, since there is substantial unused production capacity and unemployed or underemployed labor. Eventually, resource prices (including wages) rise due to scarcity, growth in final goods is outstripped by demand, and inflation picks up. Generally, goods prices inflation accelerates before services inflation does. Services CPI is classified as a lagging indicator.

In summary, long-run inflation is caused by excessive growth in money supply or by the alternative explanation of demand rising faster than output. Analysts therefore watch growth in money supply aggregates as well as variables such as the unemployment rate, capacity utilization, and the exchange value of the dollar.

KEYS TO ANALYZING THE MONTHLY REPORT
AND NEAR-TERM INFLATION TRENDS

Near-term inflation trends generally are analyzed by summing component trends once technical factors are discounted. Technical factors that create significant monthly volatility are relatively few and include seasonal adjustment problems, unseasonal weather affecting demand, temporary supply problems, and sampling problems. The pace of near-term inflation is judged by a several-month average, since some components are volatile. These issues are discussed below, primarily as related to separate commodity and services categories.

Within food, meat is a significant subcomponent because of its relative importance. Meats such as cattle and pork can be affected by adverse conditions (drought or flood) in the grain belt, since grain is a major cost in production. Interestingly, shortages of feed can lead to near-term declines in meat prices as cattle are slaughtered early, increasing retail meat supplies. But because there are lags in meat production, this year's increased slaughter reduces next year's supply, thereby raising meat prices for next year. The full impact of grain losses is not felt for at least a year.

Vegetables and fruits also are affected by temporary supply problems. Freezes can damage crops and lead to a run-up in prices for fresh fruits and vegetables when affected. However, these price changes are usually temporary, because over a year, different regions in the United States and across the world supply various fresh fruits and vegetables. For analysis of food price trends, one should track not only the United States agricultural outlook but also agricultural trends worldwide.

Energy analysis is divided into three main components: refined oil products, electricity, and natural gas. Obviously, the key motor fuel and heating oil components are affected by changes in crude oil prices as well as any taxes on these commodities.

One can easily follow market reports on spot and contract prices for crude oil. Additionally, the US Department of Energy publishes the *Short-Term Energy Outlook.* For electricity, prices are actually rates charged by utilities. Rates generally are determined on some form of cost plus profit basis, although regulators are beginning to require competitive pricing. Nonetheless, costs are based primarily on fuel expense. The fuel used most by electric utilities is coal, although environmental legislation is causing switching not only from high-sulfur coal to cleaner low-sulfur coal but also to natural gas. Analysis of electric utility trends, therefore, is dependent on trends in coal prices, natural gas prices, and changes in environmental regulations. Utilities factor in the costs of pollution abatement equipment in their rate schedules. A small but significant share of electricity output is from nuclear power plants, but they have their own unique cost structure.

The natural gas industry also is heavily regulated. Rate changes are irregular, but general industry trends can be followed in industry publications such *Oil and Gas Journal.* Spot and futures prices of natural gas are published daily in *The Wall Street Journal.*

Projecting the commodities excluding food and energy component requires tracking consumer demand trends, pricing strategies for various industries, the exchange value of the dollar, and changes in sourcing of various items by retailers. Demand affects prices of all goods and services, but some goods have demand that is relatively price sensitive. Apparel goods is the largest subcomponent of these commodities, and demand clearly affects the amount of discounting over clothing seasons. The next largest subcomponent is new passenger cars, and demand can have a significant impact on manufacturers' suggested retail prices, rebates, and dealer price concessions. Industry perceptions of demand also affect pricing strategies. Additionally, both apparel and autos generally either have significant import competition or are primarily imported. Hence, tracking the exchange value of the dollar is important. Other factors equal, a higher dollar leads to lower import prices, thereby constraining prices for domestically produced goods.

Finally, newly industrialized countries (NICs) are becoming increasingly important sources of imported goods. Latin America and Asia are growing in importance as trading partners for the United States. Due to both direct investment in these regions by the United States and other industrialized countries and internal investment in manufacturing facilities, these areas are providing low-cost goods at quality often comparable to that produced in the United States. Therefore, to project inflation for these goods, an analyst must be aware of shifts in sources of imported goods. For example, sources of imports of some consumer electronics have shifted over time from Japan to South Korea and Taiwan, even to China and other newly industrialized countries (NICs) in Asia.

Services are difficult to forecast in terms of evaluating underlying fundamentals because these underlying factors are usually very broad. Services prices generally track overall inflation pressures. Also, services differ substantially in character from subcomponent to subcomponent. Housing rent is very different from medical care services. Fortunately, services inflation changes slowly and usually with a lag relative to goods inflation. Changes in direction of goods inflation are a good leading indicator of changes in direction of services inflation.

However, since housing rental series are the largest subcomponents in this services group, it is appropriate to track indicators that affect housing rents. First, demographic factors are important. Is there a rising or declining segment of the population in the rental market (baby boomers or baby busters)? Job availability also affects whether or not household formation is strong. Vacancy rate data also indicate whether there is an excessive supply or shortage of apartments. Finally, mortgage rates and housing prices can suggest whether apartment dwellers might be interested in leaving in order to purchase a house. When housing markets are attractive, apartment rents are less likely to rise significantly. However, when using variables such as multifamily vacancy rates and housing prices to project rent inflation, one should pay close attention to the lags involved.[14]

Problems with Seasonality

Financial markets usually focus on the seasonally adjusted CPI data for analysis of current inflation pressures. Even though the CPI data are seasonally adjusted using sophisticated statistical procedures,[15] problems with seasonality can create distortions in the data. The problems are not with the seasonal adjustment procedure but are with the data: they do not have perfectly stable seasonal patterns. However, markets should be aware that the impact of seasonal irregularities can be either unsustainable (with offsets later in the season) or have a lasting impact on inflation for the year.

Seasonality can have significant effects on price changes if (1) the magnitude of seasonal discounting diverges from previous patterns due only to changes in marketing strategy (pricing) by stores, or (2) there is a significant change in demand relative to supply leaving end-of-season inventories atypically lean or overstocked. In the first instance, distortions early in the season are usually offset later in the season. In the second, the effect on inflation data remains intact with no offset.

First, one needs to be aware that not seasonally adjusted data are put into seasonally adjusted form with seasonal factors.[16] These numerical adjustments raise or lower unadjusted data to a moving average. For example, unadjusted heating oil prices are normally high in the winter and low in the summer. Seasonal factors raise unadjusted summer prices and lower winter prices to put into seasonally adjusted form. In turn, there are monthly seasonally adjusted increases or decreases in prices when unadjusted changes exceed or fall short of the changes anticipated by the seasonal factors.

However, seasonal factors, which are used to inflate or deflate unadjusted data, can exaggerate price movements when there are sharp changes in supply or demand for goods that have large seasonal swings in price and the distortion occurs during months with large seasonal factors. Such goods include motor fuel, heating oil, and fresh fruits and vegetables, among others. Continuing with the heating oil example, during a warm winter, unadjusted heating oil prices might not rise as much as normal. Unadjusted prices would be up in midwinter, but not as much as usual because of relatively slack demand. This would push seasonally adjusted prices down because the rise was not as large as anticipated by the seasonal factor. Also, since the magnitude of the seasonal factor is very large in winter, the adjusted decline also could be very noticeable.

A change in marketing strategy (that is, initial pricing in the season) can affect early seasonally adjusted price changes in a clothing season. However, if demand and supply are little changed from the previous year, then the initial effects from higher- or lower-than-usual introductory prices are usually offset in subsequent months as discounting of the necessary magnitude takes place to clear inventories. If prices start out "too high," then discounting will likely be deeper later to move merchandise. If prices start out "too low," then inventories will move earlier than usual and less discounting will be needed later in the season. Generally, with no change in supply and demand conditions, these atypical starts in pricing early in the season "wash out" later in the season.

In contrast, if Christmas sales are strong and there is little inventory for after-Christmas sales, then there is less than typical discounting. This pushes seasonally adjusted prices up, since the seasonal factor expects a specific amount of discounting that did not occur. In this situation, there are no offsetting subsequent "technical" movements in the seasonally adjusted price data. In summary, the amount of discounting is dependent upon inventories and demand. In turn, the degree of discounting compared to the past affects seasonally adjusted price movement. Less than typical discounting leads to seasonally adjusted price increases.

Occasionally one reads analysis for apparel prices stating that early introduction of clothing in a seasonal led to a price increase. However, this change in timing truly only affected the apparel data over the late 1980s when such a change did occur and was permanent. But a shift in timing of the clothing seasons distorts the seasonally adjusted data only as long as it takes for new seasonal factors to be incorporated into the data. This is for a time period of five to seven years, depending on the particular series. Since the introduction of clothing seasons are no longer being moved earlier, sharp increases in prices at the start of the season now reflect retailers attempting to pass on higher prices that may or may not be sustainable.

INDEXING SOCIAL SECURITY

For indexing government Social Security payments, the CPI-W for urban wage earners and clerical workers is used instead of the CPI-U, all urban index. Generally, these cost-of-living adjustments (COLAs) take place on January first and are based on the year-over-year percent changes for the not seasonally adjusted average level for the third quarter in the previous year. The size of the COLA is not necessarily the same as the just-mentioned year-over-year percentage, but is typically a preset percentage of the CPI rise. The CPI-W also is usually used for collective bargaining contracts.

Calculating the Percentage Changes

The financial press and electronic media report a given month's consumer price index primarily in terms of a simple monthly percentage change and in an annualized monthly percentage change. For example, for the May 1990 CPI released on June 15, 1990, the index was reported as rising a seasonally adjusted 0.2 percent or an annualized 1.9 percent. The April and May seasonally adjusted index levels were 129.1 and 129.3 respectively.[17]

As such, the simple monthly percentage change for May 1990 is calculated as follows:

$$((129.3/129.1)-1)*100 = ((1.0015492)-1)*100$$
$$=0.0015492*100$$
$$=0.15492 \text{ percent,}$$

or 0.2 percent, rounded.

The annualized (compounded), monthly percentage change for May 1989 is calculated as follows:

$$(((129.3/129.1)^{12})-1)*100 = ((1.0015492)^{12})-1)*100$$
$$= ((1.0187495)-1)*100$$
$$= (0.0187495)*100$$
$$= 1.87495 \text{ percent,}$$

or 1.9 percent annualized, rounded. This compounded percentage change is referred to as a seasonally adjusted annual rate (SAAR).

Within the above formula, the double asterisk represents an exponential function and the 12 represents the number of periods required to obtain an annual rate. In this case, with a single-period change in the data (one month's span), 12 is the appropriate amount of compounding. For quarterly data, the compounding would be for four periods. For data spanning five months (e.g., May over the previous December), the exponential figure would be 12 divided by 5.

A cumulative-to-date, annualized percentage change for May 1989 (with December 1989 being 126.3) is:

$$(((129.3/126.3)^{(12/5)})-1)*100 = ((1.023753)^{2.4})-1)*100$$
$$= ((1.057958)-1)*100$$
$$= (0.057958)*100$$
$$= 5.7958 \text{ percent,}$$

or 5.8 percent annualized, rounded.

TABLE 5–3
Analyzing the News Release: Key Insights

- What did the CPI excluding food and energy do?
- Are changes in food and energy diverging from the rest of the CPI: is the CPI excluding food and energy really a trend series for the overall CPI?
- Are changes in crude oil prices still expected to impact the CPI in coming months?
- Did a freeze or another type of agricultural problem boost food prices? Will other food-growing regions or countries be able to replenish these supplies once their growing season reaches harvest and lead to lower prices, or is the shortage for that crop going to continue all year?
- Are strong increases in feed costs likely to lead to near-term weakness in meat prices as stocks are taken to market, but then lead to higher prices later due to lower supply?
- Did passenger car prices have an unsustainably large increase? Did manufacturers' rebates affect the latest data or the previous month's data?
- Is underlying demand strong enough to support apparel prices existing at start of the season?
- Did housing components for owners' equivalent rent and for residential rent diverge from recent trends? Monthly changes in these two series are volatile but year-over-year changes move slowly. Large deviations from the average for several months generally should be discounted.
- Were there any special factors affecting seasonal demand for hotels and motels in resort areas? Lodging while out of town has very large seasonals for winter months.
- Are medical care services being affected by either new medical care plans or by expectations about passage of health care legislation?

TABLE 5–4a
Consumer Price Inflation by Expenditure Group

		Annual Average Percentage Changes		
	Total	Food and Beverages	Housing	Apparel and Upkeep
1970	5.7	5.2	7.1	4.2
1971	4.4	3.2	4.4	3.2
1972	3.2	4.1	3.7	2.0
1973	6.2	13.2	4.6	3.7
1974	11.0	13.7	11.2	7.4
1975	9.1	8.5	10.7	4.5
1976	5.8	3.2	6.1	3.7
1977	6.5	6.0	6.7	4.5
1978	7.6	9.7	8.7	3.6
1979	11.3	10.7	12.3	4.3
1980	13.5	8.5	15.7	7.1
1981	10.3	7.8	11.5	4.8
1982	6.2	4.1	7.2	2.6
1983	3.2	2.3	2.7	2.5
1984	4.3	3.7	4.1	1.9
1985	3.6	2.3	4.0	2.8
1986	1.9	3.3	3.0	0.9
1987	3.6	4.0	3.0	4.4
1988	4.1	4.1	3.8	4.3
1989	4.8	5.7	3.8	2.8
1990	5.4	5.8	4.5	4.6
1991	4.2	3.6	4.0	3.7
1992	3.0	1.4	2.9	2.5
1993	3.0	2.1	2.7	1.4

Source: Bureau of Labor Statistics.

TABLE 5–4b
Consumer Price Inflation by Expenditure Group

	Annual Average Percentage Changes			
	Transportation	Medical Care	Entertainment	Other Goods and Services
1970	5.0	6.6	5.1	5.8
1971	5.3	6.2	5.3	4.6
1972	1.0	3.3	3.0	4.2
1973	3.3	4.0	2.7	3.8
1974	11.2	9.3	7.6	7.3
1975	9.4	12.0	9.0	8.2
1976	10.0	9.5	5.0	5.8
1977	7.1	9.6	4.9	6.0
1978	4.6	8.4	5.3	6.5
1979	14.3	9.2	6.7	7.2
1980	17.9	11.0	9.0	9.1
1981	12.2	10.7	7.8	9.8
1982	4.1	11.6	6.5	10.3
1983	2.4	8.8	4.3	11.0
1984	4.4	6.2	3.7	6.7
1985	2.6	6.3	3.9	6.1
1986	−3.9	7.5	3.4	6.0
1987	3.0	6.6	3.3	5.8
1988	3.1	6.5	4.3	6.6
1989	5.0	7.7	5.2	7.8
1990	5.6	9.0	4.7	7.7
1991	2.7	8.7	4.5	7.9
1992	2.2	7.4	2.8	6.8
1993	3.1	5.9	2.5	5.2

TABLE 5–5
Annual Percentage Changes for the CPI and Selected Components

	Total	Total Less Food and Energy	Food	Energy	Commodities Less Food and Energy	Services Less Energy
1970	5.7	6.3	5.7	2.8	4.5	8.4
1971	4.4	4.7	3.1	3.9	3.9	5.6
1972	3.2	3.0	4.2	2.6	2.5	3.7
1973	6.2	3.6	14.5	8.1	2.8	4.3
1974	11.0	8.3	14.3	29.6	7.6	9.0
1975	9.1	9.1	8.5	10.5	9.3	8.9
1976	5.8	6.5	3.0	7.1	5.2	8.0
1977	6.5	6.3	6.3	9.5	5.2	7.2
1978	7.6	7.4	9.9	6.3	6.0	8.5
1979	11.3	9.8	11.0	25.1	8.4	11.3
1980	13.5	12.4	8.6	30.9	9.3	15.1
1981	10.3	10.4	7.8	13.6	7.8	13.0
1982	6.2	7.4	4.1	1.5	5.9	8.6
1983	3.2	4.0	2.1	0.7	5.1	3.0
1984	4.3	5.0	3.8	1.0	4.2	5.3
1985	3.6	4.3	2.3	0.7	2.6	5.5
1986	1.9	4.0	3.2	−13.2	1.4	5.7
1987	3.6	4.1	4.1	0.5	2.9	4.7
1988	4.1	4.4	4.1	0.8	3.6	4.8
1989	4.8	4.5	5.8	5.6	3.3	5.1
1990	5.4	5.0	5.8	8.3	3.3	5.9
1991	4.2	4.9	2.9	0.4	4.2	5.3
1992	3.0	3.7	1.2	0.5	2.9	4.1
1993	3.0	3.3	2.2	1.2	2.0	3.8

NOTES FOR CHAPTER 5

1. Data are for all the urban index (CPI-U).
2. Chapter 19, "The Consumer Price Index," *BLS Handbook of Methods,* BLS Bulletin 2414 (1992), p. 176.
3. For definition of a consumer unit, see "New Basket of Goods and Services Being Priced in Revised CPI," by Charles Mason and Clifford Butler, *Monthly Labor Review,* January 1987, pp. 3–4.
4. See Table 2, "New Basket of Goods," p. 6.
5. "The Consumer Price Index," p. 178.
6. These five largest urban areas are Chicago–Gary–Lake County, IL–IN–WI; Los Angeles–Anaheim–Riverside, CA; New York–Northern NJ–Long Island, NY–NJ–CT; Philadelphia–Wilmington–Trenton, PA–NJ–DE, MD; and San Francisco–Oakland–San Jose, CA.
7. These next 10 cities surveyed every other month are in two groups. The first group surveyed in January, March, May, July, September, and November includes Baltimore, MD; Boston–Lawrence–Salem, MA–NH; Cleveland–Akron–Lorain, OH; Miami–Fort Lauderdale, FL; St. Louis–East St. Louis, MO–IL; and Washington, DC–MD–VA. The second group surveyed in February, April, June, August, October, and December includes Dallas–Fort Worth, TX; Detroit–Ann Arbor, MI; Houston–Galveston–Brazoria, TX: and Pittsburgh–Beaver Valley, PA.
8. This survey is also more formally called the Continuing Point-of-Purchase Survey, (CPOPS). POPS is merely a more frequently used shorthand name—they are the same survey.
9. For a detailed list of expenditure classes, item strata, and entry level items, see Appendix 4, "The Consumer Price Index," pp. 221–225.
10. The 1979 to 1993 period reflects not only the impact of inflation, but also a potentially significant impact from the 1979 data being based on 1972–73 expenditure while 1993 data are based on 1982–84 expenditures.
11. The broader expenditure group of "food and beverages" differs from "food" with the inclusion of alcoholic beverages. Nonalcoholic beverages are included in the food group. By commodities and services grouping, alcoholic beverages fall under commodities excluding food and energy.
12. In fact, the slightly broader component for overall services (which includes utility gas and electricity) is one of the components in the Commerce Department's index of lagging indicators.
13. Prior to 1983, the shelter component was based on the cost of purchasing housing and included a mortgage rate component. The shelter component—and it can even be argued that the overall CPI—is a new series starting in 1983 because of the changes in definition.
14. See R Mark Rogers, Steven W Henderson, and Daniel H Ginsburg, "Consumer Prices: Examining Housing Rental Components," *Economic Review,* Federal Reserve Bank of Atlanta, May/June 1993, pp. 32–51.
15. The procedure used is ARIMA X–11.
16. However, seasonally adjusted higher levels of aggregation often reflect the sum of independently adjusted series.

17. Interestingly, the Labor Department does not release any seasonally adjusted data for the level for the overall CPI, although it does for most components. This is to prevent confusion between a seasonally adjusted level and the level for the unadjusted overall index, which is used frequently for contracts in price escalation clauses. In any given month, adjusted and unadjusted levels can differ significantly. Of course, the Labor Department releases seasonally adjusted percentage changes for the overall index and also seasonal factors, which can be used to calculate the seasonally adjusted index level.

BIBLIOGRAPHY

Henderson, Steven. "Measuring Homeownership in the CPI: The Flow of Services Using Rental Equivalence Has Replaced the Asset Approach." Paper delivered at the 65th Annual Western Economic Association International Conference. San Diego, California, July 1990.

Lane, Walter F. "Owners' Equivalent Rent in the American Consumer Price Index (CPI)." Prices Seminar Series Working Papers, US Department of Labor. Bureau of Labor Statistics. Office of Prices and Living Conditions. Working Paper 8801–1, January 1988.

Mason, Charles, and Clifford Butler. "New Basket of Goods and Services Being Priced in Revised CPI." *Monthly Labor Review*. US Department of Labor, January 1987, pp. 3–22.

McKenzie, Chester V. "Technical Note: Relative Importance of CPI Components." *Monthly Labor Review*. November 1961, pp. 1233–36.

Rogers, R Mark. "Improving Monthly Models for Economic Indicators: The Example of an Improved CPI Model." Federal Reserve Bank of Atlanta. *Economic Review*, September/October 1988, pp. 34–50.

Rogers R Mark, Steven W Henderson, and Daniel H Ginsburg. "Consumer Prices: Examining Housing Rental Components." Federal Reserve Bank of Atlanta. *Economic Review*, May/June 1993, pp. 32–46.

US Department of Labor. Bureau of Labor Statistics, *BLS Handbook of Methods*. Bulletin 2414. September 1992.

———. US Department of Labor. *Relative Importance of Components in the Consumer Price Indexes, 1992*. April 1993.

CHAPTER 6

THE PRODUCER PRICE INDEX

Probably the second most important price measure for the United States is the producer price index (PPI). It measures average changes in selling prices received by domestic producers for their output.[1] The PPI covers the mining and manufacturing sectors with some representation also in agriculture, fishing, forestry, services, and gas and electricity. The PPI's importance is that it is used in price escalation clauses and is used by government statistical agencies for deflating various goods into constant-dollar series. Also, the PPI often provides some early warning for price pressures building or receding in the consumer sector. From the financial market's perspective, this release is important because it precedes the CPI release typically by several days and provides information on likely changes in that month's CPI. From a policy perspective, the PPI also is closely monitored by the Federal Reserve Board as PPIs cover a variety of goods and services not tracked by CPI series. In addition to pricing finished goods at the producer level, there are producer price indexes for crude materials and also for intermediate materials. These indexes provide early warning signals for changes in inflation for finished goods at the producer level.

The PPI is produced by the Bureau of Labor Statistics (BLS) of the US Department of Labor. The monthly news release date is usually midmonth (the second week in the month) following the reference month. For more extensive data, the monthly detailed report is *Producer Price Indexes.* Currently, the standard base year for the producer price index is 1982, which is set equal to 100. Individual PPI series beginning after the base year use a later base. Some PPIs are available in seasonally adjusted form (depending on whether a series passes statistical tests for seasonality), but all are available as not seasonally adjusted data. Annual revisions to seasonal factors may lead to revisions to data covering the preceding five years. Monthly revisions to the data occur only once—four months after the initial release. The not seasonally adjusted data are derived from a mail-in survey, and the BLS waits for late reports and corrections for this one monthly revision to unadjusted index levels.

By definition, the PPI actually measures changes in net unit revenues received by US producers for the first significant commercial transaction within the United States. Taxes received by the government are not included. Rebates and other promotions by manufacturers affect the PPI. For example, low-interest financing plans paid by the manufacturer affect the PPI price for a car. A rebate by the manufacturer is also included since it affects net revenues, but a rebate by a dealer to a customer does not affect the PPI if no portion of the cost of the rebate is borne by the manufacturer. The PPI systematically attempts to capture actual transaction prices, not list prices.

Prices in the PPI are neither order prices nor "futures" prices. The PPI tries to measure prices for goods actually shipped in the reference month. Generally, prices are based on data for the Tuesday of the week containing the 13th of the month. There are some exceptions such as for some farm products, some refined petroleum products, natural gas, and some industrial chemicals. Most prices are reported on a free on board (f.o.b.) basis.[2]

What is now called the PPI used to be called the wholesale price index (WPI). The BLS changed the term *WPI* to *PPI* in 1978 due to public misconceptions about the meaning of wholesale. When the WPI began in 1902, the term *wholesale prices* was understood to refer to prices for goods sold in large quantities.[3] By the mid-1970s, *wholesale* was often assumed by the general public to refer to wholesalers or distributors. There never has been a BLS price measure for goods sold at the distributor level. By force of habit, the media often use the phrase *wholesale prices* when referring to the PPI.

THE SURVEY

Data for the various producer price indexes are collected by mail surveys with the reporting companies being chosen with industry-specific probability sampling procedures. The sample is chosen from establishments in the Unemployment Insurance (UI) System. The UI System covers virtually all manufacturers in the United States. The BLS updates the sample of each industry's producers every few years to take into account changes in production technology or industry structure. Usually, many of the companies that were in the sample before end up in the sample after the updating procedure. Each month, over 80,000 price quotations are used in PPI calculations. The PPI system has several major classification systems, but the indexes in all are based on data from the same pool of company reporters. The BLS does attempt to adjust reported prices for any changes in quality.

DATA ORGANIZATION

The three most important classification structures are (1) industry, (2) commodity, and (3) stage-of-processing (SOP). By far, the stage-of-processing classification is emphasized the most by the BLS and by financial analysts. First, the industry and commodity indexes are discussed briefly.

Industry Indexes

Industry PPIs measure changes in prices received for the industry's changes in prices received for that industry's output sold outside the industry or its net output. Any reference to a net output index for PPIs basically means that industry indexes are being discussed. *Net output* refers to the use of net output to derive component weights (as discussed in a following section). Series are generally calculated at the four-digit Standard Industrial Classification (SIC) industry level and often are aggregated at three- and two-digit SIC levels. Total mining and manufacturing PPIs also are calculated. Net output indexes are not available on a seasonally adjusted basis at this time.

There is no overall services index, but a number of services industries are covered by net output PPIs. These include railroads, US Postal Service, deep sea transportation, water transportation of freight, air transportation, pipelines (except natural gas), petroleum pipelines, travel agencies, tour operators, radio broadcasting, electric power, natural gas utilities, scrap and waste materials, truck rentals, and hospitals among others.

In the standard published detail PPI tables, for each industry there is the overall industry index as well as primary products, some subcomponents of primary products, secondary products and sometimes subcomponents of secondary products, and miscellaneous receipts.

Primary product indexes show changes in prices received by firms classified to be in the industry for products made primarily by that industry.[4] Such production of that product is not necessarily exclusive to that industry. Secondary products are those primarily producing in another industry. Miscellaneous receipts indexes show changes in prices of other (neither primary or secondary products) sources of revenue received by firms in the industry. An example of this might be parking lot revenues if a firm operates a parking lot as an incidental business for the use of employees or the public. Consulting services for a manufacturer would also fit into this category. All physical product series fall under either the primary or secondary product components.

Commodity Indexes

The commodity-based indexes are the traditional PPI series—those closely followed before the emphasis on stage-of-processing by BLS. The commodity PPIs are organized by end use or material composition, regardless of the industry of origin (primary or secondary) for these products. This PPI commodity system is unique and does not directly correspond to any other standard system such as SIC or the standard international trade classification (SITC). It is based on the historical availability of various PPI series and has evolved due to specific needs of various users (such as other government statistical or regulatory agencies).

There are 15 major commodity groupings in the all commodities producer price index. The all commodities index is the index that had been the overall measure of producer price inflation most closely followed prior to the introduction of the index for finished goods. For historical comparisons (especially for early this century), the all commodities index often is the only aggregate producer price series available.

The 15 major components are:

1. Farm products.

2. Processed foods and feeds.
3. Textile products and apparel.
4. Hides, skins, leather, and related products.
5. Fuels and related products and power.
6. Chemicals and allied products.
7. Rubber and plastic products.
8. Lumber and wood products.
9. Pulp, paper, and allied products.
10. Metals and metal products.
11. Machinery and equipment.
12. Furniture and household durables.
13. Nonmetallic mineral products.
14. Transportation equipment.
15. Miscellaneous products.

The first two of the components for all commodities make up the index for farm products and processed foods and feeds while the remaining 13 major components form the industrial commodities PPI. There also are a variety of other commodity groupings.

The key factors of importance for the commodity classification PPIs are that (1) they are historically based and provide some continuity with early PPI data; and (2) with further regrouping at a finer level of detail, they provide the basis for the most closely followed PPI classification—commodity-based stage-of-processing indexes.

Stage-of-Processing Indexes, Commodity-Based

The commodity-based stage-of-processing price indexes are those most emphasized by BLS. These indexes regroup commodities at the six-digit SIC level based on the class of the buyer and the amount of physical processing or assembling the products have undergone. The three stage-of-processing levels are (1) finished goods; (2) intermediate materials, supplies, and components; and (3) crude materials for further processing. There also are industry-based stage-of-processing indexes, but they are little followed at this time. Subsequent discussion is for the commodity-based SOP indexes only.

Finished Goods

Finished goods for PPI purposes are goods for sale to the final-demand user, either consumers or businesses. The two primary components for the PPI for finished goods are finished consumer goods and capital equipment. These categories roughly measure price changes at the producer level for the national income and product account (NIPA) categories for personal consumption expenditures on durables and nondurables plus utilities consumption and the producers' durable

TABLE 6–1
Producer Price Indexes by Stage-of-Processing

Relative Importance, December 1993	
Finished goods	100.000
Finished consumer goods	76.627
Finished consumer foods	22.940
Finished energy goods	13.340
Finished consumer goods excluding food and energy	40.347
Capital equipment	23.373
Manufacturing industries	6.059
Nonmanufacturing industries	17.314
Intermediate materials, supplies and components	100.000
Materials and components for manufacturing	49.060
Materials for food manufacturing	3.394
Materials for nondurable manufacturing	14.878
Materials for durable manufacturing	11.289
Components for manufacturing	19.499
Materials and components for construction	14.221
Processed fuels and lubricants	12.695
Containers	3.458
Supplies	20.567
Manufacturing industries	7.602
Nonmanufacturing industries	12.964
Crude materials for further processing	100.000
Foodstuffs and feedstuffs	44.050
Nonfood materials	55.950
Nonfood materials except fuel[5]	36.150
Manufacturing[6]	30.594
Construction	5.556
Crude fuel[7]	19.801
Manufacturing industries	4.228
Nonmanufacturing industries	15.573

Source: US Department of Labor, Bureau of Labor Statistics, *Producer Price Indexes, Data for January 1994.*

equipment component. For the consumer components, commonly followed sub-components are finished consumer foods, finished energy goods, and finished consumer goods excluding food and energy. Finished energy goods are those sold to households and include gasoline, heating oil and also what are technically services, residential electric power, and residential gas. Both finished consumer goods and capital equipment are aggregated from individual commodity series, which are available separately.

For capital equipment, the typical breakdown in the monthly releases give the aggregates for manufacturing and nonmanufacturing industries. As of December 1993, nonmanufacturing industries made up about 17 percent of the finished goods index while the manufacturing subcomponent was roughly 6 percent. Capital equipment PPIs include agricultural machinery; construction machinery; metal-cutting machine tools; metal-forming machine tools; tools, dies, jigs, fixtures, and industrial molds; pumps; and other industrial material handling equipment; electronic computers; textile machinery; paper industries machinery; paper trades machinery; transformers; communications equipment; X-ray and electromedical equipment; oil field and gas field machinery; mining machinery; office and store machines; commercial furniture; light motor trucks; heavy motor trucks; truck trailers; civilian aircraft; ships; railroad equipment; and photographic and photo-copy equipment. Cars are included in both capital equipment and consumer goods.

Capital equipment indexes are strictly limited to the civilian sector; military capital items are not included.

Intermediate Materials, Supplies, and Components

The stage-of-processing PPI for intermediate materials, supplies, and components consists of partially processed commodities as well as some nondurables that are physically complete but are used as inputs for business operations. Examples of the partially processed commodities are lumber and steel; examples of the above-mentioned nondurables are diesel fuel and corrugated boxes. The three major sub-components are intermediate foods and feeds, intermediate energy materials, and intermediate materials less foods and energy. One should note that these broad components do not correspond directly with the broad components of the finished goods categories.

The intermediate materials less foods and feeds series includes flour, refined sugar, confectionery materials, crude vegetable oils, and prepared animal feeds. Examples of intermediate energy materials are commercial electric power, natural gas to electric utilities, jet fuel, and number 2 diesel fuel. Intermediate materials less foods and energy cover a wide array of goods such as synthetic fibers, indus-trial chemicals, agricultural chemicals, plywood, miscellaneous metal products, electronic components, cement, and motor vehicle parts.

Crude Materials for Further Processing

Crude materials for further processing are unprocessed commodities not sold to consumers directly. The major subcomponents are crude foodstuffs and feedstuffs, crude energy materials, and crude nonfood materials less energy.

Crude foodstuffs and feedstuffs make up a little more than one-third of the crude materials index and are almost entirely farm products. Examples are citrus fruits, bulk dried vegetables, wheat, barley, cows, turkeys, fluid use milk, oilseeds, and raw cane sugar. Crude energy materials are about one-half of crude materials, and crude petroleum is about one-half of crude energy materials. Natural gas (to pipelines) is only a slightly smaller subcomponent. The remainder of crude energy materials consists of various specified types of coal. Crude nonfood materials other than energy span a wide variety of basic industrial and construction materi-als. A few representative series are cotton, leaf tobacco, pulpwood, carbon steel scrap, and various specified ores.

Weighting of Components

Weighting methodologies differ according to the classification system of the PPIs.

For industry series, the weights for each component are based on industry net output values of shipments. Net output values are the value of shipments from establishments classified in a particular industry to establishments classi-

TABLE 6–2
A Comparison between the PPI for Finished Goods and the CPI

PPI, Finished Goods	CPI
Covers consumer goods and capital equipment. No services.[9]	Covers consumer goods and services. No capital equipment.
Net unit revenues received by producers from first purchaser.	Prices paid by consumers.
Does not include taxes.	Includes taxes paid by the consumer.
Does not include imports.	Includes imports.
Prices generally refer to Tuesday of the week containing 13th of month.	Prices taken over most of the month.
Mail-in survey primarily.	In-store survey of retailers and a housing survey.
Includes the effects of rebates by producers but not retailers.	Includes effect of rebates by producers or retailers as long as it shows up in the price paid by the consumer.
Controls for quality changes.	Controls for quality changes.

fied in other industries. Because shipments within the industry are excluded, net output differs from gross shipment values. Due to this exclusion, net output values are dependent upon the level of aggregation. As one moves from four-digit to three-digit industry levels and higher, there are greater opportunities for intraindustry shipments. One cannot simply add up disaggregated industry net output values to get higher levels. Net output values are based on data from the *Census of Manufactures,* BEA input-output tables, and other sources.

For the traditional individual and aggregated commodity price indexes, weights are based on gross value of shipments from Census data and other sources. Since January 1987, shipments between plants owned by the same company have been counted as part of gross value. Prior to this date, they were not.

The weights using either gross shipments or net output values are based on shipments in a specified base period. Beginning with the January 1992 index month, weights are based on 1987 shipment values from the Census of Manufactures (and other sources), although the index base period remains 1982=100. From January 1987 through December 1991, PPI weights were based on 1982 shipment values. With PPI methodologies, previous weights for historical data are unchanged with updates on weights (as is also the case for the CPI).

Weights do not change over the period for which they define the mix of goods going into the index. However, the effective importance for a given good does vary over the period and even on a month-to-month basis as differing growth rates in components affect the relative standings. The weight of each component multiplied by its price increase relative to the base period and relative to the other components' price increase, since the base period is that component's relative importance in the index.[8] Basically, components with higher rates of inflation have

rising relative importance figures compared to those with low or negative inflation rates. BLS does not publish shipment values but does publish relative importance figures for December of each year.

KEYS TO ANALYZING THE MONTHLY REPORT

Market analysts each month usually focus on two primary numbers from the PPI
report: total finished goods and finished goods excluding food and energy. Data
generally are discussed in terms of simple monthly percentage changes or annualized rates. The primary use of PPI releases by financial markets is to project
the upcoming CPI release for the same reference month and to add one more piece
of information to their view of whether interest rates are priced too high or too
low or whether conditions are ripe for changes in monetary policy by the Federal Reserve.

The PPI (in this section, for finished goods unless otherwise noted) is more
volatile than the CPI—in particular the food and energy components are more
erratic in monthly movements than their CPI counterparts. Therefore, analysts are
generally predisposed to focus on the PPI less food and energy. This is often mis-
leadingly called the "core" rate of inflation and is based on the assumption that the
food and energy components are simply randomly oscillating each month and do

CHART 6–1
Producer Price Index versus Consumer Price Index

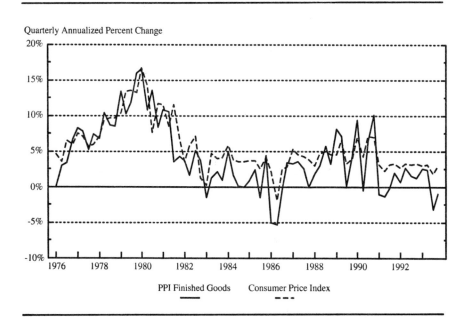

Quarterly Annualized Percent Change

PPI Finished Goods   Consumer Price Index

Source: US Department of Labor.

not have trend growth rates separate from the rest of the PPI. Of course, if food or energy has trends that are different than the trend rate for the rest of the PPI, then the trend rate for the overall PPI will be different from the PPI excluding food and energy.

For analysts interested in forecasting the CPI from the PPI, the most important factor is to use only the consumer component of the PPI.[10] The PPI has a capital equipment component that is not relevant for a CPI forecast. Also, the PPI should only be used to project durables, nondurables, and utility services for the CPI. The CPI has services comprising a little over half of its components by weight for which there are no PPI components. Also, the PPI has little lead time in predicting movement in the CPI. Studies indicate that most of the impact of changes in the PPI are seen in the same month's data for the CPI.[11]

Other than food and energy, the components that often play the largest role in affecting the PPI are for passenger cars and light trucks (10,000 lbs. and less). These components are volatile due to the introduction and ending of rebate programs and special incentives and also due to the difficulty in seasonally adjusting prices for motor vehicles. The timing of the introduction of new models varies from year to year. Also, tobacco and prescription drugs components can cause erratic movement in the PPI.

One of the broader problems with using the stage-of-processing indexes to track costs is that there often is not a uniform, one-directional flow in the production process. For various goods and even specific industries, there is not a perfect flow of materials from crude to intermediate to finished goods. Sometimes the intermediate level is skipped as is often the case with farm products or energy materials. Even intermediate goods or finished products are used in the production of some crude materials. The use of stage-of-processing indexes is best for specific commodities or industries rather than in terms of using the broad indexes to predict changes in the next stage. In particular, one should understand the direction of the production flow for specific goods and industries in order to best utilize the more detailed stage-of-processing PPIs.

Producer price indexes—all three stage-of-production indexes—are early warning signals for consumer price inflation. The finished goods index also provides information on producer prices for capital equipment. The underlying fundamentals for PPIs are similar to those as discussed in the previous chapter for consumer prices. However, producer price indexes are closely tied to manufacturing (although there are utilities components), and indicators of resource usage in manufacturing are useful for tracking and anticipating changes in PPI inflation trends. In particular, capacity utilization rates, vendor performance, and spot and futures prices for various commodities are readily available data series for detecting changes in price pressure at the producer level.

Because of their ready availability and timeliness, many market analysts like to track spot (cash) and futures prices for commodities to project changes in producer prices. A number of spot and futures prices are published daily in *The Wall Street Journal* and other financial publications.

However, a favorite series of many analysts is the Commodity Research Bureau's Futures Price Index (CRB Index). This index is calculated daily by the

CHART 6–2
Producer Price Indexes by Stage-of-Processing

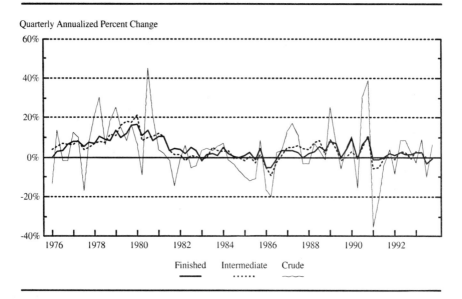

Quarterly Annualized Percent Change

Finished   Intermediate   Crude

Source: US Department of Labor.

CRB with ongoing updates during a trading day. This index currently is based on 21 commodities futures markets. The CRB publishes its index daily along with component groups for imports, industrials, grains, oilseeds, livestock/meats, energy, precious metals, and miscellaneous. The CRB index is not directly related to PPIs but contains many components similar to those in the PPI for crude materials for further processing (as well as some not included in this PPI).

When looking at these indicators, it is important to remember that these spot and futures data are a lot more volatile than PPI series. Both short-run supply and demand for these commodities are usually inelastic. Small shifts in either cause dramatic changes in prices. Only extended changes in these prices should be seen as portending a change in inflation. Frequent false signals occur from these series due to very temporary changes in supply or demand. Series such as capacity utilization rates and vendor performance are not as timely but are more reliable indicators of changing inflation pressures.

TABLE 6–3
Analyzing the News Release: Key Questions

- What did the PPI excluding food and energy do?
- For anticipating the CPI release, what were the changes in the PPI for finished consumer goods and finished consumer goods excluding food and energy?
- Are trends in food and energy diverging from the rest of the PPI: is the PPI excluding food and energy really a trend series for the overall PPI?
- Are changes in crude oil prices still expected to impact the PPI in coming months?
- Did a freeze or another type of agricultural problem boost food prices? Will other food-growing regions or countries be able to replenish these supplies once their growing season reaches harvest and lead to lower prices, or is the shortage for that crop going to continue all year?
- Did passenger car prices have an unsustainably large increase? Did manufacturers' rebates affect the latest data or the previous month's data?
- Were there any one-time, irregular changes such as for ship prices or aircraft prices, which have very lumpy changes?
- Were there any seasonal adjustment oddities (such as for passenger cars or tobacco)?

TABLE 6–4
Producer Prices by Stage-of-Processing

	Annual Percentage Changes		
	Finished Goods	Intermediate Materials, Supplies and Components	Crude Materials for Further Processing
1970	3.4	3.8	3.8
1971	3.1	4.0	2.3
1972	3.2	3.8	10.8
1973	9.1	11.0	36.6
1974	15.4	23.8	12.7
1975	10.6	10.5	0.3
1976	4.5	5.0	2.9
1977	6.4	6.6	3.3
1978	7.9	7.1	12.1
1979	11.2	12.8	17.0
1980	13.4	15.2	10.9
1981	9.2	9.2	8.1
1982	4.1	1.4	−2.9
1983	1.6	0.6	1.3
1984	2.1	2.5	2.2
1985	1.0	−0.4	−7.4
1986	−1.4	−3.5	−8.5
1987	2.1	2.4	6.8
1988	2.5	5.5	2.5
1989	5.2	4.6	7.4
1990	4.9	2.2	5.6
1991	2.1	−0.1	−7.1
1992	1.2	0.3	−0.8

Source: US Department of Labor, Bureau of Labor Statistics.

TABLE 6–5a
Producer Prices for Finished Goods

	Annual Percentage Changes			
	Total Finished Goods	Total Excluding Food and Energy	Consumer Goods	Capital Equipment
1970	3.4	na	3.2	4.7
1971	3.1	na	2.8	4.0
1972	3.2	na	3.2	2.6
1973	9.1	na	10.8	3.3
1974	15.4	11.4	15.4	14.3
1975	10.6	11.4	9.6	15.2
1976	4.5	5.7	3.8	6.7
1977	6.4	6.0	6.5	6.4
1978	7.9	7.5	7.9	7.9
1979	11.2	8.9	11.7	8.7
1980	13.4	11.2	14.3	10.7
1981	9.2	8.6	9.0	10.3
1982	4.1	5.7	3.5	5.7
1983	1.6	3.0	1.3	2.8
1984	2.1	2.4	2.0	2.3
1985	1.0	2.5	0.5	2.2
1986	−1.4	2.3	−2.3	2.0
1987	2.1	2.4	2.2	1.8
1988	2.5	3.3	2.5	2.3
1989	5.2	4.4	5.6	3.9
1990	4.9	3.7	5.4	3.5
1991	2.1	3.6	1.9	3.1
1992	1.2	2.4	1.0	1.9

Source: US Department of Labor, Bureau of Labor Statistics.

TABLE 6–5b
Producer Prices for Finished Goods

	Annual Percentage Changes			
	Total Consumer Goods	Consumer Goods Excluding Food and Energy	Consumer Foods	Finished Energy
1970	3.2	na	3.3	na
1971	2.8	na	1.6	na
1972	3.2	na	5.4	na
1973	10.8	na	20.5	na
1974	15.4	10.1	14.0	na
1975	9.6	9.2	8.4	17.2
1976	3.8	5.1	−0.3	11.7
1977	6.5	5.7	5.3	15.7
1978	7.9	7.3	9.0	6.5
1979	11.7	9.1	9.3	35.0
1980	14.3	11.4	5.8	49.2
1981	9.0	7.7	5.8	19.1
1982	3.5	5.7	2.2	−1.5
1983	1.3	3.1	1.0	−4.8
1984	2.0	2.5	4.4	−4.2
1985	0.5	2.6	−0.8	−3.9
1986	−2.3	2.5	2.6	−28.1
1987	2.2	2.8	2.1	−1.9
1988	2.5	3.8	2.8	−3.2
1989	5.6	4.6	5.4	9.9
1990	5.4	3.9	4.8	14.2
1991	1.9	3.8	−0.2	4.1
1992	1.0	2.7	−0.6	−0.4

Source: US Department of Labor, Bureau of Labor Statistics.

NOTES FOR CHAPTER 6

1. Since 1986, the PPI no longer includes imports. While imports have never had a significant role, the PPI survey currently actively filters out priced imports.
2. US Department of Labor, Bureau of Labor Statistics, *BLS Handbook of Methods*, September 1992, p. 142.
3. US Department of Labor, Bureau of Labor Statistics, *BLS Handbook of Methods*, April 1988, p. 125.
4. *BLS Handbook,* p. 143.
5. Includes crude petroleum.
6. Includes crude petroleum.
7. Excludes crude petroleum.
8. The concept of relative importance is discussed in greater detail in the CPI chapter.
9. Natural gas and electric utilities for residences are included and technically are services. While not included in the PPI for finished goods, a number of services industries are covered by producer price indexes for the net output of selected industries.
10. R Mark Rogers, "Improving Monthly Models for Economic Indicators: The Example of An Improved CPI Model," *Economic Review,* Federal Reserve Bank of Atlanta, September/October 1988, pp. 34–50.
11. Ibid., p. 39.

BIBLIOGRAPHY

Bechter, Dan M, and Margaret S Pickett. "The Wholesale and Consumer Price Indexes: What's the Connection?" *Monthly Review.* Federal Reserve Bank of Kansas City. June 1973, pp. 3–9.

Rogers, R Mark. "Improving Monthly Models for Economic Indicators: The Example of An Improved CPI Model." *Economic Review.* Federal Reserve Bank of Atlanta. September/October 1988, pp. 34–50.

US Department of Labor. Bureau of Labor Statistics. *BLS Handbook of Methods.* April 1988.

———. Bureau of Labor Statistics. *BLS Handbook of Methods.* September 1992.

———. Bureau of Labor Statistics. *Producer Price Indexes, Data for June 1993.*

CHAPTER 7

INDUSTRIAL PRODUCTION AND CAPACITY UTILIZATION RATES

The index of industrial production (IP) is compiled by the Federal Reserve Board of Governors and reflects levels of output for manufacturing, mining, and public utilities (gas and electricity). Capacity utilization rates also are estimated by the Federal Reserve and reflect the level of output relative to potential production, that is, capacity. These series are released along with IP data. Both IP and capacity utilization are important in business cycle analysis since the largest component of IP, manufacturing, is one of the more cyclical sectors of the economy. In fact, overall IP is one of four components in the Commerce Department's index of coincident indicators, which plays a key role in defining turning points in the business cycle. Since industrial production leads employment in the high-wage manufacturing sector, it also is a significant factor in cyclical changes in personal income growth. Capacity utilization rates are important as a measure of inflationary pressure and as a leading indicator for investment in the manufacturing sector.

INDUSTRIAL PRODUCTION

IP and capacity utilization rate data are released together around the 15th of each month for activity of the previous month. With each release, revisions are also made for the prior three months. The initial estimate and early revisions reflect the differing times of availability for very different types of data used to estimate production levels. This is discussed in more detail later.

The industrial production index is based on 255 basic components—the individual series—which are weighted together with a base year currently of 1987 being set equal to 100.[1] Index components are weighted by value-added shares primarily reflecting the 1987 Census of Manufactures and other sources. This is in contrast to gross-value. Each component's share discounts the cost of materials and reflects only the value added during the production process. Each industry's production represents only its contribution to a product's value. This means that as production is summed across the various stages of production, there is no double-counting.

When the IP index is rebased, the base year is determined by the most recently available Census of Manufactures and Census of Mineral Industries, which occur every five years. Annual data are benchmarked against data from these censuses.

For each component and for aggregated indexes, the index value reflects changes in physical production relative to the base year. An index value of 130.0 means that output is 30 percent higher than for the average level of output in the base year of 1987. In terms of IP's contribution to the economy, about 28 percent of real gross domestic product in 1985 was produced in the industries covered by the industrial production index.[2]

IP data are organized from two different perspectives: (1) from the supplier side with data categorized by industry and (2) from the demand side with data separately grouped by market category. The major industry sectors are, of course, manufacturing, mining, and public utilities. Public utilities include piped natural gas and electric utilities. Further divisions for industry groups are based on standard industrial classification (SIC) codes. The most familiar industry subcomponents are generally known by two- or three-digit SIC categories. As an aside, the US index of industrial production differs in one significant respect from IP indexes devised by a number of other developed countries—the US index does not include construction activity.

The reports for both sets of data now are combined into one release entitled *Industrial Production and Capacity Utilization*, also known as the Federal Reserve Board's G.17 report. Other published sources include the Federal Reserve Board's monthly *Federal Reserve Bulletin* and the Commerce Department's *Survey of Current Business*. Data are subject to preliminary revisions for three additional months following the initial release. More extensive revisions are made periodically. These revisions usually incorporate late data for monthly estimates, updated seasonal factors, and corrected errors.

IP by Industry Structure

Industrial production data for the industry groupings are based on a classification system known as the Standard Industrial Classification (SIC). This system is used by federal agencies in the United States for many economic statistics. This allows for comparisons of various statistics from differing agencies, and it also allows the statistical agencies to use the others' data in many of their own estimates. For example, the Federal Reserve Board is able to use data by industry from the Bureau of Labor Statistics on the number of hours worked in estimates for industrial output, since series are organized by comparable SIC categories. Other agencies using SIC codes for their data include, among others, the Census Bureau (new factory orders, for example) and the Bureau of Economic Analysis (such as for personal income). However, the Federal Reserve Board does not cover all industries at the four-digit SIC level (a fine level of detail). Some industries are reported with a higher level of aggregation only. The latest version of SIC codes was set in its basic form in 1972 with only minor revisions in 1977 and in 1987.[3]

Table 7–1 shows industrial production according to industry shares.

TABLE 7–1
Major Industry Groups of Industrial Production

Group	SIC Code	Proportion In 1987	In 1993
Mining and utilities	—	15.7	15.1
Mining	—	8.0	7.0
Utilities	—	7.7	8.1
Manufacturing	—	84.3	84.9
Nondurable	—	37.8	37.0
Durable	—	46.5	47.9
Mining			
Metal mining	10	0.3	0.5
Coal	12	1.2	1.2
Oil and gas extraction	13	5.8	4.8
Stone and earth minerals	14	0.7	0.6
Nondurable manufactures			
Foods	20	8.8	8.6
Tobacco products	21	1.0	0.9
Textile mill products	22	1.8	2.0
Apparel products	23	2.3	2.0
Paper and products	26	3.6	3.7
Printing and publishing	27	6.5	5.9
Chemicals and products	28	8.8	9.3
Petroleum products	29	1.3	1.3
Rubber and miscellaneous plastics products	30	3.2	3.4
Leather and products	31	0.3	0.2
Durable manufactures			
Lumber and products	24	2.1	1.9
Furniture and fixtures	25	1.5	1.4
Clay, glass, and stone products	32	2.4	2.1
Primary metals	33	3.3	3.2
Iron and steel	331,2	1.9	1.9
Fabricated metal products	34	5.4	4.9
Industrial and commercial machinery and computer equipment	35	8.5	11.1
Office and computing machines	357	2.3	4.7
Electrical machinery	36	6.9	8.0
Transportation equipment	37	9.9	9.3
Motor vehicles and parts	371	4.8	5.2
Autos and light trucks		2.2	2.6
Aerospace and miscellaneous transportation equipment	372–6,9	5.1	4.1
Instruments	38	5.1	4.8
Miscellaneous manufactures	39	1.3	1.2
Utilities			
Electric	491,3pt	6.1	6.3
Gas	492,3pt	1.6	1.7

Source: Federal Reserve Board, G.17, February 15, 1994.

CHART 7–1
Industrial Production: Durable versus Nondurable Manufacturing

Year-Ago Percent Changes

Durable Manufacturing   Nondurable Manufacturing

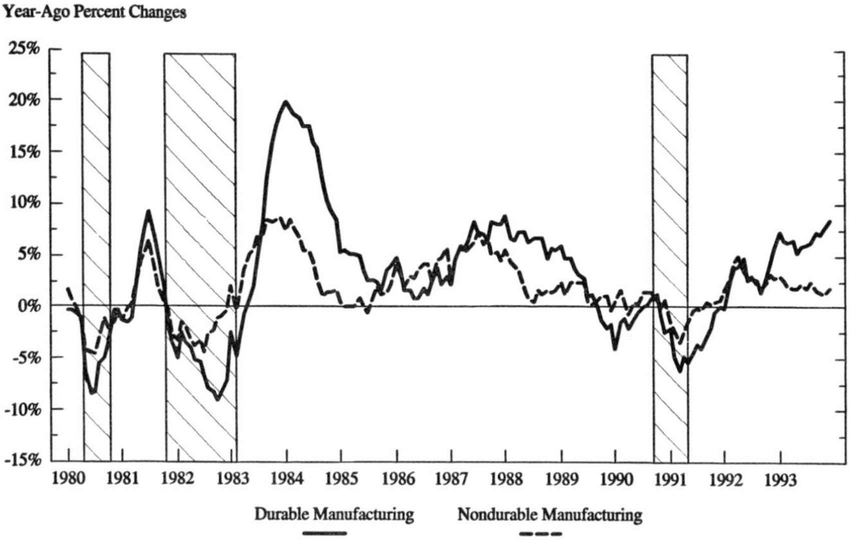

Source: Board of Governors, Federal Reserve.

IP by Market Structure

The market structure indexes for IP are based on the same 255 individual series as for the industry-based indexes. However, the market components are put together in different combinations. For example, canned and frozen foods are nondurables under industry classification as is the aviation fuel and kerosene series. By market group, canned and frozen food are nondurable consumer goods, while the aviation fuel and kerosene component is an intermediate product under business supplies for commercial energy products.

Market groups are demand-oriented with the two major groups being "products" and "materials." Products are further divided into "final products" for consumer goods and equipment and into "intermediate products." This gives a stage-of-processing or input-output approach to the data. Final products are defined as products that undergo no further processing either in the industrial or other sectors and are consumed by the consumer or government sectors or purchased as investment goods by the business sector. Intermediate and materials require further processing. However, intermediate products are used in production outside the industrial sector—such as construction, agriculture, and services—while materials remain in the industrial sector. Intermediate products are broken down into categories for construction and business supplies. Materials are subdivided into durable and nondurable materials and energy materials. Table 7–2 shows a breakdown of components by market categories.

TABLE 7–2
Major Market Groups of Industrial Production

Group	Proportion In 1987	Proportion In 1993
Total index	100.0	100.0
Products, total	59.5	59.2
Final products	44.8	45.6
Consumer goods	26.5	26.0
Equipment, total	18.3	19.6
Intermediate products	14.7	13.6
Materials	40.5	40.8
Consumer goods	26.5	26.0
Durable consumer goods	5.8	5.8
Automotive products	2.7	2.8
Autos and trucks	1.7	1.7
Auto parts and allied goods	1.0	1.0
Other durable goods	3.1	3.1
Appliances, TVs, and air conditioning	0.8	0.9
Carpeting and furniture	0.9	0.8
Miscellaneous	1.4	1.4
Nondurable consumer goods	20.7	20.2
Foods and tobacco	9.1	8.8
Clothing	2.6	2.2
Chemical products	3.6	4.0
Paper products	2.6	2.4
Energy products	2.7	2.8
Fuels	0.8	0.7
Utilities	2.0	2.1
Equipment total	18.3	19.6
Business equipment	13.2	16.0
Information processing & related	5.5	7.8
Office and computing	1.9	3.8
Industrial	3.9	4.0
Transit	2.0	2.5
Autos and trucks	1.0	1.3
Other	1.8	1.8
Defense and space equipment	4.4	2.9
Oil and gas well drilling	0.6	0.4
Manufactured homes	0.2	0.2
Intermediate products	14.7	13.6
Construction supplies	5.9	5.1
Business supplies	8.8	8.5
Materials	40.5	40.8
Durable	20.5	21.3
Consumer parts	4.1	4.2
Equipment parts	7.4	8.3
Other	9.0	8.9
Basic metals	3.1	3.1
Nondurable	9.0	9.2
Textile	1.2	1.1
Paper	2.0	2.0
Chemical	3.8	4.0
Other	2.0	2.1
Energy	11.0	10.2
Primary	7.3	6.5
Converted fuel	3.7	3.8

Source: Federal Reserve Board, G.17, February 15, 1994.

Market groups are useful for analyzing imbalances among sectors of demand. Flows can be followed from producer to user and can even take into account import/export flows with the use of end-use merchandise trade data from the Census Bureau.

Estimation Methodologies: From Initial Estimates through Benchmark Revisions

The estimation methodology varies significantly from initial estimates compared to much-later benchmark revisions. However, the initial estimation process is linked to that for revised data. Why do these processes differ? First, not all actual counts of production are available immediately for each series. Various measures of inputs—especially labor hours and electricity usage—are available sooner than output measures for many IP components. In general, less reliable input data are available sooner than output measures for many IP components. But economy watchers want estimates for IP much sooner than is possible for more accurate final estimates of production. Hence, there is a trade-off between timeliness and accuracy of the data.

The methodology used for data in each of the various stages of revision is heavily dependent upon the when the various types of data can be obtained. For estimating the IP index, there are three basic types of data series: (1) physical product, (2) production-worker hours, and (3) electric power use by industry. Electric power use data are often referred to as kilowatt hours data. Various combinations of these are used for initial estimates through benchmark revisions. The physical product series is the least available initially, but grows in importance through the revision process.

Physical product series reflect an actual count or estimates of counts of production. Output is measured in quantity—not value. Physical product is the ideal in which IP is measured. Actual counts are preferred to dollar estimates of production in calculating production since price factors are often difficult to discount. These data frequently come from industry trade sources and from government agencies such as the Department of Energy, Bureau of the Census, and others.

Data for production-worker hours for each industry come from the Bureau of Labor Statistics (BLS) and are the product of the number of production workers in a given industry and its average manufacturing workweek. Data are estimated by industry components and are used when other, more-reliable physical product data are not yet available or when physical product counts are not desirable. For example, production-worker data are used even for late revisions for industries such as defense and space where counting output may not be meaningful—especially over short time spans. Production-worker data are released by the BLS for public use the first week of the month following the reference month. Therefore, these series are available for the initial estimates for IP, which are released about 10 days to 2 weeks after the employment report.

The kilowatt-hours data—that is, electric utilities output—are collected by the District Federal Reserve banks. This is generally done with mail-in surveys, and the results are forwarded to the Board of Governors. Almost all of the kilowatt hours data are available for use in estimates of industrial production about six

TABLE 7–3
Estimated Availability of Industrial Production Data by Successive Months^5 (Percent of Value Added in 1987)

	Month of Estimate			
Type of Data	1st	2nd	3rd	4th
Physical product	14	27	32	37
Kilowatt hours (KWH)	0	27	27	27
Production-workers hours (PWH)	34	34	34	34
Federal Reserve estimates	52	12	7	2
Total industrial production	**100**	**100**	**100**	**100**

weeks after the fact. Hence, the electric power data are not used in initial estimates for IP but are first available for the second estimate (first revision).

Initial monthly estimates of industrial production are heavily based on production-worker hours from the Bureau of Labor Statistics and on judgment by the Federal Reserve staff. This judgment is largely based on incomplete industry reports and other anecdotal sources. Actual counts of production for use in the initial industrial production report are limited to a small percentage of the industries covered. Some of the key series for which hard data are usually available for the initial news release are motor vehicles, steel and other metals, and lumber and paper. By the third monthly revision, physical product data account for about 37 percent of the IP index estimate by value added. Table 7–3 shows how initial IP estimates are heavily dependent on production-worker hours directly and indirectly (for Federal Reserve Board [FRB] estimates). The indirect impact becomes less important with each revision as physical product and kilowatt hours data become available.

For the manufacturing component, annual revisions are derived from the Bureau of the Census' Annual Survey of Manufactures (ASM) with the quinquennial Census of Manufactures being used for census years. The census is a nearly complete tally of the manufacturing sector in the United States while the ASM is less comprehensive but still has a panel of over 55,000 manufacturing establishments with the reported value of shipments covering about 65 percent of manufacturing.[4]

Almost all of the mining components in the industrial production index base annual revisions on data from the Bureau of Mines in its *Mineral Yearbook*. For utilities components, annual revisions are derived from data from the Department of Energy and other sources.

KEYS TO ANALYZING THE MONTHLY REPORT

Industry Series

Industrial production is a key indicator of the current strength of the economy. Financial markets place heavy emphasis on watching this indicator. However, analysts definitely need to sort through some of the components to see the underlying strengths and weaknesses.

Manufacturing

First, manufacturing is the key component. Its weight averages around 85 percent of the total index. Analysts generally look at trends in the manufacturing component and view utilities output as tracking overall economic growth with deviations being weather-related. Mining has a larger share than utilities, but markets usually pay even less attention to it because output is more affected by relative prices of energy materials than by changes in strength of the economy. Perhaps even more importantly, there is very little employment in this sector, and there are limited spillover effects from employment and income.

When looking at the manufacturing component, one should try to discount any unsustainable fluctuations in output. This usually involves looking at the important auto industry. Often, auto output changes significantly over the course of a year due to the need to bring production in line with sales. The auto industry is notorious for not quickly adjusting output to changes in sales trends. However, the Federal Reserve Board makes it easy to take into account the oscillations of auto and light truck production. There is a special index, "manufacturing excluding motor vehicles," which is published each month.

To determine whether or not motor vehicle production is sustainable, one can look at production rates for autos and for light trucks as published in the IP release. These are easily comparable to unit sales figures put out by the Bureau of Economic Analysis (BEA) and by motor vehicle manufacturers. Production data for motor vehicles are in index form but also are published in millions of units, annualized and seasonally adjusted. This is the usual basis for comparisons between production and sales and inventories. Also automakers generally announce planned production rates one quarter ahead, and these rates are usually in millions of units annualized.

Mining

The mining component was 7.9 percent of the overall IP index in the 1987 base year and 7.0 percent in 1993. The primary subcomponents are metal mining, coal, oil and gas extraction, and stone and earth minerals. Over two-thirds of the mining component typically is oil and gas extraction. Extraction accounts for actual output of crude oil and natural gas and also natural gas liquids. Changes in the extraction of these energy goods produce most of the monthly volatility in the mining component. Oil and gas well *drilling* is a subcomponent separate from extraction. This series also is volatile but has a share under 1 percent of total IP. Data come from the Hughes Tool Company.[6]

Metal mining contains iron ores and copper ores with breakdowns also available for lead and zinc ores, gold and silver ores, ferroalloy ores, and miscellaneous metal ores. The stone and earth minerals subcomponent includes series for a stone, sand and gravel group, chemical and fertilizer materials, and a miscellaneous category.

Public Utilities

The two biggest factors affecting utility output are: (1) economic activity in general and (2) the weather. Since electricity is an input in manufacturing, utility output is indicative of industrial activity, and this, as discussed, is the rationale behind some of the Federal Reserve's estimation methodology. Of course, weather affects utility output and on a month-to-month basis is this component's chief source of volatility. The impact of weather is usually discussed in terms of residential usage, but commercial usage is also affected.

Certainly, utility output is seasonally adjusted, but this adjustment only discounts "normal" weather patterns. Unseasonal weather leads to atypical monthly utility output, and these changes in production frequently cause the overall IP index to swing sharply. When unseasonal weather returns to normal, output returns to trend and there is a technical reversal in the monthly percentage change in this IP component. For example, an abnormally severe January snowstorm would cause the utility IP to jump. Returning to a normal winter level the next month would cause a drop in output from an abnormally high level.

However, the utilities component should not be ignored by market watchers. Changes in residential utility usage are one of the key variables behind volatility in services personal consumption—a major component of gross national product (GNP) or gross domestic product (GDP).

Among IP components, the computer equipment series (or more specifically, office and computing machines) is unique in that its growth rate over extended periods of time has been maintained by technological advances. Essentially, producers probably do view their production as being not as strong in real terms as indicated by the production index. While output may be up in terms of processing capability, the number of "boxes" has been down at times. Likewise, industry revenues have experienced declines even as real production rises after adjustments for technological change.

Market Group Series

Some of the "goods" in consumer goods are not really goods that the public generally thinks of in terms for consumer products. In particular, energy products are a subcomponent of nondurable consumer goods and are further broken down into fuel and utilities. While fuel—including gasoline—is a product, it is not what one generally conceives of as a good in which production is following underlying consumer demand as might be the case for apparel or consumer electronics. This is also the case for utilities. Changes in this component may simply be weather-related rather than being indicative of production trends for general type of consumer goods. Since much of the volatility in consumer goods production for nondurables is caused by swings in energy products, one should look at subcomponent detail before making assertions about trends for the broader component. Industry series for petroleum refining and residential electric utilities often move in tandem with the market group of nondurable consumer goods or at least the energy products series.

From the market perspective, interpreting the data is more demand-oriented. A key factor in production is demand for motor vehicles. Estimation methods and allocation between various sectors of demand can affect one's interpretation of the sustainability of production in this sector. Other IP market group series may not match up with various popular concepts of demand. This is the case for some market groups containing utilities and other energy goods.

Business equipment includes autos and trucks, computers, aircraft, industrial machinery, as well as others. The motor vehicle components are important because of their relative size and monthly volatility.

Motor vehicle data for market categories begin with industry data. Auto and truck production estimates are based on figures from *Ward's Automotive News*. Physical product data for the entire month are available for the first estimate for IP. Auto and truck production by industry go into market categories of both consumer durables and business equipment. Allocation of production between these two market categories is based on the Bureau of Economic Analysis' (BEA) division of unit sales between durables personal consumption and investment in producers' durable equipment. The BEA's allocation is based on Polk registration data. Since Polk registration data are not available for two months after the fact, initial allocation by market categories reflect rough estimates based on trends and anecdotal industry information on sales trends—particularly in reference to fleet sales to car rental agencies. Automakers have developed ownership interests in many rental firms, and this does provide good information on sales to the business sector. Importantly, the roughness of the estimation of shares of production to these two market components does not change the strong reliability of the data on actual production of motor vehicles.

Defense and space production is based on production-worker hours and reflects the monthly employment data.

Intermediate products consist of construction supplies and business supplies. Intermediate products for construction closely follow building activity and indicators such as housing starts and nonresidential construction contracts. Examples of this group are lumber, flooring, plywood, and paint. Business supplies cover a wide range of goods going into business activity. A small sample of items in this group includes job printing, replacement tires for business vehicles, aviation fuel, commercial gas, and others.

Materials is the last major market group. Traditionally, materials production tracked product output. However, starting in the late 1970s, more materials were imported as foreign producers significantly increased capacity and became price-competitive. To track materials production, international commodity markets must be followed along with changes in exchange rates, subsidy policies, and even currency needs of foreign governments.

By components, durable goods materials include parts for consumer durables and for equipment as well as basic metal materials. Nondurable goods materials cover textile, paper, and chemical materials and various miscellaneous nondurables materials. Finally, energy materials are comprised of primary energy materials and converted fuel materials. Coal, crude oil, natural gas, and hydronuclear generated electricity are included in primary energy materials, while converted energy materials are industrial electricity, industrial gas, nuclear materials, coke, LPG, gas-line transmission, and residual materials.

KEY ROLES IN THE ECONOMY AND UNDERLYING FUNDAMENTALS

The index of industrial production is the primary measure of output in manufacturing, mining, and public utilities. While mining has declined in importance over the years, and public utilities output has tracked overall economic growth, manufacturing remains a very important segment of the economy. Even though employment in manufacturing has been on a secular decline, manufacturing's share of the economy's overall output has remained relatively constant. Importantly, manufacturing—particularly durables—is far more cyclical than the economy overall. Typically, manufacturing output growth must be noticeably stronger than overall economic growth during periods of expansion. Manufacturing also helps drive the consumer sector by providing high-wage jobs and also by supporting secondary service-sector and even construction-sector jobs.

Industrial production is driven by demand and inventory cycle adjustments. Changes in demand relative to output show up in unplanned changes in inventories. Unexpected declines in inventories (strong demand) lead to increased production. Unexpected increases in inventories (weak demand) result in decreased industrial production. Changes in demand (up or down) for manufacturing output are seen in changes in new factory orders. Basically, industrial production is demand-driven with imbalances between supply (production) and demand being corrected by inventory movement and resulting changes in orders to factories.

To track underlying fundamentals, one should closely watch production by market categories and corresponding demand by similar categories for personal consumption, business investment, and exports and imports. If production appears to diverge from domestic and foreign consumption of output, then one should try to corroborate these imbalances in inventory data and in orders numbers. For durables, unfilled orders data provide significant information on potential imbalances between supply and demand. For nondurables, unfilled orders data are not as strong a signal for pending production changes because few nondurables industries provide data on unfilled orders.

CAPACITY UTILIZATION RATES

Capacity utilization rates are measures of actual production relative to capacity. These series are produced by the Federal Reserve Board of Governors and are useful indicators of overall availability of manufacturing resources and of pending or actual supply bottlenecks in the US industrial sector. In turn, these series are useful in tracking changes in inflation pressures caused by supply conditions. Furthermore, these series provide information on which industries need to expand capacity and may boost planned investment. Also, for policymakers the data are useful in helping to determine if the economy is fully employed—at least from the perspective of physical capital.

TABLE 7–4
Industrial Production: Major Industries (Annual Average Percentage Changes)

	Total IP	Mining	Manufacturing Total	Durable	Nondurable	Public Utilities
1960	2.3	1.7	2.2	1.9	2.3	6.9
1961	0.7	0.7	0.3	−1.7	3.1	5.6
1962	8.4	2.9	8.8	10.9	6.1	7.6
1963	6.1	4.1	6.3	6.7	5.6	6.9
1964	6.8	4.1	6.8	7.2	6.5	8.5
1965	9.9	3.6	10.7	13.6	6.7	6.2
1966	8.8	5.4	9.1	11.1	6.3	7.6
1967	2.2	1.9	2.0	1.1	3.2	5.0
1968	5.6	3.8	5.5	4.9	6.4	8.1
1969	4.6	4.0	4.4	4.0	5.2	8.7
1970	−3.3	2.6	−4.5	−7.6	0.1	6.2
1971	1.4	−2.5	1.5	−0.5	4.0	4.8
1972	9.7	2.1	10.5	11.7	9.0	6.4
1973	8.1	0.9	8.8	11.6	5.0	3.9
1974	−1.5	−0.5	−1.5	−2.1	−0.7	−1.2
1975	−8.8	−2.2	−9.9	−12.3	−6.2	0.9
1976	9.2	0.8	10.2	10.3	10.1	4.0
1977	8.0	2.6	8.8	9.7	7.4	2.6
1978	5.7	3.1	6.2	7.7	4.2	3.0
1979	3.7	1.9	3.9	5.8	1.3	2.8
1980	−1.8	3.3	−2.6	−3.3	−1.7	0.8
1981	1.9	3.9	1.9	2.3	1.7	−1.7
1982	−4.4	−4.4	−4.6	−6.0	−2.4	−2.9
1983	3.6	−4.1	5.6	5.7	5.4	2.1
1984	9.4	6.8	10.4	15.1	4.4	3.9
1985	1.7	−2.6	2.6	3.8	0.7	2.2
1986	1.0	−7.4	2.9	2.3	3.7	−3.2
1987	5.0	−0.9	6.1	6.5	5.4	3.8
1988	4.4	1.3	4.6	6.6	2.3	4.9
1989	1.5	−1.4	1.6	1.8	1.4	3.6
1990	0.0	2.1	−0.2	−0.9	0.6	1.3
1991	−1.9	−1.8	−2.3	−3.4	−0.8	2.0
1992	2.4	−2.0	3.1	3.1	3.0	−0.1
1993	4.1	−1.0	4.6	6.7	2.0	3.4

Source: Federal Reserve Board of Governors. Based on averages of monthly seasonally adjusted indexes.

Capacity utilization rates are also available by individual industry groups. Manufacturers can track industries providing materials to their plants to see if bottlenecks are developing as well as higher prices. Following these series allows for better planning within the manufacturing sector.

There are several different concepts of capacity upon which capacity utilization rates depend. Engineering capacity reflects the idea of maximum output, but it is not a realistic concept from a business or economic perspective. Maximum engineering capacity is not practical. The Federal Reserve concept takes into account various practical operating factors.

TABLE 7–5a
Industrial Production: Major Market Categories (Annual Average Percentage Changes)

| | Total IP | Final Products | Consumer Goods | | |
			Total	Durable	Nondurable
1960	2.3	3.3	3.8	5.7	3.1
1961	0.7	0.8	2.1	−1.4	3.3
1962	8.4	8.5	6.7	13.0	4.7
1963	6.1	6.0	5.7	8.7	4.6
1964	6.8	5.6	5.6	7.5	4.9
1965	9.9	9.7	7.8	16.8	4.3
1966	8.8	9.5	5.0	5.7	4.8
1967	2.2	4.2	2.6	−3.7	5.2
1968	5.6	4.7	5.9	11.4	3.9
1969	4.6	3.2	3.8	4.4	3.4
1970	−3.3	−3.6	−1.2	−7.8	1.7
1971	1.4	0.9	5.8	13.2	2.9
1972	9.7	8.5	8.0	11.9	6.4
1973	8.1	7.4	4.4	7.7	3.0
1974	−1.5	−0.3	−3.1	−10.3	0.0
1975	−8.8	−5.8	−3.8	−9.0	−1.9
1976	9.2	7.0	9.8	17.2	7.3
1977	8.0	8.2	7.1	13.0	4.9
1978	5.7	6.3	3.9	3.8	4.0
1979	3.7	3.8	−1.3	−5.1	−0.1
1980	−1.8	1.3	−2.2	−12.8	1.6
1981	1.9	2.6	0.6	0.5	0.6
1982	−4.4	−1.5	−1.5	−7.1	0.1
1983	3.6	2.7	5.1	16.2	2.4
1984	9.4	9.7	4.6	14.1	1.8
1985	1.7	3.5	0.9	0.7	1.0
1986	1.0	1.6	3.3	3.2	3.4
1987	5.0	4.5	3.3	5.7	2.5
1988	4.4	4.8	2.8	4.6	2.3
1989	1.5	1.9	1.1	1.8	0.9
1990	0.0	0.2	−0.5	−4.0	0.5
1991	−1.9	−1.6	−0.6	−6.6	1.0
1992	2.4	2.6	3.0	7.1	1.9
1993	4.1	4.4	2.8	8.4	1.3

The capacity indexes attempt to capture the concept of sustainable practical capacity, which is defined as the greatest level of output that a plant can maintain within their framework of a realistic work schedule, taking account of normal downtime, and assuming sufficient availability of inputs to operate the machinery and equipment in place.[7]

The Federal Reserve Board's concept of capacity utilization is that changes in utilization rates should primarily reflect changes in production—not monthly changes in capacity. The Board assumes that growth in capacity is smooth. In fact, "current" estimates for capacity are based on projections from survey data of the previous year. Plant closings and openings rarely enter capacity figures and, in

TABLE 7–5b
Industrial Production: Major Industries (Annual Average Percentage Changes)

		Equipment				
	Total	Business Equipment	Defense and Space	Oil and Gas Drilling	Intermediate Products	Materials Products
1960	2.7	2.8	2.8	−6.3	0.7	1.4
1961	−1.4	−3.0	1.5	3.2	1.8	0.2
1962	11.4	8.8	15.9	6.1	6.2	8.9
1963	6.0	5.0	7.8	0.2	5.7	6.5
1964	5.7	11.8	−3.1	6.3	6.6	8.1
1965	13.1	14.6	10.6	3.4	6.4	11.4
1966	16.5	15.9	17.6	−1.0	6.1	9.0
1967	6.3	1.9	14.0	−8.5	4.1	−0.9
1968	2.9	4.4	0.2	4.3	5.7	6.6
1969	2.6	6.4	−4.8	3.4	5.4	6.0
1970	−7.1	−3.5	−15.3	−12.9	−1.5	−3.5
1971	−6.4	−5.0	−10.2	−4.3	3.0	1.5
1972	8.9	14.0	−2.8	15.0	11.7	10.2
1973	11.8	17.0	−2.3	8.2	6.5	9.5
1974	3.1	4.4	−1.5	24.4	−3.5	−2.1
1975	−8.2	−10.7	−1.9	13.5	−9.7	−12.2
1976	3.3	3.7	1.6	0.3	10.2	11.7
1977	9.7	12.0	−0.2	21.5	8.5	7.5
1978	9.2	11.2	0.6	12.3	5.6	5.2
1979	10.6	13.3	4.0	−3.1	2.7	3.9
1980	5.1	2.8	11.5	24.3	−5.1	−4.3
1981	4.8	3.5	1.9	33.1	0.0	1.6
1982	−1.5	−4.1	12.3	−6.0	−2.5	−8.3
1983	−0.3	−1.4	9.3	−13.6	6.9	3.8
1984	16.2	18.7	9.9	15.7	7.5	9.4
1985	6.3	6.7	13.4	−12.2	2.4	0.0
1986	−0.3	2.3	7.3	−45.1	4.1	−0.7
1987	5.9	7.4	4.3	−9.2	8.8	4.3
1988	7.6	10.7	−0.4	1.3	1.9	5.0
1989	3.1	4.4	0.4	−7.3	0.2	1.6
1990	1.1	1.2	−1.1	16.9	−0.8	0.1
1991	−2.8	−1.0	−7.5	−13.9	−4.3	−1.3
1992	2.1	5.6	−9.2	−17.0	2.3	2.2
1993	6.6	10.2	−9.9	5.4	3.6	4.0

turn, utilization rates until they show up in annual surveys for either capacity utilization rates or for capacity. To better understand these concepts, one should first get a brief idea of how capacity figures are derived.

Estimating Capacity and Capacity Utilization

In overview, annual figures and "current" monthly estimates are derived with somewhat different methodologies. For annual end-of-year data, the basic methodology is that capacity utilization rates are based on data from surveys and various industry sources. Meanwhile, output is measured independently as discussed in the industrial production section. Capacity then is derived as an identity from the other two series. These are preliminary estimates, however, and adjustments are made so that implied capacity figures are in line with capacity and capital stock data from various industry sources.

Official capacity utilization rates then are derived as an identity of these adjusted capacity figures and independently estimated production data. The identity is that capacity utilization is the ratio of production to capacity. One should note that capacity and capacity utilization rates are derived on an industry basis—the same as is the case for industrial production. As is discussed further below, current year monthly figures are dependent upon projections of capacity data, while annual figures for capacity are based on hard data either for capacity or for capacity utilization.

The Board's methodology for estimating capacity and capacity utilization is a multistep process that is explained and simplified below. Most of the process involves the estimation of capacity.

Step 1: Obtain Preliminary Estimates for Capacity Utilization Rates.
The board's estimates for annual capacity utilization numbers begin with capacity utilization surveys of the Census Bureau, the Department of Energy, and various industry trade associations. Since surveys that had been conducted by the BEA and McGraw-Hill/DRI (and were key providers of capacity utilization data) are no longer produced,[8] the primary source of survey data is the Survey of Plant Capacity conducted by the Census Bureau. Beginning in 1989—due to budget constraints, Census switched from an annual survey to one that takes place every two years. Surveys are conducted in the fourth quarter of even-numbered years with data obtained for both the current year and previous year. In 1990, about 9,000 industry plants participated. These surveys provide survey-based capacity utilization figures for the board to use as input in its estimates.

Step 2: Derive Preliminary Implied Capacity Estimates.
Once industrial production (already estimated by the Board of Governors) and survey-based capacity utilization rates are known, an implied figure for capacity can be derived for the year just ended. The identity or formula is: preliminary capacity equals output divided by the survey-based capacity utilization rate (see formula below). This gives an implied capacity figure that is an estimate of maximum sustainable output expressed as a percent of actual *output* in 1987. One should note that the ratio is not relative to capacity in 1987. Importantly, these preliminary capacity figures are preliminary in the sense that they are still inputs in the board's estimation procedure. These preliminary capacity figures—implied from the survey-based capacity utilization data—are never published as official data and then subsequently revised. They are merely part of the estimation process.

$$\text{Preliminary implied capacity} = \frac{\text{Output, FRB estimate}}{\text{Survey capacity utilization rate}}$$

However, the preliminary capacity figures—based on survey capacity utilization rates—are unacceptably cyclical. Preliminary capacity figures tend to rise sharply in expansion after declining in recession. Capacity tended to be "found" by survey respondents during expansion and "lost" during recovery. Apparently, plant managers can "find" capacity when they need it during periods of heavy demand. However, these extreme cyclical tendencies are not consistent with other measures of capacity growth—such as capacity in physical units, capital stock data, and capacity data from surveys in which capacity is reported directly.

Step 3: Adjust Preliminary Capacity Estimates.

Adjust preliminary capacity estimates so that their cyclical movements are in line with those for capital stock and other data but has trend growth that tracks implied capacity figures from survey capacity utilization rates. Preliminary capacity estimates are therefore adjusted to be consistent with later reported and more reliable series on capacity and related capital stock data.

> These main types of data are used to refine the year-to-year changes in preliminary capacity indexes: (1) industry capacity estimates in tons, barrels, or other physical units when available; (2) capital stock estimates; and (3) direct estimates of capacity growth provided by surveys.[9]

Of these data, the capital stock series are the primary data used for refining the preliminary capacity figures. They are used in regression procedures on an industry by industry basis. Ratios for capacity (preliminary) to capital stock are regressed against time and an error term (see Raddock [185, p. 763] for more detailed discussion of the regression specification). This regression retrends capital stock data to the growth path of preliminary implied capacity figures. The Board of Governors then uses the fitted values from the regression as the refined capacity estimates. The survey-based capacity and capacity utilization figures "disappear" at this stage in terms of deriving official data.

Nonetheless, the result of this adjustment is that refined capacity figures are still generally procyclical, following investment cycles. Refined capacity estimates broadly follow the long-term growth trends of the preliminary capacity data but have less cyclical movement based on the capital stock data (or other series if capital stock figures are not available for a given industry).

This methodology covers most industries. However, the Federal Reserve does get direct estimates of annual capacity figures from a number of industry trade sources. Industries with capacity estimated in this manner include raw steel, oil and gas well drilling, and textiles.

Step 4: Create Monthly Capacity Figures from End-of-Year Data.

Monthly capacity figures are derived using straight-line interpolation between end-of-year refined capacity estimates. Interpolation is done for individual industries. Current year monthly figures are derived as discussed further below.

Step 5: Adjust Data to Economic Capacity Concept to Series Where Needed.

Adjustments are made to some directly reported capacity estimates to make the estimates consistent with the Board of Governors' concept of economic capacity. Some data are based on engineering concepts of capacity. For example, some capacity figures from small establishments focus on maximum possible output without taking into account bottlenecks that occur within the overall economy when demand is heavy. Some of the engineering capacity is not available on an economic basis. Also, utility companies have "extra" capacity built in for heavy seasonal demand. While this extra capacity is available in an engineering sense, sustained output is not possible at levels of production seen during peak periods. Such capacity is not in use most of the time and in fact is not available for use all the time. From an economic sense, the capacity for peak loads is not excess capacity.

Step 6: Aggregation and Calculation of Capacity Utilization.
Monthly capacity indexes are aggregated into appropriate market and industry groups, using the same value-added weights as used in the aggregation of industrial production indexes.

Step 7: Calculate Capacity Utilization Rates.
An industry capacity utilization rate is defined as its individual output index divided by its capacity index. Aggregate capacity utilization rates are based on measures of aggregate output divided by aggregate capacity.

Current Year Estimates

At the end of each year, an estimate is made for capacity growth in the upcoming year. This estimate includes implicit assumptions for plant closings and openings during the upcoming year. There are no specific inputs for plant closings and openings. Growth in capacity is based on projected cyclical growth in investment net of depreciation and other factors. These estimates are made on a statistical, probabilistic basis. Monthly capacity figures are interpolated from the yearly figures. In other words, capacity is assumed to grow at this smooth annualized rate throughout the year—regardless of actual plant openings and closings during the year. Implied capacity growth at levels of aggregation higher than for individual industries can vary from month to month because of shifts in relative importance of industries in industrial production caused by differences in production growth rates. Also, yearly growth rates can be revised, and the smooth growth rates will change somewhat.

For the previous year and earlier, the Board has hard data for output and capacity utilization rates. For each month of the current year, the Board assumes a growth rate (and levels) for capacity based on various inputs and compiles hard data on output; hence:

$$\text{Current year Capacity utilization rate} = \frac{\text{Output, actual}}{\text{Capacity, FRB projection.}}$$

The inputs to the estimates include recent capital stock data, recent investment trends, and announced planned plant and equipment expenditures. Capacity projections are made on an individual industry basis.

While historical annual data use actual figures for production and utilization rates to derive capacity, "current" monthly series use actual production data together with smooth projections for capacity levels to derive current monthly figures for capacity utilization rates. Although the Board projects capacity figures from previous annual survey data, the Board makes smooth monthly estimates of capacity growth so that monthly utilization rates are oriented to reflect changes in production. The capacity utilization rate is the ratio of an output index and a capacity index. This is seen in that the numerator for this ratio, industrial production, grows at varying rates during the year, while the denominator, capacity, grows at a constant rate. Hence, whenever industrial production grows at a rate greater (or lesser) than the assumed growth rate for capacity, the capacity utilization rate rises (or falls).

The above discussion has several implications in regard to how plant closings enter capacity utilization figures. First, unexpected plant closings rarely directly enter monthly data for the current year. In fact, actual closings are not taken into account until data are revised at the end of the year and projections for the new year are made for capacity. Also, expected plant closings are not discretely discernible in the data. Furthermore, one cannot differentiate changes in utilization rates to either changes in operating rates at existing facilities (including plant closings) or to capacity expanded by new investment. As another aside, specific plants are removed from capacity (for purposes of annual data from survey questionnaires) only when equipment is removed from the inside of closed plants.

The Role of Capacity Utilization Rates as an Inflation Gauge

For policymakers, these series indicate whether or not the economy has room to grow at faster rates. They help answer the question, Does the economy need more stimulus, less, or the same? These series provide similar information for physical capital as unemployment rates provide for the workforce. What the "optimal" capacity utilization rate is usually depends on perceived inflation trade-offs. If capacity utilization rates can be boosted only through stimulus that also raises inflation rates beyond an acceptable pace, then capacity utilization rates are generally considered to be at a nonaccelerating inflation maximum. While policymakers may be interested in maintaining high capacity utilization rates, financial markets usually focus on what capacity utilization rate would lead to accelerating inflation.

Until perhaps the mid-1980s, the rule-of-thumb was that rates exceeding 80 percent for overall manufacturing capacity utilization would lead to an increase in inflation. However, this rule-of-thumb became less reliable due to the greater internationalization of the US economy. As imports played a larger role in the US economy, US capacity utilization rates have become less important relative to world capacity utilization rates. The US capacity utilization rate is still an important inflation barometer (although more so for specific industries than for the overall economy), but the focus must be spread to (1) world capacity utilization rates and (2) changes in the exchange value of the dollar.

While the aggregated capacity utilization rates are useful in evaluating potential price pressures in manufacturing, disaggregated data are even more informa-

CHART 7-2
Manufacturing Capacity and Production

1987 Production=100

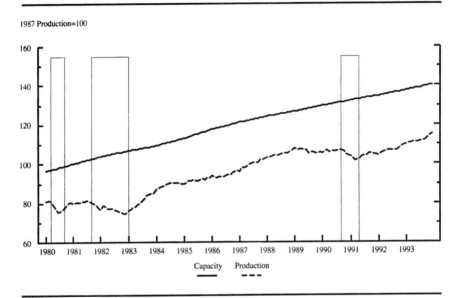

Capacity   Production

Source: Board of Governors, Federal Reserve.

CHART 7-3
Manufacturing Capacity Utilization

Percent of Capacity

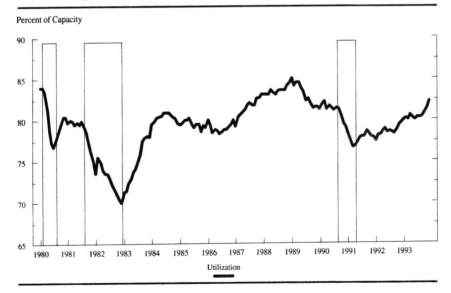

Utilization

Source: Board of Governors, Federal Reserve.

TABLE 7–6
Capacity Utilization: Manufacturing, Mining, and Utilities Percent of Capacity, Seasonally Adjusted

Item	SIC Code	1993 Proportion	1967–1992 Average	1973 High	1978–1980 High	1982 Low	1988–1989 High	1990–1991 Low
Total industry		100.0	81.9	89.2	87.3	71.8	84.8	78.1
Manufacturing		85.9	81.2	88.9	87.3	70.0	85.1	76.7
Primary processing		25.5	82.2	92.2	89.7	66.8	89.1	78.0
Advanced processing		60.4	80.6	87.5	86.3	71.4	83.3	76.0
Durable		49.4	79.0	88.8	86.9	65.0	83.9	73.8
Lumber and products	24	1.7	83.1	90.1	87.6	60.9	93.3	76.2
Furniture and fixtures	25	1.4	81.7	96.8	86.6	68.9	86.8	71.6
Clay, glass, and stone products	32	2.3	77.9	89.2	87.0	63.1	83.7	71.6
Primary metals	33	3.0	80.1	100.6	102.4	46.8	92.9	74.4
Iron and steel	331,2	1.8	79.8	105.8	110.4	38.3	95.7	72.2
Nonferrous	333–6,9	1.2	80.9	92.9	90.5	62.2	88.9	75.8
Fabricated metal products	34	5.1	77.2	87.8	83.9	62.9	82.0	72.0
Industrial and commercial machinery and computer equipment	35	10.9	80.8	96.4	92.1	64.9	83.7	71.4
Electrical machinery	36	7.9	80.4	87.8	89.4	71.1	84.9	77.3
Transportation equipment	37	10.4	74.9	83.8	82.7	56.7	84.2	70.5
Motor vehicles and parts	371	5.4	75.7	93.4	93.0	44.5	84.5	57.3
Autos and light trucks*		2.7			92.2	40.1	89.6	53.7
Aerospace and misc. transportation equipment	372–6,9	5.0	75.5	77.0	81.1	66.9	88.3	78.5
Instruments	38	5.3	82.0	89.9	92.5	79.0	81.2	76.1
Miscellaneous	39	1.3	75.6	82.9	78.7	66.1	80.1	72.9

*Series Begins in 1977.

(Table continues)

TABLE 7-6 (Continued)
Capacity Utilization: Manufacturing, Mining, and Utilities Percent of Capacity, Seasonally Adjusted

Item	SIC Code	1993 Proportion	1967–1992 Average	1973 High	1978–1980 High	1982 Low	1988–1989 High	1990–1991 Low
Nondurable		36.4	83.5	87.9	87.0	76.9	86.8	80.4
Foods	20	8.8	82.3	86.0	84.3	78.8	83.3	80.8
Textile mill products	22	1.6	86.2	92.0	91.7	73.8	92.1	78.5
Apparel products	23	2.0	81.1	84.2	86.0	78.9	84.2	74.9
Paper and products	26	3.3	89.7	96.9	94.2	82.0	94.9	86.3
Printing and publishing	27	5.9	86.5	89.7	92.2	83.0	92.3	78.5
Pulp and paper	261–3	1.5	92.2	97.1	98.2	82.1	98.1	90.2
Chemicals and products	28	9.4	80.0	87.9	85.1	70.1	85.9	79.4
Petroleum products	29	1.1	85.5	96.7	89.5	68.2	88.5	84.5
Rubber and plastics products	30	3.3	83.6	94.0	90.4	73.5	90.5	78.3
Leather and products	31	0.2	81.9	81.3	92.4	78.1	83.8	76.4
Mining		6.6	87.4	94.4	96.6	80.6	87.0	86.8
Metal mining	10	0.5	78.3	90.3	87.6	43.4	87.5	80.0
Coal mining	12	1.2	87.0	90.8	95.7	75.4	91.4	82.9
Oil and gas extraction	13	4.3	88.3	96.6	96.9	82.5	86.9	87.8
Stone and earth minerals	14	0.6	83.8	93.7	93.3	63.3	90.0	77.9
Utilities		7.6	86.7	95.6	88.3	76.2	92.6	83.1
Electric	491,3pt	5.8	88.8	99.0	88.3	78.7	94.8	86.3
Gas	492,3pt	1.7	82.5	93.2	93.6	70.8	85.5	68.3

Source: Federal Reserve Board, G.17, February 15, 1994, Table 3.

TABLE 7–7
Analyzing the News Release: Key Questions

Production

- How strong was the manufacturing component—separate from the overall index?
- Was manufacturing affected by strikes or severe weather?
- Was there a sharp change in motor vehicle assembly rates? Can this pace be maintained? In other words, are production rates too optimistic relative to sales of domestics, or are sales outstripping production?
- How strong was the special index, manufacturing excluding motor vehicles?
- Are recent overall production figures in line with growth in demand, or will production return to a more sustainable level? Are there any apparent unplanned inventory changes that must be met with changes in production?
- For utilities, did atypical weather affect production (unseasonably hot or unseasonably cold)?
- For durables manufacturing, how do changes in production compare with changes in order backlogs?

Capacity Utilization Rates

- Has production growth been trending above or below implied capacity?
- How does the latest figure for capacity utilization compare with previous periods of rising inflation?
- How does the latest figure compare to long-term averages or recent peaks or troughs?
- How do various industry capacity utilization rates compare to their own industry historical averages? Various industries have very different tendencies for standard utilization rates.
- Has capacity increased abroad as a viable substitute for capacity in the United States? Relative to the past, are foreign suppliers able to fill US demand if shortages were to occur or if prices were to rise noticeably?

---

tive. In particular, studies indicate that industries producing materials and supplies—such as textiles; paper; chemicals; stone, clay, and glass; and primary metals—have capacity utilization rates that are closely associated with changes in producer prices for those commodities.[10] These differing peak rates for various industries are shown in Table 7–6.

NOTES FOR CHAPTER 7

1. Effective with the release for the initial April 1993 industrial production and capacity utilization report that included annual revisions, the number of individual industrial production series rose to 255 from 250, netting both series added and dropped.
2. Board of Governors of the Federal Reserve System, *Industrial Production, 1986 Edition, with a Description of the Methodology,* p. 20.
3. Data are currently classified in accordance with the *Standard Industrial Classification Manual,* Office of Management and Budget, 1987.
4. *Industrial Production,* p. 46.

5. Unpublished estimates by Federal Reserve staff, December 1993.
6. *Industrial Production,* p. 132.
7. Federal Reserve Board of Governors, "Explanatory Note," *Industrial Production and Capacity Utilization,* February 18, 1993, p. 18.
8. McGraw-Hill/DRI discontinued its survey following its 1988 survey while the BEA provided data only for the 1965–1983 period.
9. Richard D Raddock, "Revised Federal Reserve Rates of Capacity Utilization." *Federal Reserve Bulletin,* October 1985, pp. 762.
10. "Recent Developments in Industrial Capacity and Utilization," *Federal Reserve Bulletin,* June 1990, p. 412.

BIBLIOGRAPHY

Armitage, Kenneth, and Dixon A Tranum. "Industrial Production: 1989 Developments and Historical Revision." *Federal Reserve Bulletin.* April 1990, pp. 187–204.

Board of Governors of the Federal Reserve System. *Industrial Production, 1986 Edition, with a Description of the Methodology.* Washington, DC. December 1986.

———. *Industrial Production and Capacity Utilization.* August 16, 1993.

Raddock, Richard D. "Industrial Production, Capacity, and Capacity Utilization Since 1987." *Federal Reserve Bulletin.* June 1993, pp. 590–605.

———. "Recent Developments in Industrial Capacity and Utilization." *Federal Reserve Bulletin.* June 1990, pp. 411–35.

———. "Revised Federal Reserve Rates of Capacity Utilization." *Federal Reserve Bulletin.* October 1985, pp. 754–66.

CHAPTER 8

MANUFACTURERS' ORDERS AND OTHER RELATED SERIES

INTRODUCTION

While industrial production is the key measure gauging the current strength of the manufacturing sector, the factory orders series are the primary indicators of the future health of this sector. The series that gets the most media attention is new factory orders, but it is only one of several related indicators compiled and released by the Census Bureau. New orders to manufacturers in seasonally adjusted dollar values are released along with figures for manufacturers' unfilled orders, shipments, and inventories. All of these series are part of the publication formally called *Manufacturers' Shipments, Inventories, and Orders,* which is part of the collection of reports put out by Census Bureau and is known as *Current Industrial Reports.* This particular orders publication is often referred to as the M3 report in technical jargon.

These indicators are also important for providing key data for estimating some of the components in other important economic indicators. These are primarily gross domestic product and the Commerce Department's composite indexes. For gross domestic product, the main components that M3 data are inputs for are producers' durable equipment and inventory investment at the manufacturing level. M3 data also contribute to estimates for two orders components in the composite index of leading indicators, the sales component in the coincident index and the inventory-to-sales component in the lagging index.

There are two release dates associated with M3. The full set of data is released near the end of the month following the reference month or sometimes the following week if holidays affect the compilation schedule. An earlier report containing only data on durables is released about three weeks after the end of the report month. The publication containing the early release is the *Advance Report on Durable Goods Manufacturers' Shipments and Orders.* In the second report, the durables data do contain generally minor revisions from the earlier release and are based on later-arriving survey data being incorporated.

Definitions

For the M3 survey, Census Bureau provides respondents with definitions for each indicator and these are used as a basis for reported dollar values. Manufacturers' new orders for M3 survey purposes reflect commitments to purchase factory goods and are defined to include only those supported by binding legal documents. Such documents include signed contracts, letters of award, or letters of intent. However, orders in some industries do not strictly adhere to this definition. This definition applies for responses to the M3 survey. Published data for new orders differ in definition and are explained later in a discussion on monthly estimates. Published data are based on both earlier benchmark figures and current survey responses.

Unfilled orders generally are defined as: "orders at the end of the reporting period are equal to unfilled orders at the beginning of the period plus net new orders less net shipments."[1]

Shipments data are based on definitions for the Annual Survey of Manufactures (ASM). The value of these shipments is "net selling values, f.o.b. plant, after discounts and allowances and excluding freight charges and excise taxes. . . . Where the products of an industry (four-digit SIC) are customarily delivered by the manufacturing establishment (such as in certain food industries—fluid milk, bakery products, soft drinks), the value is based on delivered price rather than the f.o.b. plant price."[2] For the ASM, for shipbuilding and also for aircraft produced under a cost-plus contract, shipments are based on the value of work done during the year. For aircraft produced on a fixed-price contract, shipments are reported when products are shipped.

For the ASM, shipments data are collected at the four-digit SIC level.[3] For major groups (two-digit SIC level) and higher, the shipments data contain duplication with varying degrees since the products of some four-digit SIC industries are used as inputs by other four-digit SIC industries under the same industry aggregate. This problem is most pronounced in a few industries that are highly integrated. One example is primary metals and motor vehicles and parts.

Inventories have been based on three different definitions over the course of the 1980s. Prior to the 1982 Census of Manufactures, respondents were asked to report inventories at book values. Firms would report according to the method used for tax purposes, and different respondents would use different accounting techniques. This, of course, created difficulties in aggregating inventory data. With the 1982 Census of Manufactures, last in, first out (LIFO) users were asked to report: (1) inventories prior to the LIFO adjustment, (2) the LIFO reserve, and (3) the LIFO value after adjustment for the reserve.[4]

Beginning with January 1987, inventory data have been collected on a current cost or pre-LIFO basis. Data for 1982 to 1987 have been redefined to a current cost basis.

Inventory data by stage of fabrication should be used cautiously. Response rates are low since not all companies keep this level of detail for monthly data. Also, there is some double counting since what is a finished good in one industry may be an input in another.

The Survey

Data for the M3 reports are collected by surveys that are primarily returned by mail or FAX with telephone follow-up. Seven data items are collected in each survey in dollar value for: (1) sales, (2) new orders, (3) order backlog, (4) total inventory, (5) materials and supplies inventory, (6) work-in-process inventory, and (7) finished goods inventory.[5] However, for about three-fourths of the nondurables manufactures, data for new and unfilled orders are not collected—only sales and inventory figures. Census mails the M3 report form to 3,500 reporting units. The survey covers most manufacturers with $500 million or more in annual shipments and includes selected smaller companies for additional coverage. Each company or reporting unit of a company is classified into one of 80 industry categories. This is based on the primary activity of the reporting unit. By value, the reporting units represent about 50 percent of the published dollar values. The monthly survey data are historically benchmarked against data from the quinquennial Census of Manufactures and, in between census years, to data from the Annual Survey of Manufactures. Currently, the benchmark to the ASM is released just prior to the May report. However, the benchmark is made to ASM data of two calendar years prior. Benchmarking to the quinquennial census usually takes longer than with ASM data.

Response rates do vary by industry. For shipments, about 50 percent of the estimates are based on reported data. However, at the industry category level, coverage rates vary from 20 to 99 percent.

Because of consolidated reporting by some large companies, the 80 industry categories are combined into 45 publication levels for shipments and total inventories. Low response rates lead to the need for further aggregation for published series for new and unfilled orders and for inventories by stage of fabrication.

Monthly Estimates

Following the latest census, industry levels for shipments, unfilled orders, and inventories are moved forward based on percentage changes derived from the monthly surveys. This is done by "multiplying the industry estimate for the previous month by the percentage change from the previous month for companies reporting in the current month."[6] If a particular reporting unit's data exhibit unusual movement relative to the rest of the industry, that unit's contributions are removed from the computation of the rest of the industry's percentage change, and the atypical unit's impact of the level is factored in separately.

New orders are not calculated by this ratio method. Not all companies report new orders, and some only report on new orders for specific products with long lead times in the production cycle. In the latter case, these companies exclude new orders for products shipped from inventory. To get around these problems, new orders are defined as "current month shipments plus current month unfilled orders minus prior month unfilled orders."[7]

ORGANIZATION OF THE DATA

Industry Data

Data are organized by industry and also by less publicized topical series. Industry data are divided into categories that are similar to components for industrial production for manufacturing. As with IP indexes, durables data are readily available at the two-digit SIC level for shipments, inventories, and new and unfilled orders. For general trends in durables, analysts often use broader, comprehensive special topical series discussed further below.

Within durables, the industrial machinery and equipment component deserves a little extra explanation.[8] This component includes computers and other types of information-processing equipment. These subcomponents have become more important in recent years as the use of computers and other electronic equipment have become more widespread in businesses—manufacturing and nonmanufacturing. Information-processing equipment is included in industrial machinery and equipment rather than in electrical machinery due to tradition. Originally, computers were a very minor subcomponent and functionally fit in the category for adding and accounting machines when they were mechanical rather than electronic in nature.

For nondurables, only shipments and inventories are published at the two-digit industry level. Only a small percentage of nondurables industries report unfilled orders. For the monthly estimates for new orders (based on the above-mentioned monthly methodology), this means that for these nondurable industries (those not reporting unfilled orders), new orders are defined to be the same as shipments.

The major groups for which nondurables new orders data are the same as shipments data are foods, tobacco, apparel, petroleum, rubber and plastics, and chemicals. These industries account for about three-fourths of nondurables shipments by value. Nondurables series with separate data for new orders are textile mill products, paper and paper products, printing and publishing, and leather and leather products.

Topical Series

Topical series are regroupings of the separate industry categories into: (1) market groups and (2) specially aggregated series. Market groups are similar to those for industrial production. Data for shipments, new orders, unfilled orders, and inventories are arranged in topical format.

Market categories are: (1) automotive equipment, (2) home goods and apparel, (3) consumer staples, (4) machinery and equipment, (5) business supplies, (6) construction materials and supplies, (7) defense products, and (8) other materials, supplies and intermediate products.[9] However, the market categories are aggregated more broadly than market groups for industrial production. For example, the shipments series for "home goods and apparel" would roughly correspond to the combined IP series of "home goods" and "apparel." Also the M3 market groupings are not always segregated between the consumer and business sectors. Two examples of this are for "automotive equipment" and for "other materials, supplies, and intermediate products."

Topical series also include special series. The most familiar topical series are for groupings of durables goods industries. Durables data are completely recategorized into nondefense capital goods, defense capital goods, and durables excluding capital goods.[10] Nondefense capital goods are further separated to exclude aircraft and parts.

Miscellaneous topical series include producers' durable equipment, household durable goods, information technology industries, and health care equipment and products. Except for some of the health care items, these fall under durables but do not subsume all of the durables component series. Also, some of the miscellaneous series contain components that overlap.

In the advance report for durable goods, the only topical series available are for capital goods industries and the breakdowns between defense and nondefense subcomponents and within nondefense for excluding aircraft and parts.

KEYS TO ANALYZING THE MONTHLY REPORTS

Technical Factors

New orders for durables are naturally very volatile. Contracts for items such as aircraft or various types of military goods tend to be very large and do not recur every month. This makes the new orders for durables series very "lumpy." A large increase is often followed by a decline since very large contracts do not get placed every month. Tracking unfilled orders for durables helps eliminate some of the "lumpiness" problem. Also, tracking unfilled orders eliminates the problem of some new orders data being derived from shipments data (such as with the motor vehicle industry).

Additionally, many analysts look at series excluding defense capital goods or excluding the transportation component. This is because of the volatility in these series that also tend to be "lumpy"—that is, the swings often are very sharp. However, one should remember that the transportation component and the defense capital goods components overlap. Transportation includes military aircraft as well as ships and tanks. Transportation is an industry series while defense capital goods is a special topical series.

Within transportation, motor vehicles and parts account for over half of the level of new orders for this subcomponent. Therefore, it usually accounts for some of the monthly volatility in the transportation. However, the widest swings in transportation generally are caused by aircraft orders that are usually made in very large dollar volumes—but not every month.

Key Roles as Leading Indicators: The Lead in Orders—Intuition versus Statistics

Despite the often-held belief that new orders are a leading indicator of manufacturing activity, in actual practice such is not always the case—or at least not to the degree assumed. The leading nature of orders is less true in terms of how the data are defined and in terms of the timing of data availability.

First, new orders can be filled out of inventory instead of being filled out of future production. Orders met with inventory primarily reflect current demand. Unfilled orders are better used for an indication of future production, and unfilled orders are found primarily in the durables sector—capital goods in particular.

For both durables and nondurables aggregates, Census publishes data on shipments, new orders, and inventories for the industries that report unfilled orders. For the nondurables aggregate, the unfilled orders data are not as meaningful simply because for most nondurables industries, unfilled orders are not reported. Over the business cycle, industries reporting shipments and not reporting unfilled (or new) orders may strengthen faster than those reporting unfilled orders. In this situation, the ratio of unfilled orders to shipments would fall. At first glance, once might interpret this decline as a sign of nundurables weakness, but if it is caused by certain industries having rapid gains in shipments and new orders, but no reported unfilled orders, then the decline in this ratio is actually an indication of improvement in nondurables manufacturing.

One important, specific example of the new orders data having little leading information is for motor vehicles. New orders for this are basically derived from shipments data reported to Census by motor vehicle manufacturers. For any given month, the impact of this orders information has already shown up in the Federal Reserve's production figures for that industry since its production and shipments are closely tied.

As has already been discussed, much of the new orders data is based on shipments data. This precludes many goods from being produced after the order statistically is recorded. Also, the Census M3 reports for a given month are released to the public about two weeks following the release of industrial production for the same month. However, these circumstances do not mean that these data are not useful for tracking and projecting manufacturing trends, but the orders and production data do not follow the "intuitive" cycle of orders leading production. In regard to the tardiness of the monthly report of M3 data relative to industrial production, one should remember that the M3 data are hard data from surveys of manufacturers. The initial IP data for most components are to a large degree rough estimates—largely based on econometric models and various inputs, especially employment data.

Nondurables: Any Lead?
Extracting useful information out of nondurables data is a little more difficult than with durables. This is primarily because most nondurables orders have no leading information. Nondurables new orders—that is, shipments—are basically an indicator of current demand. As long as inventories are stable, nondurables orders also are a good measure of current production. On a monthly basis, much of the volatility in nondurables data is price-related. This is particularly true for petroleum products.

Shipments' Role in Investment Estimates

For estimating investment in producers' durable equipment in GDP, the Bureau of Economic Analysis (BEA) uses Census M3 data on shipments from capital goods industries. In the past, most private analysts used shipments for nondefense capital goods as a close estimate for the series used by the BEA; the monthly data provided early estimates for that component in the GDP release (for its PDEs estimate, the BEA also incorporates figures on business purchases of motor vehicles and capital equipment exports and imports). Similarly, private analysts would use new and unfilled orders for nondefense capital goods as an indicator of future investment in business equipment or producers' durable equipment (PDEs) in the national income and product accounts. Until 1991, this was the best series to follow for PDEs. In 1991, Census calculated a broader topical measure for producers' durable equipment. This Census topical measure was given the title of producers' durable equipment and uses the same components that the BEA uses from the M3 report as inputs into its calculations for PDE expenditures in GDP. However, the BEA uses different weights for the M3 PDE components.

TABLE 8–1
Analyzing the News Release: Key Questions

- For new orders, what has been the trend over the last three months (since the data are so volatile)?
- How much were data for the previous two months revised?
- How strong were new orders excluding the very volatile aircraft series (or the broader transportation component that includes aircraft)?
- Within nonelectrical machinery, was much of the movement for computers?
- How strong were new orders excluding the volatile defense capital goods component (this and aircraft overlap)?
- For a longer run perspective, are unfilled orders rising or declining?
- If unfilled orders are little-changed, are shipments and new orders trending upward or downward together, thereby portraying changes in underlying strength for manufacturing that unfilled orders miss?
- For nondurables orders, did changes in oil prices appear to have an impact?
- For helping to estimate the producers' durable equipment component in *current* quarter GDP, how strong were *shipments* of nondefense capital goods orders (or more specifically, the topical series for PDEs)?
- To get an idea of future spending on business equipment investment, how strong were new and unfilled orders for nondefense capital equipment?

TABLE 8–2
M3 Shipments, Orders, and Inventories (Levels in Billions of Current Dollars[11])

Year	Shipments	New Orders	Unfilled Orders	Inventories
		Durables		
1970	335	326	100	67
1971	356	355	100	66
1972	405	418	113	70
1973	472	508	149	81
1974	526	558	182	101
1975	520	500	162	103
1976	604	613	170	112
1977	707	730	193	121
1978	813	868	248	138
1979	911	954	291	161
1980	929	953	315	175
1981	1,004	1,003	315	186
1982	950	936	301	200
1983	1,026	1,059	333	200
1984	1,175	1,201	360	221
1985	1,214	1,227	372	218
1986	1,238	1,242	377	212
1987	1,296	1,328	409	221
1988	1,415	1,456	450	241
1989	1,458	1,497	489	256
1990	1,466	1,480	503	260
1991	1,430	1,415	488	249
1992	1,506	1,470	452	238
1993	1,629	1,597	420	236

Source: US Department of Commerce, Bureau of the Census. Shipments and new orders are annual totals of monthly seasonally adjusted data. Unfilled orders and inventories are December data seasonally adjusted.

TABLE 8–3
M3 Shipments, Orders, and Inventories (Levels in Billions of Current Dollars)

		Nondurables		
Year	Shipments	New Orders	Unfilled Orders	Inventories
1970	296	296	5	35
1971	312	312	5	36
1972	348	350	6	38
1973	400	401	7	43
1974	487	486	6	56
1975	516	518	8	57
1976	578	579	8	63
1977	648	649	9	68
1978	710	712	11	74
1979	817	818	12	81
1980	924	924	12	90
1981	1,013	1,013	12	97
1982	1,009	1,009	11	111
1983	1,045	1,048	14	113
1984	1,113	1,113	14	118
1985	1,118	1,119	15	117
1986	1,097	1,099	17	111
1987	1,178	1,183	22	117
1988	1,266	1,266	22	126
1989	1,332	1,332	22	131
1990	1,404	1,404	22	139
1991	1,396	1,397	23	137
1992	1,426	1,426	23	142
1993	1,471	1,470	22	141

TABLE 8–4
M3 Shipments, Orders, and Inventories (Year-over-Year Percent Changes)

		Durables		
Year	Shipments	New Orders	Unfilled Orders	Inventories
1970	−4.2	−8.5	−8.8	3.2
1971	6.1	9.2	−0.2	−0.8
1972	13.9	17.6	12.8	5.9
1973	16.5	21.6	32.0	15.9
1974	11.5	9.9	21.7	25.0
1975	−1.1	−10.4	−10.9	1.1
1976	16.2	22.5	5.1	9.2
1977	17.0	19.2	13.8	7.9
1978	15.0	18.8	28.4	14.3
1979	12.0	9.9	17.3	16.3
1980	2.1	0.0	8.2	8.7
1981	8.0	5.3	−0.2	6.7
1982	−5.4	−6.7	−4.4	7.5
1983	8.1	13.1	10.7	−0.3
1984	14.4	13.5	8.0	10.7
1985	3.4	2.1	3.4	−1.4
1986	2.0	1.3	1.2	−2.8
1987	4.7	6.9	8.5	4.1
1988	9.2	9.6	10.1	9.3
1989	3.1	2.8	8.6	6.1
1990	0.5	−1.1	2.9	1.5
1991	−2.5	−4.4	−3.0	−4.2
1992	5.3	3.9	−7.3	−4.6
1993	8.2	8.6	−7.1	−0.6

TABLE 8–5

M3 Shipments, Orders, and Inventories (Year-over-Year Percent Changes)

Year	Shipments	Nondurables New Orders	Unfilled Orders	Inventories
1970	2.3	2.3	10.0	4.2
1971	5.5	5.5	9.3	4.2
1972	11.7	11.9	25.7	4.5
1973	14.7	14.6	16.5	13.8
1974	22.0	21.2	−24.9	29.6
1975	5.9	6.8	42.7	1.8
1976	12.1	11.6	4.9	9.7
1977	12.1	12.1	5.2	7.7
1978	9.5	9.8	25.1	8.9
1979	15.0	14.9	12.7	10.8
1980	13.1	12.9	−0.5	11.1
1981	9.6	9.6	−3.1	7.2
1982	−0.4	−0.4	−6.3	14.9
1983	3.5	3.9	27.7	1.0
1984	6.6	6.2	−2.0	5.0
1985	0.4	0.6	8.6	−1.4
1986	−1.9	−1.9	11.4	−5.1
1987	7.4	7.7	29.2	6.0
1988	7.5	7.1	1.2	7.4
1989	5.2	5.1	−1.2	3.8
1990	5.4	5.5	1.2	6.3
1991	−0.6	−0.5	5.9	−1.3
1992	2.2	2.1	−1.3	3.1
1993	3.2	3.1	−5.5	−0.3

NOTES FOR CHAPTER 8

1. U.S. Department of Commerce, Bureau of the Census, "Description of Survey," *Current Industrial Reports, Manufacturers' Shipments, Inventories, and Orders: 1982–1990*, p. XI.
2. U.S. Department of Commerce, Bureau of Census, Chapter 2, *Current Industrial Reports, Manufacturers' Shipments, Inventories, and Orders: 1982–1988*, p. XIX.
3. In the SIC manual, a four-digit SIC is an industry, a three-digit SIC is an industry group, and a two-digit SIC is a major industry group or major group for short.
4. U.S. Department of Commerce, Bureau of the Census, "Description of Survey," p. XI.
5. U.S. Department of Commerce, Bureau of the Census, "Appendix A, Sample of M3 Report Form," *Manufacturers' Shipments, Inventories, and Orders: 1982–1990*. One should note that the 1982–1990 version inadvertently includes an old report form that still requests inventories on a LIFO basis. The M3 report now requests inventories on a current cost basis.
6. Chapter 2, p. XVII.
7. Ibid., p. XVIII.
8. Prior to the 1987, revision to SIC classifications, the industrial machinery and equipment component, was known as nonelectrical machinery. Both are the equivalent of SIC major group 35.
9. In more detail, consumer staples include meat products, dairy products, fats and oils, beverages, other food, cigars and cigarettes; chewing and smoking tobacco and snuff; miscellaneous converted paper products; newspapers, periodicals, and books; other publishing and printing products; drugs, soaps, and toiletries; and petroleum refining products. Home goods and apparel include knitting mills, carpets, and rugs; apparel and other finished textile products, household furniture, rubber and plastic footwear; hose, belting, gaskets, and other rubber products; leather products, kitchen articles and pottery; stone, clay, and glass products; cutlery and hand tools; refrigeration, heating, and service industry machinery; household appliances, household audio and video equipment; ophthalmic goods, watches and clocks, jewelry, silverware, toys and games, miscellaneous goods, and caskets.
10. Nondefense capital goods industries include ordnance and accessories; steam, gas and hydraulic turbines; internal combustion engines; construction, mining, and material handling equipment; metalworking machinery; special industry machinery; general industrial machinery; computer and office equipment; refrigeration, heating and service industry machinery; electrical transmission and distribution equipment; electrical industrial apparatus; communications equipment; aircraft, missiles, space vehicles, and engines and parts; ships and tank components; railroad equipment; and search and navigation equipment.

    Defense capital goods industries include ordnance and accessories; communications equipment; aircraft, missiles, space vehicles, and engines and parts; ships, tanks and tank components; and search and navigation equipment. Source: footnotes to topical series tables in monthly M3 report.
11. For durables and nondurables, shipments and new orders are annual sums of seasonally adjusted monthly data. Unfilled orders and inventories are the December values for seasonally adjusted monthly data. From 1982 forward, the inventory data are on a current cost basis while prior to this period they are on a book value basis.

Source of data: U.S. Department of Commerce, Bureau of the Census.

BIBLIOGRAPHY

U.S. Department of Commerce. Bureau of the Census. *Current Industrial Reports, Manufacturers' Shipments, Inventories, and Orders: 1982–1988.*

————. *Current Industrial Reports, Manufacturers' Shipments, Inventories, and Orders: 1982–1990.*

CHAPTER 9

BUSINESS INVENTORIES AND SALES

The business inventories and sales series are the last major monthly indicators to be released for a given month. Even though data are released two months after the fact, financial markets do not give these indicators the attention they deserve. In terms of the business cycle, inventories keep sales and production in line with each other. Unplanned declines in inventories lead to higher production while unplanned increases lead to cutbacks in output. Inventory change is the "tail that wags the dog" in manufacturing.

Similarly, inventories play a key role in the GDP accounts. The monthly inventory data are used as input for the inventory investment component in GDP, the change in business inventories series. This series has the greatest quarterly volatility of any GDP component. Also, analysts watch this GDP component to help determine the sustainability of GDP growth. Ironically, financial analysts pay more attention to the less timely inventory investment component in GDP than to the monthly inventories data, even though the monthly figures are inputs into the GDP figures.

Monthly business inventories and sales figures are produced by the Census Bureau and are part of the release entitled *Manufacturing and Trade Inventories and Sales*. This report is largely a compilation of data from three earlier reports for retail sales, wholesale trade, and manufacturers' sales and inventories. However, for the most recent reference month, the retail inventories numbers have not been released until this publication.

The release date generally is midmonth, two months after the reference month. Revisions are directly incorporated from series prepared separately for manufacturing, wholesale trade, and retail trade.

The Wholesale Trade Report

Manufacturers' orders, inventories, and sales as well as retail trade have already been discussed in other chapters, whereas the report wholesale trade has not. Most analysts consider this to be a minor report, based on the premise that wholesale sales are driven by retail sales and also because wholesale inventories are the smallest of the three levels.

The monthly wholesale trade report covers only a specific portion of the wholesale trade sector. Conceptually, wholesale trade as broadly covered by the 1987 Economic Census includes establishments.

selling merchandise to retailers; to industrial, commercial, institutional, farm, or professional business users to other wholesalers; or acting as agents or brokers in buying merchandise for or selling merchandise to such persons or companies.[1]

These establishments can be merchant wholesalers; sales branches of manufacturers; or various agents, brokers, and commission merchants. However, the scope of the monthly wholesale trade survey and report is narrowed to only merchant wholesalers due to budgetary constraints and the greater difficulties involved in obtaining a survey sample of properly defined nonmerchant wholesalers.[2]

The primary defining characteristic of merchant wholesalers is their ownership of inventories. Merchant wholesalers take title to goods they sell. These establishments include:

wholesale merchants or jobbers, industrial distributors, voluntary groups wholesalers, exporters, importers, cash-and-carry wholesalers, drop shippers, major distributors, retailer cooperative warehouses, terminal elevators, and cooperative buying associations.[3]

To get perspective on the size of merchant wholesale activity, at the end of 1992, merchant wholesale inventories stood at $214.5 billion in current dollars, compared to $25.9 billion for nonmerchant wholesalers (based on data in the GDP accounts). There are small accounting differences between the national income and product account (NIPA) figures and the Census figures for merchant wholesale inventories; the Census estimate for December 1992 was $204.8 billion.

The wholesale data for initial estimates are based on a monthly sample of establishments drawn by the Census Bureau from (1) all employer identification numbers issued by the Internal Revenue Service for merchant wholesalers and from (2) a list of all establishments of known (from Social Security and other agencies) multiestablishment firms. Rotating panels of wholesalers are used except for very large businesses that report each month. As with the retail sales procedure, there are three rotating panels with each month's panel providing data for two months—the current month and previous month. Each month's first estimate is a composite of: (1) the current month's change in the reporting panel's sales and inventories (35 percent weight) and (2) a ratio estimate based on the previous month's estimate (from a separate panel) being multiplied by the current month's ratio to the previous month (65 percent weight).[4]

The final estimate—which is also the first revision—is released the next month and is a weighted average of: (1) the preliminary composite estimate (70 percent weight) for the given reference month and (2) the unbiased estimate (30 percent weight) for the reference obtained from the following month's panel that reports the next month's preliminary estimate and figures for the month being revised.

Annual revisions usually are released with the report for March with sales and inventory data adjusted to reflect estimates from the Census Bureau's Annual Trade Survey for the calendar year of two years prior. Benchmark revisions are based on and follow quinquennial censuses of wholesale trade.

Data are classified by kind-of-business categories. Durables subcomponents are motor vehicles and automotive parts and supplies; furniture and home furnishings; lumber and other construction materials; professional and commercial equipment and supplies; metals and minerals, except petroleum; electrical goods; hardware, plumbing, and heating equipment, and supplies; machinery, equipment, and supplies; and miscellaneous durable goods. Nondurables include: paper and paper products; drugs, drug proprietaries, and druggists' sundries; apparel, piece goods, and notions; groceries and related products; farm-product raw materials; chemicals and allied products; petroleum and petroleum products; beer, wine, and distilled alcoholic beverages; and miscellaneous nondurable goods.

KEYS TO ANALYZING THE MONTHLY REPORT

The primary uses of monthly inventory data are to anticipate inventory effects on industrial production and to project the nonfarm inventory investment component in real GDP.

The Importance of Monthly Inventories: Is Accumulation Planned or Unplanned, Imported or Domestic?

The primary importance of the inventory data is its use in evaluating the status of the production cycle. A key question in business cycle analysis is whether inventory movement is planned or unplanned. Essentially, production responds to undesired or unplanned changes in inventories. If inventories fall below desired levels, then firms respond by raising production levels. If inventories exceed desired levels, then production is reduced. Subsequently, employment and income are affected as well as aggregate demand. Unplanned changes in inventories lead to oscillations in business activity or—if large enough—create changes in the business cycle.

Sometimes one comes across analysis of inventory data that implies that simply because inventories rose sharply during a given month or quarter, production will have to be cut back. Similarly, some assume that if inventories decline, then production will rise to rebuild inventories. This type of analysis is erroneous to the extent that there has been no determination of whether desired inventory levels have changed. Inventories may be rising, but desired levels may be also. In fact, if desired inventory-to-sales ratios remain constant, then an expanding economy requires an uptrend in desired inventory levels.

However, the monthly inventory data measure "actual" inventories (taking into account that these actual inventory figures include both sampling and non-sampling errors). They are not broken down between planned and unplanned inventory changes. Properly analyzing inventory movements relative to their impact on the business cycle requires making some assumptions about how much of the changes are desired or not.

Over the business cycle, desired inventories change with businesses' view of the economy. As the end of recession nears and a rise in demand appears to be imminent, then businesses typically add to inventories. This rise does not portend a later decline in production. In fact, moderate inventory stocking normally helps fuel economic growth during the early stages of recovery. Often, it is when the economy is sluggish— late in expansion—that a sharp rise in inventories leads to a slowdown in production.

Similarly, if firms accurately anticipate a drop in demand, inventories can be drawn down and if demand remains weak, then the drop in inventories may not be followed by a near-term increase in production.

Over the 1980s and 1990s, the United States has become more of an open economy. Increasingly, consumers and businesses have purchased goods and equipment from abroad. While analysts easily remember that consumers are buying more imports and analysts are starting to understand the importance of imports in capital equipment, the fact that significant portions of inventory needs are met with imports is often overlooked.

Importantly, if imports meet a noticeable share of inventory needs, then as inventory adjustments are made in the overall economy, domestic production generally is less affected than if there were no imports. For example, when auto demand falls (for both domestics and imports) and inventories are "too high," auto dealers cut back on orders to manufacturers. Since some inventories are imports, the order reductions affect foreign producers as well as domestic producers. In turn, domestic production declines by less than the overall inventory adjustment. The reverse also is true when demand rises. Inventory stocking is met partially by imports, and domestic production does not receive all of the benefit of higher demand. Essentially, the foreign content of inventories has moderated the inventory cycle for domestic producers.

How does one determine the impact of imports on domestic production through inventory adjustments? That is, if an inventory adjustment is underway, how much of inventories is imported and how will this impact changes in orders to domestic and foreign producers?

The answers to these questions do not come easily or precisely. Just as inventory data are not designated as planned or unplanned, inventories are not classified as being imported or domestic. Only inferences can be made from various data series. For complete analysis (which is heavily subjective), one must track the flow of demand, production, and inventories. Essentially, one must compare data series by market categories for consumer spending, business investment for equipment, industrial production, and merchandise trade. The industrial production data indicate where domestic strengths and weaknesses likely are in inventories, while merchandise trade data suggest what inventories are likely to be imported. After becoming familiar with production and trade data, one can examine more detailed inventory figures and ask the basic question: Are the various goods in the inventory change more likely domestically produced or imported? For example, if inventories of consumer electronics rise, there is a high probability that much of the inventories were imported. On the other hand, if aircraft inventories are up, it is almost a certainty that these are domestically produced.

Inventory Investment in Real GDP

For estimating current quarter inventory investment, one needs to look at business inventory data that have been deflated into constant dollar terms and then put into quarterly averages to evaluate quarter-to-quarter absolute changes. Of course, when the initial quarterly GDP estimate is released, only two months of business inventory data are available. The missing month must be projected. However, since unit auto inventories are available for the missing month, this information can be used in making the projection. Nonetheless, because of the missing month of data and because of the complexities of deflating nominal inventory figures—using both consumer price indexes (CPIs) and producer price indexes (PPIs)—it is difficult to project the nonfarm inventory component in current quarter real GDP. Also, the BEA makes various accounting adjustments to the monthly data and makes independent estimates for nonmerchant wholesale inventories, since the monthly report does not provide data for nonmerchant wholesale inventories.

TABLE 9–1
Analyzing the News Release: Key Questions

- Are inventories rising (declining) faster than demand (sales)?
- Are inventory-to-sales ratios changing? Are firms implementing tighter inventory controls?
- Are auto manufacturers running special incentives to move inventories?
- Do inventory changes (increases or decreases) appear to be planned?
- If accumulation or rundown appears to be unplanned, is it for goods that are produced primarily domestically or are they generally imported? *Note:* inventory data are not classified as either imports or domestic—inferences can be made only through comparisons with production and import detail.
- Are auto sales noticeably above or below expectations, leading to sharp inventory changes?

TABLE 9–2
Business Inventories (End-of-Period, Monthly SA) Billions of Dollars

	Total	Manufacturing	Retail	Merchant Wholesale
1980	510.126	265.215	121.078	123.833
1981	547.181	283.413	132.719	131.049
1982	575.504	311.852	134.628	129.024
1983	591.875	312.379	147.833	131.663
1984	651.551	339.516	167.812	144.223
1985	665.835	334.799	181.881	149.155
1986	664.624	322.669	186.510	155.445
1987	711.725	338.075	207.836	165.814
1988	767.538	367.422	219.581	180.535
1989	813.637	386.911	238.160	188.566
1990	837.120	399.068	241.117	196.935
1991	832.852	386.348	245.042	201.462
1992	841.831	379.238	253.836	208.757
1993	865.584	377.425	271.573	216.586

Source: US Department of Commerce.

NOTES FOR CHAPTER 9

1. U.S. Department of Commerce, Bureau of the Census, *Revised Monthly Wholesale Trade, Sales, and Inventories, January 1986 through March 1992*, p. 4.
2. There are a few minor exceptions, with the most significant being the inclusion of sales and inventories of manufacturers' sales branches of ferrous metals service centers with inventories, as part of SIC 505 (metals and minerals, except petroleum).
3. *Wholesale Trade*, p. 4.
4. Ibid., p. 3.

BIBLIOGRAPHY

US Department of Commerce. Bureau of the Census. *Revised Monthly Wholesale Trade, Sales and Inventories, January 1986 through March 1992.*

CHAPTER 10

THE PURCHASING
MANAGERS' INDEX

The purchasing managers' index is a composite index based on data from a
monthly report, *The Report on Business,* compiled and released by the National
Association of Purchasing Management (NAPM) based in Tempe, Arizona. This
report is the only one given a chapter in this book that is not compiled by a government statistical agency. The importance of this report is based on its broad coverage of the US manufacturing sector and on its timeliness. The NAPM report is
released the first business day following the reference month and is used by financial analysts to help project government-produced economic indicators related to
manufacturing—industrial production in particular.

Methodology

The purchasing managers' index is based on data from a survey mailed to about
300 NAPM members. The survey is mailed by midmonth of the reference month,
and responses are tallied around the 21st. The response rate varies each month, but
it is not published. The questionnaires are distributed by industry according to
value-added shares in US production. However, response rates vary each month
by industry, and this affects how well the index sample is stratified.

Survey members are asked to provide information on various facets of their
firm's manufacturing activity. Questions cover five key categories: production,
new orders, inventories of purchased materials, employment, and vendor deliveries.[1] For most categories, the possible answers essentially are equivalent to "better," "no change," or "worse." For vendor performance, replies are in terms of
"faster," "same," and "slower." For supplier deliveries, slower is a positive for
this component.

For each category, the NAPM tallies the number of positive, negative, and no
change responses and publishes them in terms of percentages of total responses
per category. From this information, the NAPM computes a diffusion index, indicating the broadness of worsening or improving conditions among surveyed members. This approach is in contrast to other surveys (such as those conducted by the
US Commerce Department's Bureau of the Census), which measure actual levels
by components for series like new orders, inventories, and shipments.

By the NAPM's own definition, an overall index above 50 indicates an expanding manufacturing sector, and a number below 50 suggests a generalized contraction.

These conclusions are based on the component indexes being equal to the percent responding "better" plus one-half of the percent indicating no change.

$$\text{Index} = \% \text{ increase} + (1/2 * \% \text{ same})$$

The NAPM index is thus ordinal, not cardinal: the index does not report precise levels of activity but instead indicates whether a given month is better or worse than the preceding one. Diffusion indexes such as the NAPM series have the merit of being highly correlated with growth rates, but they are not as precise as surveys that measure actual production levels from period to period. This is not to say that the NAPM survey is wrong in any sense by design but simply that a diffusion index does not measure growth rates based on precise levels of activity. Because the NAPM index is designed to gauge whether manufacturing is expanding or contracting in industries represented in the survey, forecasters believe that it reasonably reflects "current" conditions in manufacturing. That is, respondents' views are seen as similar to actual production as measured in the Federal Reserve Board's index of industrial production—in technical terms, the two are correlated.

The NAPM Composite Index

The overall NAPM composite index is derived from five component diffusions indexes. Published data originally were limited to percentages for each answer category. The data were first put into composite form in February 1982, based on the work of Theodore Torda, an economist at the Department of Commerce.

Component diffusion indexes are derived from not seasonally adjusted percents. Then, component diffusion indexes are seasonally adjusted before being combined into a composite index. The Commerce Department seasonally adjusts the indexes and provides the seasonal factors to the NAPM. The composite index components and their respective weights (out of 100 percent) are as follows: new orders, 30; production, 25; supplier deliveries, 15; inventories, 10; and employment, 20. Table 10–1 shows how each month's data are combined into a composite index.

The supplier deliveries' component requires a little elaboration. It is also known as vendor performance. This series reflects how quickly suppliers to man-

TABLE 10–1
Putting Together the NAPM Composite Index:[2] (December 1992)

Component	Diffusion Index, SA		Weight in Index		Component Contribution
New Orders	64.4	*	.30	=	19.32
Production	59.4	*	.25	=	14.85
Supplier deliveries	52.1	*	.15	=	7.82
Inventories	44.8	*	.10	=	4.48
Employment	47.1	*	.20	=	9.42
Composite index					55.9
(rounded to one decimal place)					

ufacturers deliver factory inputs. Slower deliveries suggest shortages of supplies—possibly due to heavy demand. Quicker deliveries suggest the opposite. Therefore, this component is the sum of the percent of companies reporting *slower* deliveries and half of the percent reporting the same delivery speed. A decline in vendor performance—reflecting slower deliveries—is a positive for the index.

Revisions

The NAPM does not revise monthly data on an ongoing basis. Late reports are not carried over for revisions with the next month's release. The only revisions are for new seasonal factors for both diffusion indexes for individual series and the composite index based on these component series. Annual revisions usually cover the previous three calendar years and are released with each year's report for January. The NAPM first began seasonally adjusting the data in late 1988. Deriving the seasonal factors is done by the Commerce Department, and this is their only contribution to the data.

Problems with the Data

Two of the key problems with NAPM data are closely tied to their primary benefit. The data are diffusion indexes that are based on questions that are quick to answer, compile, and publish. However, the data are not as precise as data published by the Federal Reserve Board or by the Census Bureau. No NAPM component explains more than half of the variation in the corresponding government data series for the month. Timeliness creates another problem. The surveys are mailed out early in the reference month and are tabulated around the 21st of the reference month. In effect, survey respondents must base answers partly on information from weeks prior to the reference month. Studies show that industrial production in month t is as closely related to NAPM data in month $t+1$ as in month t.[3] In other words, January industrial production is as statistically related to the later February NAPM as to the concurrent January NAPM index.

KEYS TO ANALYZING THE MONTHLY REPORT

How Is the Monthly Report Used by the Markets?

The purchasing managers' index, first, is used as a direct gauge of the strength of the manufacturing sector. Analysts look to see if the composite index suggests any change in the perceived strength or weakness in the manufacturing sector. Because of the construction of the composite from its component diffusion indexes, the index level of 50 is said by NAPM to be the break-even point between expansion and contraction in manufacturing. The component diffusion indexes are supposed to represent the percentage of firms reporting increases—even though it really is the sum of positive responses plus one-half of those reporting no change. Nonetheless, if the percentage of positive responses equals that of negative responses (regardless of the share of those answering no change), then the diffusion indexes produce a value of 50. A diffusion index value above 50 indicates that more firms are reporting increases than those with decreases—hence, above 50 indicates expansion.

However, this index level of 50 as a neutral point is strictly a definitional one related to the NAPM's survey. It does not necessarily mean that an index level of over 50 in a given month means that actual manufacturing activity for the United States is in expansion. Statistical analysis of NAPM data and more definitive government data are necessary to determine what NAPM index level is related to a break-even point for all of manufacturing. In fact, econometric studies indicate that 50 is not the exact break-even point for industrial production or even the manufacturing component within industrial production.

Standard Regression Models Using NAPM Data

Analysts usually use NAPM data to forecast the upcoming industrial production release produced by the Federal Reserve Board of Governors. Modelers want to project the change in industrial production, specifically the monthly percent change. Since the NAPM index is a diffusion index, its *level* is associated with the *rate of growth* in manufacturing. A low index level (near but still above 50) is associated with low growth rates, and a high index level is associated with high growth rates. There are similar relationships between NAPM index levels below the break-even point and how strong declines are for manufacturing. Therefore, in simple regression models, the NAPM composite index in levels is used as an explanatory variable for predicting the percent change in industrial production.

$$\%IP = \beta * NAPM + constant + error\ term$$

There are a number of variations of this model. Some forecasters choose to use initial estimates of the data for one or both the dependent and independent variables while others use revised data. Also, some analysts prefer to predict only the manufacturing component of industrial production (and exclude mining and utilities) since the NAPM data cover only manufacturing.

Table 10–2 presents the output of one NAPM-based model. The monthly percent change for manufacturing IP is regressed against the level for the purchasing managers' composite index and a constant. Data for both the dependent and independent variables are from initial releases. The model has only modest predictive power with an adjusted R^2 of 0.36 and a mean absolute error of the regression of 0.40 percentage points, compared with the mean of the absolute value of the dependent variable of 0.55 percentage points.

However, the model does have the expected signs for the coefficients. For each index point change in the index, the initial manufacturing IP changes by 0.006 percentage points minus the constant of 2.87. The purchasing managers' composite index is positively correlated with manufacturing IP, as expected, and the *t*-statistics are greater than the rule of 2 (absolute value) for statistical significance.

The degree of confidence one can place in the reliability of the estimate for the coefficients is indicated by *t*-statistics. The *t*-statistic is the ratio of the coefficient value to its standard error. The greater the coefficient to its standard error

TABLE 10–2
An NAPM-Based Model for Monthly Industrial Production⁴

Dependent variable: Monthly percent change in industrial production for manufacturing, initial release.

Regression Period: January 1982–November 1991

Independent Variables	Coefficient	Standard Error	T-statistic
NAPM index, initial	0.06	0.0075	8.03
Constant	−2.87	0.39	−7.44

Number of observations:	119	R²:	0.36
Mean absolute percent change		Adjusted R²:	0.35
of dependent variable:	0.55	Durbin-Watson:	1.87
Standard error of regression:	0.58	Standard deviation	
Mean absolute error (MAE):	0.40	of MAE:	0.41
Root mean square error:	0.57		

(ignoring the sign of the coefficient), the greater the confidence that the coefficient is significantly different from zero. If the coefficient is not significantly different from zero, then that variable does not "explain" changes in the dependent variable.

This model might best be interpreted by setting the model solution equal to zero and solving for the index for the "no change" value. Values for the NAPM greater than this solution value would tend to be associated with increases in industrial production (as measured by the Federal Reserve Board's index), while lower index levels would suggest declines in industrial production.

$$\%IP_{mfg} = \beta * NAPM + constant$$
$$0 = 0.06 * NAPM - 2.87$$
$$47.83 = NAPM.$$

This model shows that "no change" in manufacturing IP is statistically associated with a value of 47.83 for the purchasing managers' index over the 1982–90 period. Thus zero is the point estimate (forecast) for IP manufacturing when the NAPM equals 47.83. The constant is negative because index numbers below 47.83 are associated with declines in production. This figure is somewhat below the level of 50 identified by the NAPM as associated with a generalized decline in the manufacturing sector. Although the difference is not statistically significant, regressions using different periods consistently estimated break-even values of below 50.

Importantly, the NAPM data do not forecast industrial production as well as a model using aggregate production hours data from the BLS. However, adding the NAPM index as a variable to production hours models improves its accuracy to a noticeable degree. Also, NAPM data are available earlier than the hours data.

The other primary modeling use of the NAPM data is to project payroll employment (or just the manufacturing portion) for the same month's employment report. The structure of these models is similar to that for industrial production. The level of the NAPM diffusion index for employment is used as an explanatory variable to predict the percent change in employment. To a lesser degree, component series are used in regression models for new orders and for inventories.

Break-Even Points for Monthly Analysis.   A study by Ethan S. Harris of the Federal Reserve Bank of New York confirms that breakeven points for NAPM component diffusion indexes relative to their government statistical counterparts are not exactly 50 as implied by the NAPM methodology.[5] There are better, statistically derived rules-of-thumb for evaluating the monthly NAPM data. This study used revised data for dependent and independent variables. The Census Bureau's new orders data were deflated with implicit deflators for shipments. The statistically derived break-even points are shown below in Table 10–3.

Using these statistically derived break-even points should provide a clearer idea of what each month's report suggests for pending economic releases.

These break-even points suggest that there are biases in the data due to either a sample bias or due to certain tendencies by the respondents. Except for the price series, all break-even points are below 50. This general tendency may be due to the NAPM survey being sent to older, larger, and more established firms. These firms remain in the sample even during stages of decline and into bankruptcy. Firms are replaced when closed (or they drop out from lack of interest), and the replacement firm usually is a mature firm. New, smaller, and faster-growing firms do not make it into the survey although the government industrial production, orders, and employment data are more likely to be inclusive of these or use adjustment factors to account for them.

For inventories and prices, special biases appear to be built in. The inventory series' break-even point is the lowest of all components, and this may be the result of firms' partly reporting desired inventories instead of actual inventories. The

TABLE 10–3

	Break-even Point	
Series Explained with	Using Data Covering:	
NAPM Components	1959–91	1980–91
Industrial production	51.5	49.3
Payroll employment	49.1	47.4
New orders	51.4	49.3
Materials inventories	44.7	47.0
Crude producer prices	56.3	56.1
Series Explained with		
NAPM Composite Index		
Industrial production	49.0	46.9
Real GNP	44.4	44.5

purchasing managers filling out the survey may not always check actual inventory levels before answering the qualitative response deemed appropriate. For materials prices, manufacturers may be influenced by the fact that they almost always have more types of materials inputs than goods produced. Purchasing managers may focus on a tendency for more input prices to be rising than output prices. Also, manufacturers' tendency to see input prices rising is consistent with their ongoing worries about cost.

While the intent of a diffusion index survey with qualitative responses is to reduce the reporting burden and to speed up processing, an unintended consequence is that respondents may not be compelled to check precise levels of indicator activity. Qualitative surveys have the flaw of more easily allowing respondents' biases into the data—as is suggested by the statistically derived break-even points for inventories and materials prices.

NAPM Data as Leading Indicators.   While the NAPM index is helpful in interpreting changes in the business cycle, it is not definitive. The composite index leads the business cycle, but the lead prior to peaks and troughs varies significantly from cycle to cycle. The index also tends to send numerous false signals. Because the NAPM index is a diffusion index that correlates with growth rates, the composite index will peak as economic growth decelerates, but still remains in the positive growth range for some time before turning negative. Essentially, a diffusion index peak represents a peak in growth rates. The NAPM lead is quite long because slower growth in a business cycle occurs well before the level of activity peaks and then declines. Any moderate rebound in growth rates will then cause the index to rise to another peak. Hence, prior to official business cycle peaks and troughs, the NAPM index typically will peak several times. One cannot know which NAPM peak is correctly predicting a business cycle downturn and which is a false signal of recession—portending only slower growth instead.

If NAPM data are examined in terms of the timing of crossing the break-even points shown in Table 10–3, the data generally still lead government statistics. However, the false signal problem remains as during periods of sluggish activity the NAPM data tend to cross break-even points several times before an official turning point occurs. Over the business cycle, the NAPM data are best used to confirm cyclical movements rather than to anticipate them.

THE COMPOSITE INDEX: A MIXED INDEX OF CURRENT AND FUTURE ACTIVITY

The NAPM's composite index is advertised as an indicator of the current strength of manufacturing. And it also—as discussed above—is touted as a leading index. There is some truth to both of these claims since the composite index includes some components that are measures of current activity and some that are indicative of future activity. Additionally, the inventory component can be interpreted in two ways—at times it is a measure of current strength, and at others it portends pending changes in output. How does the composite index do all this?

First, of the five components, two—production and employment—are generally considered to reflect current conditions. The corresponding government statistics are part of the Commerce Department's composite index of coincident indicators. A third component, new orders, generally leads production while the supplier deliveries component—also known as vendor performance—is one of the components of the Commerce Department's index of leading indicators. However, the coincident and predictive nature of these components relative to government statistics is somewhat hampered by the survey's early compilation deadlines that force respondents to partially rely on the previous month's data.

The inclusion of the inventory component in the composite index also creates a special problem for evaluating the manufacturing sector's strength with this index. Inventory changes can be either planned or unplanned. Importantly, it is the unplanned changes—when actual levels differ from desired levels—that lead to changes in planned production. Yet, this NAPM component does not indicate whether inventory changes are desired or not for the current month (this also is the case with government data on inventories). The implication is that if the inventory component rises to meet *anticipated* demand, it should be construed as a positive for that month. In contrast, if inventories rise due to a drop in demand (orders and shipments), then the accumulation of unwanted stocks is a negative in terms of the impact on pending production. Therefore, the movement of the inventory component should be carefully interpreted in terms of whether it is a plus or minus for gauging strength in manufacturing through the use of the current month NAPM composite index.

RELATED SURVEYS

There are other surveys covering the manufacturing sector similar to the NAPM survey that are useful for complementing the NAPM data or even in some instances of predicting the NAPM release. First, the Chicago purchasing managers' index—published by the Purchasing Management Association of Chicago—is released at the end of the reference month, thereby preceding the national index's release.

Additionally, three regional Federal Reserve banks produce manufacturing surveys. These regional banks are for Philadelphia, Richmond, and Atlanta. However, the reference period definitions and release dates vary. Each Fed's survey is produced independently.

The longest running of the Fed surveys, the Philadelphia Fed's *Business Outlook Survey,* is generally released during the third week of a reference month. The historical series goes back to 1968. Answers by respondents are essentially based on about three weeks of data from the prior month plus one week's worth of information from the reference month. The Philadelphia Fed's release does provide some prior information before the NAPM release which is 10 days to two weeks later. The NAPM index is processed in the third week of the reference month and is based on about two weeks of information from the reference month.

The Richmond Fed's survey of business conditions is the only one of the three Federal Reserve surveys that is not monthly. Their survey is timed to be processed just prior to each of the Federal Open Market Committee (FOMC) meetings and is published eight times a year. Historical data go back to mid-1986.

The Atlanta Fed's *Survey of Southeastern Manufacturing Conditions* is the recent newcomer with official data starting with December 1991. Their survey is mailed out late in the reference month (around the 25th) and is tallied early the following month. The Atlanta survey is published the second business day after the 10th of the month immediately following the reference month. Respondents' answers are based on a little more than three weeks' worth of information on actual data and planned activity for the reference month. Hence, data for the Atlanta reference month more closely correspond to the calendar month than do the NAPM or other Fed surveys.

TABLE 10–4
Analyzing the News Release: Key Questions

- To get an indication of whether manufacturing growth is positive or negative, is the composite index above or below the break-even point (index levels are associated with growth rates for corresponding government indicators)?
- To get an indication of whether growth is accelerating or decelerating, is the composite index rising or falling?
- How does the latest month's composite index compare to statistically derived break-even points rather than to the definitional break-even point of 50?
- Is one component in particular causing most of the movement in the latest month's composite index?
- How is the production trend relative to the employment trend to get an idea of changes in productivity?
- Do the components paint a different picture of future production relative to current production? Are new orders healthy even though production may have been weak for the same month?
- Is the inventory component playing a large role in moving the composite index for the month? Is the inventory movement "perverse"? Does a decline in inventories portend a rise in production even though it is a negative in the composite index?

NOTES FOR CHAPTER 10

1. There also are questions on commodity prices, quantity of purchased materials, buying policy, and (in recent years) new export orders. However, these components do not enter into the composite index.
2. Source of data: "December U.S. Purchasing Managers' Index Summary Data," *Market News,* December 31, 1992.
3. See Harris (1991) and Rogers (1992a).
4. R. Mark Rogers, "Forecasting Industrial Production: Purchasing Managers' versus Production-Worker Hours Data," *Economic Review,* Federal Reserve Bank of Atlanta, January/February 1992, p. 28.
5. Ethan S. Harris, "Tracking the Economy with the Purchasing Managers' Index," *Quarterly Review,* Federal Reserve Bank of New York, Autumn 1991, p. 63.

BIBLIOGRAPHY

Bell, John, and Theodore Crone. "Charting the Course of the Economy: What Can Local Manufacturers Tell Us?" Federal Reserve Bank of Philadelphia. *Business Review.* July/August 1986, pp. 3–16.

Chmura, Christine. "New Survey Monitors District Manufacturing Activity." *Cross Sections.* Federal Reserve Bank of Richmond. Winter 1987/88, pp. 9–11.

Harris, Ethan S. "Tracking the Economy with the Purchasing Managers' Index." *Quarterly Review.* Federal Reserve Bank of New York. Autumn 1991, pp. 61–69.

National Association of Purchasing Management. *The Report on Business: Information Kit,* 1990.

Rogers, R Mark. "Forecasting Industrial Production: Purchasing Managers' versus Production-Worker Hours Data." *Economic Review.* Federal Reserve Bank of Atlanta. January/February 1992, pp. 25–35.

———."Tracking Manufacturing: The *Survey of Southeastern Manufacturing Conditions.*" *Economic Review.* Federal Reserve Bank of Atlanta. September/October 1992, pp. 26–33.

CHAPTER 11

MONTHLY INTERNATIONAL TRADE

The monthly report on international trade, entitled *US International Trade in Goods and Services,* is important because it is the most timely publicly available data on the US foreign trade sector. The data are viewed as important by the financial markets because they reflect the strength of domestic demand for imports to the United States relative to foreign demand for exports of US goods. In turn, perceptions of the strength of these trade flows affect the value of the dollar and other currencies in foreign exchange markets.

The flow of goods through the foreign sector also helps to determine how much changes in domestic demand impact changes in domestic production. In other words, if domestic demand is rising but a greater share than in the past is being met with imports, then gains in domestic production will lag import growth. Similarly, if foreign demand for US products is rising faster than domestic demand, then US production would likely rise more rapidly. In a world economy that is becoming more integrated, these considerations are of growing importance.

Financial effects also are more complex. As foreign exchange markets react to changes in the international flow of goods, money and credit markets move also. For example, if the dollar depreciates due to a rapid buildup in imports, then (assuming no other factors change) US interest rates are bid higher by foreign holders of US currencies. This is to offset their losses in asset values from dollar depreciation. Dollar depreciation also generally is associated with a near-term rise in price levels due to higher import costs and less competitive price pressure on domestic producers.

In contrast, if there is a strong upward trend in export growth for the United States, then one would likely see the opposite effects. The dollar would appreciate, imports would become cheaper, inflation pressures would ease, and US interest rates would decline—at least relative to foreign rates. These scenarios are generalized, but in sum, changes in international trade trends can have significant effects on domestic production and employment. There also can be resulting changes in exchange rates, interest rates, and even long-run inflation rates, although international financial flows generally overwhelm the effects of real trade flows.

From a political perspective, these trade data are significant because they are used in international trade negotiations such as the General Agreement on Tariffs and Trade (GATT). The data also are used to meet a number of legal and regulatory requirements, including import duties and quotas and export restrictions.

Finally, in terms of statistically measuring the strength of the economy, the monthly merchandise and services trade data are the key inputs for the foreign accounts in both gross domestic product (GDP) and in the quarterly balance-of-payments accounts. These are discussed in a later section. The monthly international trade report is the first each month of the various releases on US trade flows.

Publication, New Format, and Timing of Releases

Prior to 1994, monthly international trade data were published only for merchandise components. Monthly merchandise trade data were compiled and published by the US Bureau of the Census. The monthly report was simply entitled *US Merchandise Trade* and was technically referred to as the FT-900 publication of Census Bureau. Beginning with the March 22, 1994, release of trade data for January, the Census Bureau combined its FT-900 report with the Bureau of Economic Analysis' report for balance-of-payments data. This report combines two of the three major types of trade data for the United States—the third being national income and product account (NIPA) net exports (in GDP). The Census, balance-of-payments, and NIPA data are produced for different purposes. The Census data are primarily taken from U.S. Customs tabulations with data collected for Customs' needs. Balance-of-payments data are estimated with the intent of tracking international financial flows. The NIPA data are oriented toward estimating domestic output. These differences are discussed in greater detail further below.

Added to the Census basis merchandise trade data were monthly balance-of-payments basis data for merchandise trade as well as monthly components for services exports and imports in the balance-of-payments accounts. Previously, all balance-of-payments data were on a quarterly basis. The Commerce Department discontinued its quarterly merchandise trade report on a balance-of-payments basis following the fourth quarter 1993 report, released March 3, 1994. The differences between Census basis and balance-of-payments basis data are discussed later.

The change in format of monthly international trade data is very useful to economists and financial analysts trying to gauge the strength of the economy. The data on a balance-of-payments basis puts the figures in a format closer to the GDP data than are the Census basis data. This is discussed in greater detail in a later section. Also, the addition of services in the monthly report provides an earlier glimpse of the strength in services exports and imports than was the case when the first estimate of balance-of-payments services data were released after the advance release of real GDP for a given quarter.

While the new monthly report includes balance-of-payments data for services, not all balance of payments categories are covered. Income components and unilateral transfers are not included in the monthly report. The full-scale balance-of-payments report, entitled *Summary of US International Transactions,* also includes components for income transactions and unilateral transfers. However, as discussed later, the monthly balance-of-payments components for merchandise and services provide coverage similar to the merchandise and services components within GDP exports and imports.

TABLE 11–1
Merchandise and Services Exports and Imports, Balance-of-Payments Basis
(Millions of Dollars)

	1990	1991	1992	1993
Exports of goods and services	**537,605**	**579,599**	**619,848**	**643,559**
Merchandise, adjusted, excluding military*	389,303	416,937	440,138	456,766
Services#	148,302	164,260	179,710	186,792
Transfers under US military agency sales contracts	9,698	10,545	11,015	11,259
Travel	43,007	48,384	53,861	56,501
Passenger fares	15,298	15,854	17,353	17,849
Other transportation	21,954	22,326	22,773	23,508
Royalties and license fees	17,069	18,479	20,238	20,414
Other private services	40,608	47,982	53,601	56,434
US government miscellaneous services	668	690	869	827
Imports of goods and services	**615,986**	**609,117**	**659,575**	**720,358**
Merchandise, adjusted, excluding military*	498,336	490,739	536,276	589,244
Services#	117,650	118,378	123,299	131,114
Direct defense expenditures	17,531	16,396	13,766	12,286
Travel	37,349	35,322	39,872	42,329
Passenger fares	10,530	10,012	10,943	11,256
Other transportation	23,401	23,297	23,454	24,511
Royalties and license fees	3,168	4,203	4,986	4,748
Other private services	23,753	27,035	27,988	33,595
US government miscellaneous services	1,919	2,114	2,290	2,388

*Adjusted for timing, valuation, and coverage to balance-of-payments basis; excludes exports under US military agency sales contracts and imports of US military agencies.
#Includes some goods that cannot be separately identified from services.

Sources: US Department of Commerce, *Survey of Current Business*, June 1993, pp. 70–71. *US International Transactions: Fourth Quarter and Year 1993*, March 15, 1994.

Because the methodologies for the new monthly services series have not been fully explained in published detail, this chapter concentrates on the methodologies and formats behind the pre-1994 Census merchandise trade data along with how the balance-of-payments data differ from Census basis data. This provides a link between the more familiar Census data and the new monthly balance-of-payments data. Differences between balance-of-payments data and NIPA (GDP) data are then discussed. Finally, available information on monthly services components are explained at the end of the chapter.

As was the case with the old merchandise trade report, the new *U.S. International Trade in Goods and Services* is released the third week of the month, two months following the reference month.

The FT-900 Report

Prior to 1994, the monthly merchandise trade release was called the FT-900 report. The old FT-900 provide historical data with comparable series in the new report. The following discussion in reference to the FT-900 report explains the Census basis merchandise trade data. Even though the FT-900 has been incorporated into the joint Census/BEA release, the published Census data are the same series as in the earlier FT-900 data. For merchandise trade, the primary components are for major end-use categories. Discussion of major end-use categories for Census data carries over to the new format for balance-of-payments figures since they also are categorized by major end-use categories.

Concerning available Census basis data, the FT-900 includes seasonally adjusted and not seasonally adjusted series for major end-use commodity categories. For the seasonally adjusted end-use categories, data are provided in current dollars and constant 1987 dollars. Tables are also included for some not seasonally adjusted detail by selected countries and geographic areas and by principal standard international trade classification (SITC) commodity groupings. Finally, special tables are presented for imports of energy-related petroleum products and for exports and imports of advanced technology products. For the energy-related petroleum products table, imports are tracked in value, quantity (barrels), and unit price (dollars per barrel).

The FT-900 Supplement provides detail for standard industrial classification (SIC)-based product codes, which differ from SITC codes. Also included are general imports of crude petroleum by country, SITC export and import data by broad commodity sections, and greater detail (than in the FT-900) for exports and imports by country and area. Figures are also tabulated for the origin of movement of US exports by state, by SIC-based product code groupings. All of these series in the supplement are in not seasonally adjusted form. Finally, historical data are given for the overall trade balance, exports, and imports in both adjusted and not seasonally adjusted form. The Census Bureau also publishes a number of other detailed reports on foreign trade.

For Census basis data, each month revisions are made only for the previous month's data to incorporate statistics arriving too late to be included in the transaction month. Therefore, each month's recorded data do not exactly reflect the actual transactions that occurred—although the difference between the two are small. Not all published data series are revised—only those for seasonally adjusted aggregate (nominal and constant dollar); unadjusted aggregates for exports, imports, and trade balance; and end-use totals. SITC and country detail are not revised monthly, but the timing adjustments in the relevant tables reflect the difference between originally reported and revised data.

Annual revisions are usually published in May and include information received after the monthly revisions. These revisions are available in the FT-900 Final Report (informally referred to as the 13th month report). However, these revisions usually are only applied to totals, end-use, SITC, and country summary data. Annual revisions also incorporate updates for seasonal factors, where applicable, and go back as far as 1979 for some series. New seasonal factors that are published generally go back two calendar years. Seasonal adjustment—for series adjusted—is done at the five-digit end-use level.

Methodology

In contrast with other economic statistics compiled by the Census Bureau, the Census basis merchandise trade figures are not derived from surveys. Data on exports from the United States to countries other than Canada come from Shipper's Export Declarations (SEDs). Filing an SED is mandatory under federal law, and these are collected by the US Customs Service at the port of export. In turn, the US Customs Service electronically transmits SED data directly to the Census Bureau. For exports to Canada (as a final destination), the United States substitutes Canadian figures for imports from the United States. Similarly, Canada uses US data on Canadian imports for estimates of its exports. Finally, for exports, some specific grants in aid from the Defense Department are reported directly to the Census Bureau.

Census' US import data are compiled primarily through the US Customs Automated Commercial System. Other data come from various documents filed with the US Customs Service as required by law.

In summary, the Census basis US merchandise export and import data are obtained from three basic sources, in descending order of importance: the US Customs Service, Canadian Customs via Statistics Canada, and the US Department of Defense.

Coverage and Definitions

The Census basis monthly merchandise trade data reflect movement into and out of US Customs' jurisdictions. This means that the data not only reflect goods to and from foreign countries into and out of the 50 states and the District of Columbia but also into and out of Puerto Rico, the US Virgin Islands, and US Foreign Trade Zones. Essentially, the monthly trade data are not defined by US national boundaries but by US Customs' geographic authority. Shipments by both nongovernment and government entities are included. However, shipments that do not represent a shift in use of merchandise between US Customs area residents or government and those of foreign countries generally are excluded from the data.

> The statistics used to compile the Census basis merchandise trade balance exclude the following types of transactions:
>
> a. United States trade with US possessions, trade between US possessions, and trade between US possessions and foreign countries (except Puerto Rico and the US Virgin Islands).
>
> b. Merchandise shipped in transit through the United States from one foreign country to another.

c. Shipments to the US Armed Forces, including post exchanges, for their own use, as well as US merchandise returned by the US Armed Forces for their own use.

d. Monetary gold and silver.

e. Issued monetary coins (in current circulation) of all component metals.

f. Bunker fuels and other supplies and equipment for use on departing vessels, planes, or other carriers engaged in foreign trade.

g. Shipment of furniture, equipment, and supplies to US government agencies as well as such merchandise when returned to the United States.

h. Imports of articles repaired under warranty.

i. Some other transactions not considered to be of statistical importance, such as shipments of personal and household effects of travelers and certain temporary exports and imports.[1]

Exports and imports are defined as follows:
Exports measure the total physical movement of merchandise out of the United States to foreign countries whether such merchandise is exported from within the US Customs territory or from a US Customs bonded warehouse or a US Foreign Trade Zone.

Imports of merchandise include commodities of foreign origin as well as goods of domestic origin returned to the United States with no change in condition or after having been processed and/or assembled in other countries.[2]

The Census basis monthly merchandise trade balance is simply US merchandise exports based on fas values less US general imports based on Customs values. For exports, the fas (free alongside ship) value includes all inland costs incurred to get the merchandise placed alongside the carrier at the port of exportation. This includes inland freight, insurance, and other charges but does not cover the cost of loading the merchandise on the carrier nor the cost of transportation beyond the port of exportation.

General imports include the total physical arrivals of merchandise from abroad regardless of whether the imports are for immediate consumption or not. Merchandise imports are classified as for immediate consumption if the goods are duty-free merchandise or if duty is paid on arrival.[3] Merchandise imports that are not classified as for immediate consumption either go into bonded warehouses or Foreign Trade Zones under Customs custody.

Customs import value is based on Customs appraisal standards and generally is the price actually paid or payable for merchandise ready for export from the exporting country. It includes the cost of getting the merchandise to the carrier (not on) but excludes US import duties, freight, insurance, and other costs of transporting the goods to the United States. While not currently used to derive the merchandise trade balance, Census also reports imports on a cif basis (cost, insurance, and freight). This basically is the landed value of imported goods at the first port of arrival in the United States and does not include US import duties. For imports from Canada and Mexico, customs values typically do not include inland freight expenses—that is, the costs of moving goods from plant of origin to the US border.

Recent Trends

Over the last few decades, the foreign trade sector has grown dramatically in importance worldwide with the United States included. In 1960, as a percentage of nominal GDP, merchandise exports and imports[4] were 4 percent and 3 percent, respectively. By 1993, merchandise exports and import shares had risen to over 7 percent and 9½ percent, respectively. Domestic demand has increasingly been met by imports while exports have become a more significant factor underlying growth in manufacturing output.

What does the United States export and import? In 1993, by principal end-use categories, exports were led by capital goods excluding autos and with second place held by industrial supplies and materials[5]. The most imports were for industrial supplies and materials followed by automotive vehicles, parts and engines. Table 11–2 gives export and import shares by principal end-use categories. End-use categories are the primary classification of Census trade data.

Export and import flows between various trading partners have changed significantly since the end of World War II. Though still important, western Europe no longer dominates as the United States' primary trading region. For exports, Canada is by far the most important buyer of US goods. However, Japan has nudged Canada out of first place as the number one foreign supplier of goods to the United States. Table 11–3 shows the top 10 trading partners of the United States for exports, imports, and balance.

Over the 1990s, international trade will likely grow worldwide. For the United States, Latin America probably will resume its importance as a trading bloc due to the implementation of the North American Free Trade Agreement (NAFTA) with Canada and Mexico. Many foreign trade analysts expect for this agreement to be expanded to include most of South America and the Caribbean. Over the 1970s, Latin America was a significant buyer of US exports, but trade dwindled due to the debt problems over the mid-1980s through early 1990s

TABLE 11–2
Export and Import Shares for Census Merchandise Trade by Principal End-Use Categories, 1993 Data

	Exports	Imports
Foods, feeds, and beverages	8.7	4.8
Industrial supplies and materials	24.1	25.0
Capital goods, except automotive	39.4	26.3
Automotive vehicles, parts and engines	11.1	17.6
Consumer goods (nonfood), except automotive	11.5	23.1
Other merchandise	5.2	3.2
Total	100.0	100.0

TABLE 11-3
Top Ten U.S. Merchandise Export/Import Trading Partners in 1993 (Millions of Current Dollars)

Exports to	Rank	Value	Percent of Total	Imports from	Rank	Value*	Percent of Total
Canada	(1)	100,444.3	21.6	Canada	(1)	111,216.4	19.2
Japan	(2)	47,891.5	10.3	Japan	(2)	107,246.4	18.5
Mexico	(3)	41,581.1	8.9	Mexico	(3)	39,917.4	6.9
United Kingdom	(4)	26,438.3	5.7	China	(4)	31,539.9	5.4
Germany	(5)	18,932.2	4.1	Germany	(5)	28,562.1	4.9
Taiwan	(6)	16,167.8	3.5	Taiwan	(6)	25,101.5	4.3
South Korea	(7)	14,782.0	3.2	United Kingdom	(7)	21,730.1	3.7
France	(8)	13,266.8	2.9	South Korea	(8)	17,118.0	2.9
Netherlands	(9)	12,838.5	2.8	France	(9)	15,279.3	2.6
Singapore	(10)	11,678.0	2.5	Italy	(10)	13,215.6	2.3
Total Merchandise Imports		465,091.0	100.0	Total Merchandise Exports		580,659.4	100.0

Trade Surplus	Rank	Value		Trade Deficit	Rank	Value
Netherlands	(1)	7,395.2		Japan	(1)	−59,354.9
Australia	(2)	4,979.2		China	(2)	−22,777.1
United Kingdom	(3)	4,708.1		Canada	(3)	−10,772.1
Belgium	(4)	3,729.4		Germany	(4)	−9,629.9
Argentina	(5)	2,570.0		Taiwan	(5)	−8,933.7
Turkey	(6)	2,231.4		Italy	(6)	−6,751.9
Egypt	(7)	2,154.8		Thailand	(7)	−4,775.4
Mexico	(8)	1,663.7		Malaysia	(8)	−4,498.6
Russia	(9)	1,227.0		Nigeria	(9)	−4,406.7
Spain	(10)	1,176.2		Venezuala	(10)	−3,549.7

*Imports are on a customs value basis.

Source: US Department of Commerce, Bureau of the Census, *US International Trade in Goods and Services: Annual Revision for 1993.*

for many Latin American nations that constrained their ability to pay for foreign-produced goods. Over the mid- to late 1990s, Latin America is expected to be a big purchaser of US capital equipment and consumer goods. Similarly, eastern Europe will likely be heavily dependent on capital from abroad—including the United States.

Newly industrialized countries will likely specialize in producing goods that are not capital-intensive and require a work force that is not as technologically advanced as in the developed nations. These nations increasingly will export more consumer goods, such as apparel, to the United States and worldwide.

KEYS TO ANALYZING THE MONTHLY CENSUS TRADE DATA

End-Use Categories

Understanding the key subcomponents in each major end-use category is important to making sense of the trends in trade. Table 11-4 shows export, import, and balance levels for the major end-use categories. As discussed below, the major

TABLE 11-4

Merchandise Trade: Principal End-Use Categories, Census Basis (Millions of Current Dollars)

Exports

	Total	Foods, Feeds and Beverages	Industrial Supplies and Materials	Capital Goods, except Automotive	Automotive Vehicles, Parts and Engines	Consumer Goods (Nonfood), except Automotive	Other Merchandise
1990	393,592.3	35,077.4	104,435.8	152,679.5	37,394.7	43,270.4	20,734.4
1991	421,730.0	35,696.7	109,718.0	166,663.2	40,044.7	45,943.8	23,663.7
1992	448,163.6	40,209.3	109,307.3	176,708.6	47,080.4	50,381.6	24,476.4
1993	464,767.2	40,421.2	112,004.5	182,952.1	51,690.5	53,408.0	24,290.8

Imports

	Total	Foods, Feeds and Beverages	Industrial Supplies and Materials	Capital Goods, except Automotive	Automotive Vehicles, Parts and Engines	Consumer Goods (Nonfood), except Automotive	Other Merchandise
1990	495,310.5	26,649.1	143,202.8	116,389.6	87,313.5	105,666.4	16,089.1
1991	488,453.0	26,466.7	131,596.2	120,737.0	85,691.3	108,022.2	15,939.6
1992	532,664.8	27,857.2	138,273.0	134,192.9	91,779.4	122,972.6	17,589.8
1993	580,554.2	28,055.0	145,126.8	152,701.0	102,441.1	133,867.5	18,352.6

Balance

	Total	Foods, Feeds and Beverages	Industrial Supplies and Materials	Capital Goods, except Automotive	Automotive Vehicles, Parts and Engines	Consumer Goods (Nonfood), except Automotive	Other Merchandise
1990	-101,718.2	8,428.3	-38,767.0	36,289.9	-49,918.8	-62,396.0	4,645.3
1991	-66,723.0	9,230.0	-21,878.2	45,926.2	-45,646.6	-62,078.4	7,724.1
1992	-84,501.2	12,352.1	-28,965.7	45,515.7	-44,699.0	-72,591.0	6,886.8
1993	-115,787.0	12,366.2	-33,122.3	30,251.1	-50,750.6	-80,459.5	5,938.2

end-use categories are: (1) food, feeds, and beverages; (2) industrial supplies and materials; (3) capital goods except autos; (4) consumer goods except autos; (5) automotive vehicles, parts, and engines; and (6) other merchandise.

The foods, feeds, and beverages end-use category is usually in surplus due to the United States' large volume of agricultural exports. Large swings can be caused by drought in agricultural areas abroad or in the United States. In recent years, the surplus has been eroded by greater US dependence on imports on vegetables and some meats. Grain is still the primary source of export strength. The United States primarily exports foods and feeds that use economies of scale—for example, wheat and corn—which are made possible by wide expanses of arable land and by the ability to use farm equipment extensively. Food imports generally are for crops that are labor-intensive or simply those imported during the United States' off season. Many off-season crops come from Latin America.

Foods, feeds, and beverages are primarily categorized between agricultural and nonagricultural components. For exports, listed agricultural components are grains and preparations (largely wheat and corn), soybeans, meat products and poultry; vegetables, fruits, nuts, and preparations; and other agricultural foods, feeds, and beverages. For imports, the listed agricultural components are the same except for the deletions of grains and preparations and soybeans and the additions of coffee, cocoa, and sugar; and wine and related products. Of course, there are minor quantities of many of these goods in both exports and imports, but these are not specifically listed categories. Exported or imported goods that do not fall into listed categories go under "other" agricultural. For both exports and imports, nonagricultural goods are primarily fish and shellfish along with distilled beverages and other miscellaneous categories.

The import component for industrial supplies and materials often swings sharply due to the inclusion of oil imports. Oil exports, of course, are negligible. This also causes this end-use component usually to be in a sharp deficit. On the import side, industrial supplies and materials are largely petroleum and products, metals, and metallic products. For exports, this component is led by chemicals, nonferrous metals, paper, petroleum and products, and coal. A critical factor in analyzing this end-use category is being able to take into account both price and volume changes in oil imports. Nominal data can be difficult for translating into estimates for real net exports for real GDP. This component also includes nonmonetary gold and occasionally reflects large shipments for numismatic reasons even though the gold is still in bullion form.

Petroleum imports do get special attention in the merchandise trade reports. Petroleum imports are listed in the monthly publications in tables by dollar value and by the volume of barrels imported. Also published is the average price per barrel of imported oil.

The capital goods except autos component is generally in surplus, since the production of capital goods is one of the United States' significant comparative advantages. In contrast, the consumer goods except autos component and the automobile and parts components are usually in deficit as newly industrialized countries have tended to specialize in consumer goods—including autos.

Capital goods, except automobiles, is led in exports by civilian aircraft; computers; semiconductors; industrial machinery; and oil drilling, mining, and construction machinery. Because aircraft shipments can be very large when they take place, this end-use category for exports is often volatile due to the inclusion of subcomponent. Very large swings in this end-use export component are usually attributable to aircraft. For imports, this end-use category is led by nonelectrical machinery—especially computers and semiconductors.

The "other merchandise" component primarily includes military goods and low-value shipments. Exports valued under $2,501 (as of 1993) per commodity classification per shipment do not have to be documented, and the Census Bureau makes estimates for this component. For exports to Canada, the Canadian import exemption level is used. For imports to the United States, only shipments valued $1,251 and higher generally require formal reports. An exception is textile imports under certain textile programs. Otherwise, imports under $1,251 per shipment are low value and are estimated by the Census Bureau. The dollar value definition of what is low value has changed over time.

On the export side, the other merchandise end-use category also includes an adjustment for exports to Canada as documented by Canadian Customs. Import data are usually better documented than export information. The difference between US estimates for exports to Canada and Canadian estimates for US imports to Canada is entered as a subcomponent in this end-use export category. This is first done with the first monthly revision to merchandise trade data. In the initial report, the adjustment is assumed to have a zero value. There is no equivalent adjustment on the import side for the other merchandise component.

End-use components are very useful in analyzing the supply and demand flow for US goods production and consumption. Data are available on similar basis for production and consumption as for end-use exports and imports. Imports are now an important factor in meeting demand for consumer goods and business equipment as well as for playing a key role in keeping inventories at desired levels. Exports are now a growing source of demand for industrial production.

The impact of changes in export or import flows cannot be determined by simply looking at aggregate values. There must be an understanding of flows by end-use categories and even finer detail. For example, does a monthly surge in imports mean that domestic production will falter? It might if these imports directly compete with goods also produced in the United States, such as automobiles or apparel. However, a jump in imports of consumer electronics probably would not, since most such goods purchased in the United States are no longer produced domestically.

Somewhat detailed analysis of end-use trade categories also helps to explain events in other demand sectors. If inventories unexpectedly rise, does this imply a downturn in domestic production? Production cutbacks are not likely if inventory accumulation is fueled by imports—foreign production will slip instead. However, inventory data are not maintained by domestic or import status, and import shares can only be inferred by analysis of US production by types of goods and by trends in consumer and business consumption and in exports and imports by types of goods.

Other Insights into the Monthly Data

For the trade data, the levels are as important to focus on as the percent changes in exports and imports by components. The levels define the surplus or deficit, and for some components there are significant or even dramatic differences between the export and import levels where the United States has a large comparative advantage or disadvantage. Additionally, it is whether the trade balance is improving or growing worse that affects growth rates in the economy in the near term—not whether the trade balance is in surplus or deficit. However, the size of the surplus or deficit does affect the economy in the medium and longer run through delayed effects on the dollar and other financial markets.

On a monthly basis, financial analysts use the Census data to project the current quarter net exports component of real GDP, since the Census data are published before the GDP data. This process has been made easier since Census began publishing monthly constant dollar (1987) seasonally adjusted export, import, and balance data beginning with January 1990 statistics and with data going back to January 1989. Even though Census figures are already seasonally adjusted at highly aggregated levels, the monthly data must be summed and then annualized for estimates of GDP trade components. When estimating NIPA net exports and components, Census data should only be used to project the merchandise trade portion of GDP net exports. Services data in the NIPA trade figures should be estimated separately. Nonetheless, there are definitional differences between NIPA trade data and Census data, and these lead to differences in dollar levels. However, the changes in the Census data from quarter to quarter give a good estimate of the changes in the NIPA data. The definitional differences are discussed in a following section. The balance-of-payments data also can be used for estimating net exports, but these series are not in constant dollar terms.

Broader Perspectives

It is important to note that it is hard to say what level various statistics actually indicate when a nations' trade flow is in balance. First, services surpluses can balance deficits in merchandise. Also, even though theoretically the sum of all nations' merchandise trade balances should equal zero (an import by one nation should be claimed as an export by another), this does not work out in practice in terms of statistical measures. Statistically, there is a worldwide merchandise trade deficit. This largely is due to the fact that every nation has more incentives to more closely monitor imports than exports. Generally, governments tend to tax imports while exports are taxed little or not at all. Domestic producers for each nation want to keep track of import competitors and lobby their politicians to maintain various restrictions. And, finally, trade statistics are used in trade negotiations, and each nation finds it to be advantageous to understate exports but not imports.

Each month, the monthly international trade figures provide one of the last pieces of the GDP puzzle for the current quarter (inventories are last). Certainly, the strength for the current quarter is partially determined by whether or not the deficit is widening or narrowing. However, for the longer run—or even the next quarter—a broader perspective is needed. For example, a surge (or sharp drop) in imports in the last month of a quarter does not necessarily mean that it is part of a change in trend. Basic questions must be asked about the data. These include: Can domestic demand continue to absorb imports at current growth rates or even at current levels, or will imports sit in inventories and cause a slowdown in coming months? Similarly, for exports one must ask: Are foreign economies capable of absorbing or demanding US exports at current rates? Are they strong enough, or is the latest data merely a blip due to the timing of shipments?

One of the keys to interpreting international trade trends is to remember that trade patterns change slowly due to the long lags caused by the time between contracts being signed and shipments being made. True changes in trend are caused by long-term factors such as significant exchange rate movements, changes in tariffs or export subsidies, changes in income domestically or abroad, changes in relative costs separate from exchange rates (financial capital and labor), and changes in availability of products abroad (capacity). Trade data are not significantly changed by these factors on a month-to-month basis.

On a final note, it should be apparent that many factors affect trade trends, but the value of the dollar is often the focus of attention and analysis of its impact is frequently misunderstood. It is often overlooked that focusing on bilateral exchange rates or certain composite dollar indexes ignores the impact of changes in trade patterns on the overall level of exports and imports. Even though the dollar depreciated sharply against a number of traditional trading partners in the early 1990s, US retailers and manufacturers imported goods and materials increasingly from newly industrialized countries that had currencies that showed little or no appreciation against the dollar. Traditional dollar indexes often missed this facet of emerging trade patterns and many forecasts underestimated the strength of imports over the period when the dollar fell according to these traditional measures.

CENSUS DATA AS INPUT IN OTHER FOREIGN TRADE STATISTICAL REPORTS

The monthly Census/BEA merchandise trade report provides data that are key inputs into other reports on foreign trade published by US statistical agencies. There are two other major reports in which the monthly data play significant roles. These are the summary of US international transactions or current account report and the net export portion of the national income and product accounts, or real GDP, report. Both reports are produced by the Bureau of Economic Analysis, although the first is under the direction of the Balance-of-Payments Division of the BEA while the second is published by the National Income and Wealth Division. Table 11–5 compares the levels of Census, balance of payments, and NIPA trade data.

The Current Account Reports

Both of these reports are part of what is known as the balance-of-payments accounts. These accounts are designed to be a comprehensive measure of the financial position of the United States with other nations in the world, and they have similar accounts. While the emphasis is on financial flows, the flow of physical goods is an important part of international financial transactions as merchandise trade balances affect financial standings. That is, exports and imports of goods are exchanged for either a monetary payment or a promise to pay.

The monthly Census data are used as direct inputs into monthly figures for monthly exports and imports on a balance-of-payments basis. There are three basic categories of adjustments made to Census foreign trade data for the figures to conform with other international transactions in the balance of payments data: timing, coverage, and valuation.[6]

First, timing adjustments are made to correct for documentation lags that result in exports and imports not being reported in the month of actual transactions.

Next, coverage adjustments reflect a variety of changes to incorporate a broader sphere of financial transactions, to substitute more reliable sources of data for the later published balance-of-payments data (relative to Census data), to fill in minor gaps in coverage, and to eliminate known sources of double-counting in the data.

There is a coverage adjustment for nonmonetary gold transactions made by the Federal Reserve Bank of New York on behalf of foreign governments and the International Monetary Fund (IMF). This adjustment is necessary because these transactions do not show up in Census documents since there is no movement across borders. Next, the Balance-of-Payments Division substitutes data on Department of Defense (DOD) exports and imports from a special comprehensive report it receives. The data the Census Bureau receives are not as detailed, and the Census-based data on DOD exports/imports are excluded to prevent double-counting. These transfers under US military agency sales contracts are excluded from the Census merchandise trade data and are not part of the merchandise portion of the trade data on a balance-of-payments basis. The more detailed DOD data enter the balance-of-payments accounts under services.

Until January 1989, an adjustment was made for electrical energy exports and imports to and from Canada with historical data coming from Statistics Canada. Beginning in January 1989, Census began including this data for electrical energy transactions with Canada. There is also a continuing adjustment for electrical energy trade with Mexico with the source of the data being the US Department of Energy. This adjustment is small.

A variety of other coverage adjustments are made for:

- Shipping vessels purchased or transferred by US persons—including any change of flag.
- Excluding exposed movie film as an offset to the inclusion of royalties and fees.
- Some double-counting in the repair of US vessels and aircraft.

- Repairs and alterations of equipment exported from and imported into the United States.
- Grain shipped by the United States to other countries through Canada.
- Gift parcel post exports.
- Canadian reconciliation of trade statistics.
- Sales of fish caught in US territorial waters by both US and foreign vessels and exported directly without landing in the United States.
- Imports of petroleum into Guam.[7]

The valuation adjustment is made for trade with Canada and Mexico and is made to correct for inland freight charges not included in customs import estimates. Some estimates for imports to the United States are shipments valued at f.o.b. plant rather than including the cost of bringing the merchandise to the border.

Table 11–5 compares the dollar values of Census basis merchandise trade figures and the data on a balance-of-payments basis and NIPA basis. The levels differ somewhat but the changes from year to year are close. The exclusion of military transfers is the largest adjustment to Census exports and is the reason why balance-of-payments data are lower for exports than Census data. On the import side, the biggest adjustment is for inland freight to Canada, and this raises the value of imports on a balance-of-payments basis relative to the Census basis. Adjustments also are made for Mexico but they are not as large as for Canada. The only significant offset is the exclusion of merchandise imports of US military agencies, but the value of this adjustment usually is less than half of the addition of the inland freight adjustment. The only other sizable adjustments (but still minor) are for private gift remittances and nonmonetary gold exports and imports.

The current account report incorporates information, not just on merchandise trade, but also on transfer payments by individuals and by governments, travel expenditures, royalties and license fees, various private and government services, and income to and from abroad, such as income on direct investment and income on financial investments (government and private securities). The monthly merchandise trade data on a balance-of-payments basis are combined with similar figures for services, income, and unilateral transfers to get a complete current account report. Table 11–5 also shows the dollar values of merchandise trade to overall trade in the balance of payments data.

From Monthly Balance-of-Payments Data to NIPA Net Exports in Gross Domestic Product

The monthly balance-of-payments data are inputs into the international trade components of exports and imports in gross domestic product (GDP). However, the National Income and Wealth Division of the BEA does not use the Balance-of-Payment Division's trade data directly. This division of the BEA receives both merchandise and services trade data as adjusted for the balance-of-payments accounts (BPAs), and the data in this form provide the basis for the foreign transactions series in the national income and product accounts (NIPAs). Still, there are a few definitional and statistical differences between the BPA and NIPA data.

TABLE 11–5
Foreign Trade Data: Census, Balance-of-Payments Accounts, and NIPA Basis
(Billions of Current Dollars)

	Census Merch.	BPA Merch.	NIPA Merch.	BPA Total	NIPA Total
			Exports		
1990	393.6	389.3	398.7	688.8	557.1
1991	421.7	416.9	426.4	708.5	601.5
1992	448.2	440.1	448.7	730.5	640.5
1993	464.8	456.8	461.5	753.9	661.7
			Imports		
1990	495.3	498.3	509.0	746.8	628.5
1991	487.1	490.7	500.7	723.4	621.1
1992	532.7	536.3	544.5	764.0	670.1
1993	580.5	589.2	592.1	830.6	725.3
			Balance		
1990	−101.7	−109.0	−110.3	−58.0	−71.4
1991	−65.4	−73.8	−74.3	−14.9	−19.6
1992	−84.5	−96.1	−95.8	−33.5	−29.6
1993	−115.7	−132.4	−130.6	−76.7	−63.6

Note: The nonmerchandise components in the BPAs include both services and income receipts/payments on income. The lower overall export and import levels for GDP relative to the BPAs are primarily due to the BPA's inclusion of income receipts/payments.

Sources: U.S. Department of Commerce, Bureau of the Census, *U.S. Merchandise Trade, 1991 Final Report* and *1992 Final Report,* Exhibit 1; *Survey of Current Business,* June 1993, p. 71, Table 1; *Survey of Current Business, August 1993, U.S. International Trade in Goods and Services,* February 1994: *U.S. International Transactions-Fourth Quarter and Year 1993: Gross Domestic Product: Fourth Quarter 1993 (Final).*

The differences between the NIPA and BPA entries, called reconciliation items, . . . reflect different publication and revision schedules, different definitions of the United States, and—most importantly—different treatment of certain transactions. The first source of difference arises because the NIPA estimates incorporate BPA revisions with lags. The second arises because the NIPAs exclude Puerto Rico and US territories from the definition of the United States, while the BPAs include them. The third arises because the two sets of accounts serve different purposes and, therefore, treat certain types of transactions differently.[8]

In more detail, BPA data are typically revised in a number of ways prior to when the revisions are made to NIPA data. Each year, annual revisions are made first to BPA series and then to NIPA figures. Additionally, BPAs may be benchmarked earlier or incorporate a new methodology prior to NIPA data (or be based on new source data for some services components).

For balance-of-payments data, Puerto Rico, US territories and possessions are included in the definition of the United States. For NIPA data, they are not included. Therefore, territorial adjustments are made to merchandise series. Exports to other countries from US territories and Puerto Rico are subtracted from the BPA data, and exports from the 50 states and the District of Columbia to US territories and Puerto Rico are added. Similar adjustments are made for imports.

Limiting discussion to merchandise components, the only difference in the treatment of transactions between BPAs and NIPAs is for gold. For background, as already discussed, Census data ignore monetary gold transfers. BPA data make a distinction between monetary and nonmonetary gold, and adjustments are made to incorporate monetary gold transactions for BPAs. Industrial-use gold enters BPA accounts through standard Census data for exports and imports. However, official transactions between monetary authorities and/or governments take place in capital accounts in BPAs. Beginning in 1975, gold sold to private foreigners by the US Treasury is recorded as exports, and gold purchased by private US residents from the International Monetary Fund and foreign official agencies is counted as imports. This background helps explain the focus in the GDP account for gold in terms of production of industrial-use gold and changes in holdings of industrial-use gold—other uses are generally extraterritorial.

> In the NIPAs, US gold production is included in GNP, and transactions in nonmonetary gold held for industrial use are recorded as any other commodity in the expenditure components of GNP. Nonmonetary gold held for nonindustrial use, however, is treated as if it were in the foreign sector in the same manner as monetary gold owned by the US Treasury, because purchases of nonindustrial gold have an investment aspect that would make their inclusion in the domestic expenditure components problematic for many types of analysis.[9]

Essentially, the gold subcomponents in the BPA exports and imports are removed. Then an entry is made in imports for gold on a NIPA basis. The replacement entry for gold in NIPA net exports is the difference between domestic gold production and the change in holdings of industrial gold. This entry incorporates movement of industrial-use gold between US residents and foreigners and also shifts between industrial and nonindustrial use by US residents. Because of inadequacies in the data, exports and imports of gold are not measured separately. NIPA exports of gold are set equal to zero, and net exports of gold are defined as imports (with the sign reversed). There is no NIPA gold component in exports.

The biggest adjustments to BPA exports and imports to get corresponding NIPA merchandise series are the adjustments for US territories and Puerto Rico. As shown in Table 11–4, these adjustments raise the levels of exports and imports relative to BPA levels. The adjustments for gold are a distant second in magnitude, and the exclusion has a lowering effect—but not enough to offset the territorial adjustments.

For services exports and imports, the only major adjustment to BPA data to get NIPA series is a bottom-line adjustment each for exports and imports to take into account territorial differences. The adjustment is "bottom line" in that adjustments are not made to individual components. There are other minor adjustments in these adjustment line items, but the dollar values are very small.

THE SERVICES COMPONENTS IN THE MONTHLY REPORT

Table 11–1 shows the balance-of-payments services components. The importance of these series is that they give a direct indication of the BEA's view for trends in these services exports and imports—which are major inputs in GDP services exports and imports. However, estimates for current year services exports and imports are very preliminary. Estimates are based on annual trends plus partial information on prices and quantities from sources such as travel agencies, trade sources, Customs data, and the Treasury reporting system. Annual data are based on more complete sources.

Annual data for balance-of-payments services from a variety of voluntary and mandatory surveys, as well as sources such as US Treasury Department data, data from other US government agencies, and private trade sources. Voluntary surveys include the Survey of US Travelers Visiting Canada and also Expenditures of United States Travelers in Mexico. These BEA surveys are distributed continuously at border points. Mandatory surveys cover ocean freight revenues and foreign expenses of US carriers; US airline operators' foreign revenues and expenses; foreign ocean carriers' expenses in the United States; foreign airline operators' revenues and expenses in the United States; and other private services, royalties, and license fees. Other private services cover services ranging from computer processing, telecommunications, performing arts, accounting, legal services, mining services, and insurance. Services components are discussed in further detail in the chapter on gross domestic product.

Analyzing the News Release: Key Questions

- To determine the impact on real GDP—that is, real net exports for merchandise—is the constant-dollar monthly merchandise trade deficit improving or worsening, regardless of the level of the balance?
- When imports surge, does this surge represent a sustainable rise in domestic demand or merely special timing factors?
- Are imports up in late summer due to earlier-than-usual shipments for Christmas inventory needs?
- Is an increase in imports only temporary due to pending import restrictions? Similarly, is a drop in imports due to reaching import restrictions such as voluntary import restrictions on motor vehicles?
- Were imports up due to replenishing needs for oil inventories through increased oil imports?
- Are capital goods exports unusually high because of the timing of shipments of aircraft out of inventories?

NOTES FOR CHAPTER 11

1. US Department of Commerce, Bureau of the Census, *Guide to Foreign Trade Statistics, 1991 Edition*, Section 2, p. 3.
2. Ibid., pp. 3–4.
3. The term *consumption* is unrelated to the term in NIPA categories. These imports can be used for purchases by consumers, businesses, and government; for inventory accumulation; or for inputs as crude or intermediate products.
4. Exports and imports are on a NIPA basis. Census data are not consistent series back to 1960.
5. For both exports and imports, this category includes petroleum products.
6. The following discussion on adjustments to Census data to put into balance-of-payments form is based on *The Balance of Payments of the United States: Concepts, Data Sources, and Estimating Procedures*, May 1990, U.S. Department of Commerce, Bureau of the Census, pp. 31–35.
7. The full list appears in The *Balance of Payments of the United States: Concepts, Data Sources, and Estimating Procedures*, May 1990, U.S. Department of Commerce, pp. 33–35.
8. U.S. Department of Commerce, Bureau of Economic Analysis, *Foreign Transactions, Methodology Papers: U.S. National Income and Product Accounts*, BEA-MP-3, May 1987, p. 7.
9. Ibid.

BIBLIOGRAPHY

U.S. Department of Commerce. Bureau of Economic Analysis. *The Balance of Payments of the United States: Concepts, Data Sources, and Estimating Procedures*, May 1990.

———. *Foreign Transactions, Methodology Papers: U.S. National Income and Product Accounts*, BEA-MP-3, May 1987.

———. *Guide to Foreign Trade Statistics, 1991 Edition*.

———. *U.S. Merchandise Trade: 1991 Final Report*.

———. *U.S. Merchandise Trade: 1992 Final Report*.

CHAPTER 12

MONTHLY CONSTRUCTION INDICATORS

Construction tends to be a very cyclical activity that can have a very significant impact on the national economy and even more so on various local economies. Construction activity has a significant impact on local employment due to secondary effects on construction supply and services industries. While there are many construction statistics produced and released each month by the federal government, the two most watched are housing starts and housing permits. They are followed for two key reasons: (1) starts and permits are key indicators of the near-term health of the housing industry, and (2) these data series tend to be leading indicators for the overall economy.

Of lesser notoriety are new single-family homes sales and the monthly construction outlays series. This sales series, of course, is a closely watched indicator of housing demand, while outlay data are broader in scope. They cover not only residential activity but also nonresidential and public-sector construction spending. These data are important for monitoring the level of current construction activity—as opposed to potential future activity—and more specifically because the data are important inputs in the GDP accounts.

In overview, permits and starts reflect plans for construction activity, sales reflect demand, and outlays are a measure of actual production in the construction sector.

CURRENT CONSTRUCTION REPORTS

The source for each of these series is the Census Bureau of the US Department of Commerce. They are part of Census' publications known as *Current Construction Reports*. This chapter focuses only on four of the reports. Each report is referred to in shorthand by the number of the construction report publication number. For example, the housing permits report is known as C40. The reference numbers and official titles of these publications are:

C20, Housing Starts.

C21, New Residential Activity in Selected Standard Metropolitan Statistical Areas.

C22, Housing Completions.

C25, New One-Family Houses Sold.

C30, Value of New Construction Put in Place.

C40, Housing Units Authorized by Building Permits.

C50, Expenditures for Residential Improvements and Repairs.

HOUSING PERMITS

The housing permit series is officially known as new privately owned housing units authorized and is published by the Census Bureau in the C40 construction report. Preliminary permit data are released to the public at the same time as housing starts. This is generally the third week of the month following the reference month. The housing permit series is an indicator of planned construction activity in the residential sector. Permit authorization is one of the first steps in the construction process taken by builders, with later steps including the start, continuing outlays, and then completion. The importance of the permit data is evident in that this is the only construction indicator in the Commerce Department's index of leading indicators.

Permit authorization is given by local governments such as cities and counties. Housing permit data no longer incorporate publicly owned housing. This component was last published at the national level in 1986 due to the difficulty in getting the data from the US Department of Housing and Urban Development and due to the declining significance of publicly owned housing.

The housing permit series represents only new housing units intended for occupants on a housekeeping basis. Hotels, motels, nursing homes, and dormitories are excluded. Mobile homes also are not included in the permit data.

Statistics for these series are derived from reports by local building permit officials in response to a mail survey by Census. For reports that are not returned, Census replaces the missing data either with information from its Survey of Use of Permits (SUP)—which is used to collect data for estimates of housing starts—or an indirect estimate is used. The SUP survey is much more limited in sample coverage for permit-issuing places than the mail survey. Where the SUP survey cannot substitute for missing data, the estimate is based on the assumption that the ratio of current month authorizations to those of a year ago are the same for both reporting and nonreporting places. That is, nonreporting places have the same year-ago change in permits as reporting places, and this ratio is applied to known year-ago data for nonreporting places.

With each month's initial release, only the prior month is revised. Annual revisions to seasonal factors are made for the release of data for the reference month of April and cover the previous two calendar years. However, monthly permit data are not benchmarked to annual survey levels. Therefore, pure annual figures do not equal the sum of monthly permit data.

The Sample

The current version of the housing permit series is based on data from a sample of about 8,300 permit-issuing places that were chosen from a universe of approximately 17,000 places. Estimation of the permit data from a sampling technique applies only to the statistics at relatively high levels of aggregation—for the United States, the Census regions, and for the individual states. Lower-level statistics (such as for MSAs) are not based on samples but on actual reported data. There is complete enumeration of all permit-issuing places in selected metropolitan areas and certain states with a small number of permit-issuing places. The rest of the sample is stratified by state with large permit-issuing places chosen with certainty and other places selected at a rate of 1 in 10. The definition of *large* varies by state and was set to ensure a minimum reliability for each state. Estimates for the United States, the Census regions, and most states are based on techniques applicable to samples.

Due to the constantly changing number in actual permit-issuing places, the Census Bureau chooses a fixed universe for the data series. Changes include adding new permit-issuing places and deleting places no longer issuing permits. A chosen, fixed universe keeps the data consistent. The universe is used only for the annual data, while a sample of this universe is used for the monthly estimates. The monthly sample for the current 17,000 universe is roughly 8,300 places.

Monthly permit levels are estimated from the 8,300 sample. First, about 7,500 places are selected with certainty; these are the places issuing greater numbers of permits—essentially metropolitan areas. Permit levels from these places are entered directly into monthly estimates. These 7,500 are not just representative of themselves in the 17,000 sample but are equivalent. The remaining 800 reporting places in the monthly sample are representative of the places that are not selected with certainty in the monthly sample. To obtain the appropriate level of permits in the monthly sample, the data for the remaining 800 places are weighted by a factor of 10.

For the places selected with certainty, the criteria differ somewhat from state to state due to the need to maintain a sufficiently large sample for each state in order to publish state data that are statistically meaningful.

The number of permit-issuing places that define the permit series has changed over time. This has changed the size of the sample and essentially changed the definition of permit data at specific times. Permit data from the Census Bureau originally were based on 13,000 permit-issuing places with the data starting in 1967 and going through December 1972. In January of 1973, data were reported that were based on 14,000 permit-issuing places with data starting in 1973 and ending in December 1977. The sample size was increased to 16,000 in April 1979 and then to 17,000 in 1985, which is the current size. Data based on the 16,000 sample run from 1978 through 1984. Overlap data are available for the first year of each series.

KEYS TO ANALYZING THE MONTHLY PERMITS DATA

The housing permit series is a leading indicator of the economy. This is due to permit issuance being the initial stage of housing activity and because of the leading nature of the housing sector. Housing typically leads the economy because of its interest rate sensitivity. Also, decisions to make housing purchases are highly dependent on consumer confidence—including expectations of income. Changes in housing activity also lead to significant secondary effects in other industries. Housing demand also affects demand for goods such as appliances, furniture, and carpeting. Analysts of these industries closely watch housing data. Interestingly, booms in new housing later lead to booms for replacement appliances as much original equipment wears out over a common time span. That is, air-conditioning and heating units and carpeting each need replacing a certain number of years after being installed in new housing. The new housing boom in the 1970s later led to a rise in demand for replacement goods in the late 1980s and early 1990s.

Permits represent planned construction—they are potential activity rather than actual outlays. They do not represent starts or the amount of construction having taken place. Also, permit data differ from starts in another aspect: permits reflect coverage in permit-issuing places, whereas starts include activity in both permit-issuing and nonpermit-issuing areas. Of course, the issuance of a permit does not necessarily mean that a start or further construction must occur.

Housing permit data—like other housing statistics—are very seasonal and volatile on a monthly basis even after seasonal influences have been accounted for statistically. Housing data for winter months are heavily influenced by seasonal factors, and reports of unusually large increases or declines (after seasonal adjustment) should be viewed warily until a several-month trend is established. The Census Bureau acknowledges this by charting the data in the construction report series, typically with a four-month moving average as well as with one-month actual data.

Seasonal factors for permit data for the United States are derived indirectly.

> The seasonally adjusted building permits estimates are computed using a procedure similar to that used for housing starts . . . The seasonally adjusted US total is the sum of six seasonally adjusted components: single-family structures in each of the four regions, US total for two-to-four unit structures, and US total for structures with five units or more. Also, the unadjusted data for the four regions are seasonally adjusted and subsequently modified so that the seasonally adjusted US total derived from the regions equals the seasonally adjusted US total derived from the structures.[1]

Therefore, for total permits (and starts), there are only implied seasonal factors at the national level—no directly derived seasonal factors.

Permits also can be heavily influenced by changes in regulations. For example, California passed legislation in the fall of 1985 that changed building codes for handicap access. Multifamily permits for that state surged prior to the new codes' effective date and even led to a large increase in the US totals.

For use in the index of leading indicators, the data in the index typically do not quite match the levels in the most recent official release for permit data. The reason is that the BEA has access to late-received data that end up in the revised numbers in the next C40 release.

CHART 12–1
Housing Permits

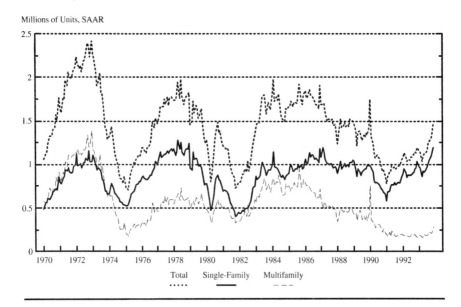

Millions of Units, SAAR

Total	Single-Family ———	Multifamily – – –

Source: US Bureau of the Census

HOUSING STARTS

Housing starts, or, formally, new privately owned housing units started, measure when construction activity begins. For privately owned housing, the start of construction is "when excavation begins for the footings or foundation of a building."[2] Beginning with the September 1992 release, the estimates for both starts and permits also include units in structures being totally rebuilt on an existing foundation.[3] This definition of starts covers buildings intended for "housekeeping purposes"— that is, excluding group homes such as dormitories and nursing homes. Residential structures such as hotels also are excluded. For multifamily buildings such as apartments and condominiums, all housing units in the building are counted as being started when the excavation has begun. As with permit data, starts no longer include publicly owned housing units.

Housing units are defined to exclude mobile homes. Data for mobile home shipments are published in the C20 report but represent an entirely different data series. However, the starts data do include prefabricated, panelized, componentized, sectional, and modular housing units in addition to the conventional "stick-built" units.[4]

With each month's initial release, the two prior months are revised. Three-year seasonal adjustment revisions are published with the release of data for the reference month of January.

Derivation of Starts Estimates

Housing starts estimates are based on permit data for permit-covered areas and on separate on-site surveys for other areas.

For the 17,000 permit-issuing places, a mail-in survey is sent to a sample of 8,300 to estimate the number of permits issued. Next, the Census Bureau sends interviewers on-site to an 840 representative subset of the 8,300 sample to determine which units were started for a particular month. This survey of 840 is the Survey of Use of Permits (SUP). Follow-up interviews are made if a unit is not started by the end of the month.

From the data gathered with the interview process, ratios are calculated (by type of structure—single-family, etc.) of the number of units started to units covered by permits. These ratios, called starts rates, are calculated for each month following (and including) the month of permit issuance. For units with permit authorization, starts estimates are derived by applying the starts rates to permits authorized over the appropriate number of months and by structure type.

The above methodology only covers starts for units that received permit authorization. In permit-issuing places, some starts take place without permit authorization. To take this into account, the Census Bureau makes an upward adjustment of 3.3 percent to the number of single-family structures started with permits. This figure is based on a study during the 1970s on the number of starts covered by permits in permit-issuing places. Adjustments are also made to account for units started before permit authorization in permit-issuing places and for late reports.

Given the sample design, approximately 95 percent of start activity typically occurs within permit-issuing places. In nonpermit-issuing places, a small sample of the land area is surveyed to provide an estimate of starts. These small sample data are then used to derive starts for the total area not covered by permits. Finally, this estimate of starts in nonpermit-covered areas is added to the estimate of starts in the 17,000 permit-issuing places to get an estimate of total private housing starts.

KEYS TO ANALYZING THE MONTHLY STARTS DATA

Housing starts data generally closely track housing permit data in terms of changes in levels. It is normal for starts levels to exceed permit levels because not all areas require permits for a start. While not all permits are started, the percentage not started is very small due to the expense of obtaining a permit.

The primary factors causing temporary divergent movement between permits and starts include weather (delaying or accelerating starts), expected changes in permit regulations, and perceived changes in housing demand by builders— particularly in reference to whether home buyers anticipate changes in mortgage rates.

CONSTRUCTION EXPENDITURES

Construction expenditures data are published in the C30 construction report and are more formally known as Value of New Construction Put in Place. In contrast to permit and start information, construction expenditures refer to actual con-

CHART 12–2
Housing Starts versus Fixed-Rate Mortgage Rates

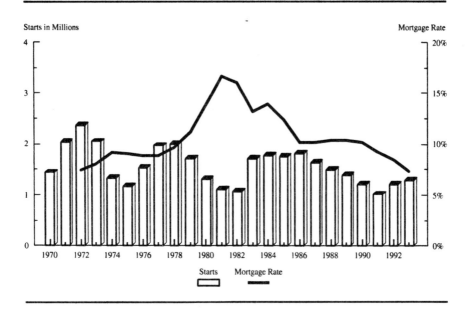

Source: US Department of Commerce and FHLMC

CHART 12–3
Single-Family Starts versus Demographic Trends

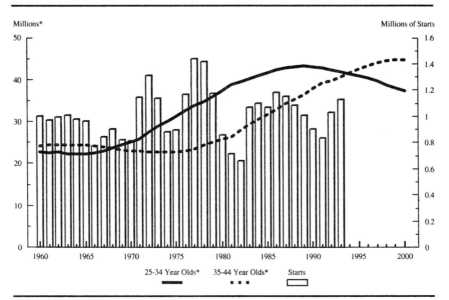

Source: US Bureau of the Census

TABLE 12–1
Housing Data: Permits and Starts (Levels in Thousands)

Year	Permits Total	Single-Family	Multi-Family	Start Total	Single-Family	Multi-Family
1970	1,351.5	646.8	704.8	1,433.6	812.9	620.7
1971	1,924.6	906.1	1,018.6	2,052.2	1,151.0	901.2
1972	2,218.9	1,033.1	1,185.8	2,356.6	1,309.2	1,047.5
1973	1,819.5	882.1	937.5	2,045.3	1,132.0	913.3
1974	1,074.4	643.8	430.5	1,337.7	888.1	449.7
1975	939.2	675.5	263.7	1,160.4	892.2	268.3
1976	1,296.2	893.6	402.6	1,537.5	1,162.4	375.1
1977	1,690.0	1,126.1	564.0	1,987.1	1,450.9	536.1
1978	1,800.5	1,182.6	617.9	2,020.3	1,433.3	587.0
1979	1,551.8	981.5	570.2	1,745.1	1,194.1	551.0
1980	1,190.6	710.4	480.2	1,292.2	852.2	440.0
1981	985.5	564.3	421.2	1,084.2	705.4	378.8
1982	1,000.5	546.4	454.1	1,062.2	662.6	399.6
1983	1,605.2	901.5	703.7	1,703.0	1,067.6	635.5
1984	1,681.8	922.4	759.4	1,749.5	1,084.2	665.4
1985	1,733.3	956.6	776.7	1,741.8	1,072.4	669.5
1986	1,769.4	1,077.6	691.9	1,805.4	1,179.4	626.0
1987	1,534.8	1,024.4	510.4	1,620.5	1,146.4	474.0
1988	1,455.6	993.8	461.8	1,488.1	1,081.3	406.8
1989	1,338.4	931.7	406.8	1,376.1	1,003.3	372.8
1990	1,110.8	793.9	316.9	1,192.7	894.8	297.9
1991	948.8	753.5	195.2	1,013.9	840.4	173.5
1992	1,094.9	910.7	184.2	1,199.7	1,029.9	169.7
1993	1,214.2	1,004.6	209.6	1,287.6	1,125.7	161.9

Annual figures are not seasonally adjusted totals.

Source: U.S. Department of Commerce, Bureau of the Census, C40 and C20 Reports.

struction rather than planned or just initiated activity. In essence, construction expenditures are a measure of current production in the construction sector. Importantly, these data series cover nonresidential and public sectors as well as residential construction.

This "value of new construction put in place" is a measure of the value of construction installed or erected at the site during a given period. For an individual project, this includes:

1. Cost of materials installed or erected.
2. Cost of labor (both by contractors and force account) and a proportionate share of construction equipment rental.
3. Contractor's profit.
4. Project owner's overhead and office costs.
5. Cost of architectural and engineering work.

6. Miscellaneous costs chargeable to the project on the owner's books.

7. Interest and taxes paid during construction.[5]

Expenses do not include the cost of land.

For public construction, there are two main components: building and non-building. In nominal terms, over the late 1980s and early 1990s, the buildings component has been about 40 to 45 percent of public expenditures, with educational buildings the largest subcomponent. The nonbuilding subcomponent overwhelmingly consists of highways and streets, with sewer systems and water supply facilities being distant second and third largest components.

Private construction includes two major components—residential buildings and nonresidential buildings—plus a number of minor series. Residential construction includes new private housing and also improvements. For new housing units, included are new houses, apartments, condominiums, and town houses. Other types of residential construction that are generally for nonhousekeeping or institutional purposes (hospitals, dormitories, hotels, etc.) are included in nonresidential construction. New private housing units are classified as "1 unit" or "2 or more units."

Private nonresidential construction put in place includes a variety of familiar components as well as a number of components not typically assumed to be in a series defined as nonresidential. The best-known private nonresidential component is for nonresidential buildings, with other components being farm nonresidential, privately owned public utilities, and "all other."

As might be expected, the nonresidential buildings component includes industrial, office buildings, and "other commercial"—such as shopping centers, banks, service stations, warehouses, and other categories. Also falling under the nonresidential heading are religious, educational, hospital and institutional, and "miscellaneous nonresidential" building.[6] These subcomponents are only for private construction.

Rounding out the private construction component are farm nonresidential, public utilities, and "all other private." These are generally of a nonresidential nature but are not part of nonresidential buildings. Farm nonresidential construction is a relatively minor component and includes structures such as barns, storage houses, and fences. Land improvements such as leveling, terracing, ponds, and roads also are a part of this subcomponent. Data for farm nonresidential construction reflect activity only for establishments having annual agricultural sales of $1,000 or more.

Privately owned public utilities construction is categorized by industry rather than by function of the building or structure. This component includes expenditures made by utilities for telecommunications, railroads, petroleum pipelines, electric light and power, and natural gas. Also, the public utilities category includes some nonresidential and nonbuilding expenditures (office building and parking lots, for example) when such construction is for the utilities' own use.

"All other private" includes privately owned streets and bridges, parking areas, sewer and water facilities, parks and playgrounds, golf courses, airfields, and similar construction.

METHODOLOGIES FOR ESTIMATING CONSTRUCTION EXPENDITURES

Residential Expenditures

Residential expenditures for one-unit houses are based on estimated final construction costs and a predetermined pattern for the distribution of the total cost over the construction period. The construction cost is estimated using data from the Census Bureau's Housing Starts Survey and Housing Sales Survey, while the distribution patterns is based on historical data on typical monthly distributions of construction progress from start to finish. The Census Bureau publishes a table showing the assumed progress by percent completed each month. There is a separate distribution pattern for each month that new units are started.

For units built to be sold or rented and units built by the owner, construction cost is estimated separately. For units to be sold or rented, estimates are based on the average sales price at the time of the start and then discounted to take into account the cost of nonconstruction items such as raw land, marketing costs, closing costs, and movable appliances. For units built for the owner, the cost is based on the contract value at the time of the start with a minor net upward adjustment to eliminate nonconstruction items but also to add the value of land development done by the developer.

For multifamily units, a subsample of the Census Bureau's Housing Starts Survey is used to estimate construction progress. About 1,800 projects are in the survey. Owners are to report construction progress until the project is completed.

Estimates of value put in place are derived from the sum of the adjusted reported value for all projects. Upward adjustments are made for architectural, engineering, and miscellaneous costs (which are not reported monthly in the survey).

Residential improvements are derived from Census surveys using household interviews in a representative sample for owner-occupied units and a mail-in survey of owners of rental or vacant properties. Data from these surveys are oriented for quarterly estimates and substantially lag the monthly estimates of expenditures on new construction. As a result, monthly figures for total residential improvements are usually forecasted from incomplete data. Estimates based on complete data are first used in the May publication for revisions to the previous year.[7]

Private Nonresidential Expenditures

Private nonresidential expenditures are based on a monthly Construction Progress Reporting Survey with the survey primarily choosing the sample based on reports from the F.W. Dodge Division of the McGraw-Hill Information Systems Company for projects valued at $50,000 or more in the United States except Hawaii. Census uses building permit notifications for sample projects in portions of Hawaii. Census also seeks sample projects in areas not covered by building permit systems or reported by Dodge. Monthly progress reports are requested from the owners of selected projects until the project is completed. About 4,600 projects are in the survey.

Estimates for value put in place are derived by the summed weighted reported values of the projects with upward adjustments for architectural, engineering, and miscellaneous costs. An upward adjustment is also made for undercoverage of projects not reported by F.W. Dodge.

Other Private Construction Categories

Farm nonresidential construction expenditure estimates are extrapolations from the annual US Department of Agriculture report, *Income and Balance Sheet Statistics*. These expenditures are not reported separately on a monthly or quarterly basis.

For utility construction, a variety of sources are used. Data are derived and organized by industry. Actual monthly construction progress reports are available for telephone and telegraph components of telecommunication construction. Annual reports from federal regulatory agencies and various private organizations are used for annual construction put-in-place estimates for TV cable, electric light and power, gas, railroad, and petroleum components. Monthly estimates for railroads are derived from quarterly estimates by the Interstate Commerce Commission. Other monthly figures are based on forecasts primarily from industry sources.[8]

Public Construction

State and local public construction expenditures are based on progress reports from a stratified survey. The survey is created from information from F.W. Dodge. Federal construction expenditures are reported almost entirely by each federal agency. For the few agencies not reporting, information is obtained from the federal budget with annual expenditures prorated to derive monthly figures.

KEYS TO ANALYZING MONTHLY CONSTRUCTION OUTLAYS

Broad Cyclical Trends

The construction outlays data basically reflect the value of construction that has taken place over a given time period. Data are for current production, however. Over the business cycle, different components of outlays exhibit differences in cyclical timing. First, residential outlays are a leading series. Housing outlays are interest rate sensitive and tack housing starts and permits with a short lag. Most new houses are completed within three or four months of a start.

Over the business cycle, the nonresidential outlays series is a lagging indicator. Business investment in structures is interest rate sensitive, but nonresidential outlays typically lag investment in producers' durable equipment. Businesses expand equipment investment first because it is quicker to boost production capacity with purchases of machinery than with new plant construction. Also, structures investment is more costly in absolute dollar size, and it is riskier in terms of demand remaining strong long enough to pay off the cost of the structures investment.

Public construction is primarily state and local outlays. State and local construction is dependent on revenue growth (or decline) and therefore sometimes lags the peaks and troughs in the business cycle. Perhaps more importantly, secular trends are also largely affected by changes in federal funding for various types of infrastructure improvement programs. Federal grants-in-aid show up in state and local outlays and at times counterbalance the cyclical changes in other state and local revenues. Over the long run, public construction outlays are largely affected by population growth—which affects highway, sewer, and waterline types of construction—and by the size of the school age population—which affects construction of education buildings.

Use as Source Data for GDP

Construction outlays series are measures of output and are primary inputs in several key expenditure series in GDP—for nominal and constant 1987 dollars. For nonresidential fixed investment in GDP, construction outlays are the main inputs for nonfarm buildings, utilities, and "other nonfarm structures." GDP estimates for residential investment rely heavily on C30 data for permanent-site single-family and multifamily housing. However, quarterly changes in broad categories of residential and nonresidential outlays do not precisely match movement in corresponding GDP components because not all of the GDP subcomponents are based on C30 data. For nonresidential structures investment, other sources are used to estimate: oil and gas well drilling and exploration; construction of mine shafts and exploration; and broker commissions. For residential investment, subcomponents not based on Census outlays figures include mobile homes, brokers' commissions, and the producers' durable equipment component[9] of residential investment.

For the public sector, value put-in-place figures are used for estimates for the state and local structures subcomponent of government purchases within GDP data.

NEW SINGLE-FAMILY HOME SALES

The new single-family home sales series is published in the Monthly Current Construction Report, *New One-Family Houses Sold and for Sale*—otherwise known as C25. The Housing Sales survey is conducted by the Bureau of the Census under contract with the U.S. Department of Housing and Urban Development. Data are published for sales, inventory, median and average prices for houses sold, and months on the market for houses sold and for sale. Data are organized by Census region and generally are seasonally adjusted at that level of detail and higher. This report is usually released to the public near the end of the month following the reference month of the first week of the second month following the reference month. With each initial release, monthly revisions cover the previous three months. Seasonal adjustment revisions normally occur with the release for data for the reference month of January (usually released in early March) and affect data for the previous three calendar years.

A sale takes place when a home buyer signs a contract or makes a deposit. Land must be included in the sale or the house is assumed to be for the landown-

TABLE 12–2
Construction Outlays (Billions, Current Dollars)

	Total	Private Residential Buildings	Private Non-residential Buildings	Farm Non-residential	Public Utilities	All Other Private	Public Construction
1970	100.727	35.863	23.008	1.875	11.127	0.946	27.908
1971	117.311	48.514	24.204	1.916	11.985	0.992	29.699
1972	133.318	60.693	26.568	1.785	13.301	0.941	30.030
1973	146.826	65.085	30.683	2.525	15.272	0.912	32.348
1974	147.476	55.967	32.195	3.249	16.933	1.000	38.132
1975	145.623	51.581	28.397	3.731	17.553	1.068	43.293
1976	165.441	68.273	27.936	3.971	20.204	1.077	43.979
1977	193.126	92.004	30.871	4.431	21.437	1.301	43.083
1978	230.178	109.838	39.135	5.209	24.567	1.283	50.146
1979	259.839	116.444	51.732	5.588	27.978	1.452	56.646
1980	259.746	100.381	58.290	5.274	30.905	1.250	63.646
1981	271.950	99.241	68.450	4.612	33.688	1.268	64.691
1982	260.594	84.676	73.953	3.672	33.942	1.269	63.064
1983	294.945	125.521	70.438	3.255	30.817	1.464	63.450
1984	348.817	153.849	87.493	3.161	32.191	1.905	70.217
1985	377.366	158.474	103.455	2.197	32.692	2.726	77.823
1986	407.693	187.148	98.674	2.072	32.931	2.275	84.593
1987	419.366	194.656	100.933	2.605	27.916	2.628	90.628
1988	432.304	198.101	106.994	2.350	27.949	2.121	94.788
1989	443.605	196.551	113.988	2.449	30.030	2.460	98.128
1990	442.143	182.856	117.971	2.670	28.228	2.957	107.460
1991	403.440	157.835	97.841	2.563	32.354	2.943	109.904
1992	436.043	187.819	87.241	2.211	36.418	3.570	118.785
1993	470.118	208.092	91.471	na	na	3.281	127.166

Source: U.S. Department of Commerce, Bureau of The Census, C30 Reports.

er's use. The monthly sample used for this housing survey excludes owner-built houses, contractor-built houses, houses built to be rented, nonresidential buildings, and mobile homes.

The reason for these exclusions is to keep the permits selected by Census to a common cost basis for residential, single-family housing. The Census Bureau basically seeks a sample of speculatively built single-family housing—which includes both land and structure costs in the transaction. If land is not included, as with owner-built and contractor-built[10] houses, then there is typically a 20 percent discrepancy in the sales price. This difference is around 25 percent in the Northeast and west Census regions. The above exclusions are the primary reason for the level of the Census Bureau's new one-family houses sold being lower than one-family starts or permits.

The housing sales survey sample is a subset of the sample used for building permit and housing starts data. About 840 permit-issuing places are selected—based on proportions of permit activity—and used for selecting sample permits for determining if the unit is for sale. Interviewers call to check on whether a chosen permit meets the criteria for this survey. Nonpermit areas are taken into account with Census interviewers canvassing selected areas for one-family houses started. For 1989, the Housing Sales Survey's average monthly sample size was 12,000 sample cases.[11]

The sales sample consists of the one-family houses found to be either sold or for sale. Even though the basic sample used is permit-based, overall estimates of new houses sold include estimates for new houses sold before issuance of building permits in permit-issuing places and new houses sold prior to start in non-permit places.[12] There is no follow-up to see if sales are actually completed. If a buyer makes a deposit on a house but later backs out, it is still counted as a sale for this report.

The one-family houses for sale series does include a small number of houses not actively being marketed. Some of these include model or sample houses being used as temporary offices by builders, houses involved in bankruptcy procedures, and houses in estate settlements.[13]

The tables in the C25 report include among others:

Table 1: Houses for sales and months' supply at current sales rate.

Table 2: Houses sold and for sale, by region.

Table 3: Houses sold and for sale, by stage of construction. The stages of construction are: (1) completed, (2) under construction, and (3) not started.

Table 4: Houses sold, by sales price. This table includes median and average sales prices.

Table 6: Median number of months on sales market. This is for houses sold and for sale.

There also are tables listing seasonal factors and detailing the monthly variability of the series.

KEYS TO ANALYZING THE MONTHLY NEW HOME SALES AND PRICE DATA

As with other construction data, deviations from seasonal norms for weather can cause significant month-to-month volatility. This is particularly true for winter months when seasonal factors are very large. The very seasonal nature of housing sales—and other monthly housing data—is seen in the data shown in Table 12–3.

Changes in mortgage rates are certainly another factor affecting sales as lower rates generally lead to higher sales; and higher rates, lower sales. However, expectations can lead to the opposite effect in the short run. Sales can jump if mortgage rates rise and further increases are expected. The reverse may hold for declining mortgage rates if buyers wait for lower rates.

The months' supply concept is analogous to an inventory-to-sales ratio. On a not seasonally adjusted basis, it is the ratio of houses *for* sale divided by the number of houses sold. However, sales are usually annualized, and for monthly figures on months supply, annualized sales data must be divided by 12 to get the correct number. For seasonally adjusted figures, the series is not calculated as the seasonally for sale divided by seasonally adjusted sold. Instead, actual unadjusted months supply data are seasonally adjusted in this form directly. Therefore, published adjusted numbers for months supply differ slightly from numbers calculated with published adjusted sales and inventories data.

TABLE 12–3

Comparison of Monthly Housing Data: Not Seasonally Adjusted to Seasonally Adjusted Data (Thousands of Single-Family Units)

1992	Permits NSA	SAAR	Starts NSA	SAAR	New Houses Sold NSA	SAAR
January	55.4	913	58.4	989	48	667
February	60.8	946	69.2	1,109	55	627
March	82.1	907	90.9	1,068	56	555
April	88.9	873	93.5	933	53	546
May	82.9	879	100.2	1,019	52	554
June	91.4	872	102.7	999	53	583
July	83.6	879	93.2	956	52	616
August	76.7	877	91.8	1,042	56	627
September	80.4	913	91.4	1,051	51	671
October	80.8	959	96.1	1,077	48	618
November	63.5	955	74.1	1,090	42	617
December	66.1	1,045	68.2	1,130	41	656

NSA = Not Seasonally Adjusted.
SAAR = Seasonally Adjusted at an Annual Rate.

Sources: U.S. Department of Commerce, Bureau of the Census. Press release, Housing Starts and Building Permits in December 1992, January 22, 1993. Also, Bureau of the Census, C25 Section (for sales), which were released on February 2, 1993.

Months' supply is a cyclically volatile series. A slowdown in sales can lead to a sharp rise in "overhang." However, at the start of recovery in the business cycle, months' supply should not be interpreted in terms of ratios based on very weak actual sales. Instead, "true" overhang might better be based on a ratio assuming a reasonable, improved sales pace that would be reflective of lower mortgage rates once the recovery is underway. In other words, once sales have picked up, how long will the supply of houses for sale last?

For the home price data, one must use caution in interpreting price trends because the prices are not for a constant set of features for homes sold. Changes in the median and average prices reflect changes in costs as well as changes in the types of homes sold. For example, if during distressed economic times, the "low end" of the market has weak demand due to layoffs and fears of layoffs, then sales prices will more than on average be influenced by buyers of more expensive houses, regardless of what is happening to the costs of building these houses. Also, recessions and expansions are not even throughout the United States. For example, in 1993 California and Hawaii were roughly 40 percent of the West—not 60 percent as was the case in 1987. This 20 percent difference has the impact of lowering the west average and median prices over what they would have been with a constant share.

CHART 12–4
New Single-Family Home Sales

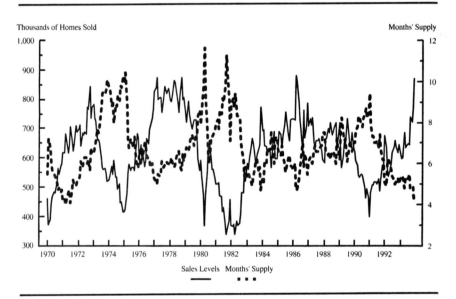

Source: US Bureau of the Census

TABLE 12–4

Housing Data: New Single-Family Houses Sold and for Sale

	Houses Sold (000s)	Houses for Sale (000s)	Months' Supply	Average Sales Price	Median Sales Price
1963	560	265	8.5	$19,300	$18,000
1964	565	250	7.6	20,500	18,900
1965	575	228	6.1	21,500	20,000
1966	461	196	8.5	23,300	21,400
1967	487	190	6.2	24,600	22,700
1968	490	218	6.9	26,600	24,700
1969	448	228	8.1	27,900	25,600
1970	485	227	6.2	26,600	23,400
1971	656	294	6.7	28,300	25,200
1972	718	416	8.9	30,500	27,600
1973	634	422	14.1	35,500	32,500
1974	519	350	14.4	38,900	35,900
1975	549	316	8.1	42,600	39,300
1976	646	358	7.7	48,000	44,200
1977	819	408	8.0	54,200	48,800
1978	817	419	8.3	62,500	55,700
1979	709	402	11.6	71,800	62,900
1980	545	342	10.3	76,400	64,600
1981	436	278	9.5	83,000	68,900
1982	412	255	7.8	83,900	69,300
1983	623	304	6.3	89,800	75,300
1984	639	358	9.4	97,600	79,900
1985	688	350	7.5	100,800	84,300
1986	750	361	7.4	111,900	92,000
1987	671	370	10.0	127,200	104,500
1988	676	371	8.8	138,300	112,500
1989	650	366	9.2	148,800	120,000
1990	534	321	10.9	149,800	122,900
1991	509	284	7.9	147,200	120,000
1992	610	267	6.4	144,100	121,500
1993	666	295	5.8	147,700	126,500

Sales are annual totals. Houses for sale and months' supply are December data. All data are not seasonally adjusted.

TABLE 12–5

Analyzing the News Releases: Key Questions

Construction Data in General

- Did atypical weather (more or less favorable) affect activity?
- What are general expectations for interest rates in order to take into account their impact on current and future demand?
- Are there pending regulatory or tax changes that will affect the industry?
- How are demographic trends impacting activity?

Housing Starts and Permits

- How is strength or weakness divided between single-family and multifamily components?
- How are vacancy rates affecting multifamily construction?
- Did an expected change in government regulations affect permits?

Construction Outlays

- How were changes in outlays allocated between the public and private sectors?
- After making assumptions for any missing months in the current quarter, what do current quarter growth rates imply for real residential and nonresidential investment in real GDP?
- After making assumptions for any missing months in the current quarter, what do current quarter growth rates for real public outlays imply for the structures component of state and local government purchases in the GDP accounts?
- Has there been a shift in residential expenditure growth relative to recent start and permit activity that suggests concern over a possible change in demand? For example, builders may slow construction if sales are below expectations and inventories are higher than desired.
- For analysts with access to *Dodge* construction data, what does recent contract activity suggest for near-term outlays?

New Single-Family Home Sales

- Are expectations of a change in interest rates leading to an acceleration or delay in sales (for expected higher or lower rates, respectively)?
- Are inventories low or high, thereby likely encouraging or discouraging further starts in the near term?

NOTES FOR CHAPTER 12

1. US Department of Commerce, Bureau of the Census, *Housing Starts,* April 1993, p. 14.
2. *Construction Reports,* C20–86–1, January 1986, p. 13.
3. This change in definition was due to the extensive rebuilding in south Florida following Hurricane Andrew in late August 1992. The impact on the data was negligible at the national level. See "Housing Starts and Building Permits in September 1992," news release, US Department of Commerce, Bureau of the Census, October 20, 1992.
4. *Construction Reports,* p. 13.
5. US Department of Commerce, Bureau of the Census, *Value of New Construction Put in Place,* June 1993, p.2.
6. For greater detail of component definitions, see *Value of New Construction Put in Place,* the May issue of each year, which includes annual revisions.
7. *Value of New Construction,* May 1993, p. B–2.
8. Ibid., p. B–3.
9. This subcomponent of residential investment is purchases by landlords of movable appliances. These are purchases for structures intended for rental purposes only. Similar purchases made by homeowners are classified as durables personal consumption.
10. Contractor-built primarily refers to custom-built houses where the owner of land arranges for a general contractor to build the house.
11. Appendix A, Description of Monthly Housing Sales Survey Report, Current Construction Reports, *New One-Family Houses, Sold and for Sale,* January 1993, p.11.
12. The methodology for estimating these "presales" changed with the initial estimate for December 1992 data. Previously, a historical ratio of presales to sales after permit issuance (or after start) was used for the initial estimate. This ratio generally was constant over the business cycle. This changed with the release of the initial December 1992 estimate. Over the 1992 recovery, the Census Bureau estimates were regularly low due to a cyclical increase in presales—a phenomenon that also occurred in 1983. Initial estimates were regularly revised up as permits were eventually taken out on presales. These upward revisions would show up one to three months after the initial estimate. Currently, the Census Bureau uses a moving average of this ratio for initial estimates—with judgment determining the length of the moving average (generally four to six months).
13. Appendix A, Description of Monthly Housing Sales Survey Report, Current Construction Reports, *New One-Family Houses, Sold and for Sale,* January 1990, p. 9.

BIBLIOGRAPHY

US Department of Commerce. Bureau of the Census. *Construction Reports.* C20–86–1. January 1986.

———. *Housing Units Authorized by Building Permits.* Appendix: Description of Survey and Supplementary Information. November 1990 and February 1994.

———. *New One-Family Houses, Sold and For Sale.* Appendix A. Description of Monthly Housing Sales Survey. January 1993 and March 1994.

———. *Value of New Construction Put in Place.* May 1993.

———. *Value of New Construction Put in Place.* June 1993 and February 1994.

CHAPTER 13

GROSS DOMESTIC PRODUCT

Gross domestic product or GDP is the broadest measure of the health of the US economy. Real GDP is defined as the output of goods and services produced by labor and property located in the United States.[1] This series generally lags other indicators' release dates. As such, other indicators "build up" to the market's anticipation of how the GDP numbers describe the state of the economy.

Real GDP is an important indicator to track because it provides the greatest and broadest sectoral detail of any other series. Data reflect income as well as expenditure flows. Sectoral coverage includes durable and nondurable goods, structures, and services. Also, price data by sector are available for detailed subcomponents. Because of the detail available in the GDP reports, this series provides comprehensive information on supply and demand conditions, including information for various types of developing imbalances over the business cycle.

Real GDP is a quarterly figure, but is released on a monthly basis with an initial estimate—referred to as the "advance" estimate—and two subsequent revisions over the following two months. The Bureau of Economic Analysis (BEA) produces the GDP figures and releases the advance estimate generally during the fourth week of the first month following the reference quarter. That is, the first quarter advance estimate is published in late April, and subsequent first estimates are released in July, October, and January. The first revised estimate for a given quarter is known as the "preliminary" estimate, and the third estimate for a given quarter is called the "revised" or "final" estimate. Annual revisions are usually released in July with the first figures for the second quarter. They cover the three prior calendar years plus the quarter(s) already published in the current year. Benchmark revisions occur about every five years with the base year tied to a recent quinquennial economic census such as the Census Survey of Manufacturers.

WHY GROSS DOMESTIC PRODUCT INSTEAD OF GROSS NATIONAL PRODUCT?

The switch in emphasis by the BEA in December 1991 to GDP from GNP as the key measure of aggregate economic activity in the national income and product account(s) (NIPA) was made for several reasons. First, the move was part of a long-run objective of the BEA to make the US accounts more consistent with those of most other countries that use the United Nations System of National Accounts (UNSNA or SNA for short).[2] The SNA emphasizes GDP instead of GNP. As a practical matter, when the BEA prepares initial estimates for GDP, there are little or no reliable data on net income from the rest of the world (factor income), which is used to derive GNP from GDP. With the switch in emphasis to GDP, the BEA no longer provides an initial estimate of GNP at the same time as the initial release of GDP. The first release of GNP is now with the first revision of GDP for a given quarter. Finally, GDP is more of a measure of domestic production than is GNP. Therefore, it more closely tracks other measures of domestic economic activity such as industrial production or employment. Gross national product is more of a measure of income since it reflects income from domestic production (GDP) plus net income from abroad.

> Domestic measures relate to the physical location of the factors of production; they refer to production attributable to all labor and property located in a country. The national measures differ from the domestic measures by the net inflow—that is, inflow less outflow—of labor and property incomes from abroad.[3]

Essentially, gross domestic product includes production within national borders regardless of whether the labor and property inputs are domestically or foreign owned. In contrast, gross national product is the output of labor and property of US nationals regardless of the location of the labor and property. Gross national product includes income earned by the factors of production (assets and labor) owned by a country's residents but excludes income produced within the country's borders by factors of production owned by nonresidents.

The estimates for GDP and GNP are derived from the same expenditure measures with the difference being income (net) from foreign sources. Gross national product is equal to gross domestic product plus receipts of factor income from the rest of the world less payments of factor income to the rest of the world. As is the case for the United States, GNP exceeds GDP when a nation is earning more from its businesses, financial investments, and labor that are overseas than US nonresidents are earning on businesses in the United States that they own, plus returns on US financial investments, plus labor income for nonresidents in the United States. Receipts of this factor income consist largely of receipts by US residents of interest and dividends and reinvested earnings of foreign affiliates of US corporations. The payments are largely those to foreign residents of interest and dividends and reinvested earnings of US affiliates of foreign corporations.

For the United States, the dollar difference between GDP and GNP is very small—about one-half of 0.1 percent of real GDP in 1993. The difference between the nominal data was negligible. Hence, growth rates for these aggregates in the United States typically are very similar.

GDP BY PRODUCT OR EXPENDITURE CATEGORIES

Gross domestic product is a measure of production within the national income and product accounts. There are three alternative ways of deriving GDP: sum of expenditures, sum of incomes, and sum of value added (either by industry, by firm or by establishment, depending on what data are available). In theory, GDP as measured by all three methods should be the same. This would be the case if perfect data were available. In actual practice, of the two methods primarily followed by the financial markets, it is easier to obtain reliable estimates for expenditures than for income components. Basically, expenditures are measured more directly than income.[4]

This chapter focuses on the expenditure components for GDP since the expenditure approach is most closely followed by markets. This is partly due to most expenditure data being more readily available than some of the income data. While quarterly personal income data are released with the advance GDP release, corporate profits are not available until the following month.[5] The expenditure approach to estimating GDP clearly is the method most closely followed by the financial markets. The major expenditure components are personal consumption (C), gross private domestic investment (I), government purchases (G), and net exports (X-M); they form the familiar identity of:

$$GDP = C + I + G + X - M.$$

As already mentioned, the export and import components no longer include income from abroad (in the old identity for GNP, X and M included factor income from abroad).

The following sections discuss key series in each expenditure component, data sources, unusual methodological factors, and various cyclical and secular trends.

Personal Consumption Expenditures

The components for personal consumption—durables, nondurables, and services—have already been discussed in detail in the chapter on monthly personal income. The monthly personal income data and personal consumption figures are part of the NIPA framework, and the quarterly personal consumption numbers in GDP are merely quarterly averages of the monthly data. Monthly personal consumption levels are already seasonally adjusted and are on an annualized basis. The sources for personal consumption estimates are also discussed in the chapter on personal income.

Without going into the same detail as in the earlier chapter, durables are the most volatile and services are the most stable. Durables are dependent on interest rates, which are cyclical, while both nondurables and services are more dependent on population trends. Overall personal consumption expenditures (PCEs) make up about two-thirds of GDP. However, this is somewhat of an awkward comparison, since some GDP components such as net exports and inventory investment are negative on an occasional basis.

Gross Private Domestic Investment

The broad category of gross private domestic investment covers several categories—both nonresidential and residential. Also, most of the investment is fixed investment, although a portion is not. These definitions and overlapping classifi-

TABLE 13–1
Gross Domestic Product (Billions of 1987 Dollars)

	1990	1991	1992	1993
Gross domestic product	**4,897.3**	**4,861.4**	**4,986.3**	**5,136.0**
Personal consumption expenditures	**3,272.6**	**3,258.6**	**3,341.8**	**3,453.2**
Durable goods	443.1	426.6	456.6	490.0
Nondurable goods	1,060.7	1,048.2	1,062.9	1088.1
Services	1,768.8	1,783.8	1,822.3	1875.2
Gross private domestic investment	**746.8**	**675.7**	**732.9**	**820.3**
Fixed investment	741.1	684.1	726.4	806.0
Nonresidential	546.6	514.5	529.2	591.8
Structures	179.5	160.2	150.6	151.5
Producers' durable equipment	367.0	354.3	378.6	440.2
Residential	194.5	169.5	197.1	214.2
Change in business inventories	5.7	−8.4	6.5	14.3
Nonfarm	3.2	−8.6	2.7	19.7
Farm	2.5	0.2	3.8	−5.3
Government purchases	**932.6**	**946.3**	**945.2**	**938.9**
Federal	384.1	386.5	373.0	354.9
National defense	283.6	281.3	261.2	242.4
Nondefense	100.4	105.3	111.8	112.5
State and local	548.5	559.7	572.2	584.0
Net exports of goods and services[6]	**−54.7**	**−19.1**	**−33.6**	**−76.5**
Exports	510.5	543.4	578.0	598.3
Merchandise	368.9	396.7	422.7	440.5
Services	141.6	146.7	155.4	157.8
Imports	565.1	562.5	611.6	674.8
Merchandise	461.4	463.9	511.9	571.4
Services	103.7	98.5	99.7	103.4

Source: US Department of Commerce, *Survey of Current Business,* August 1993. Press release, *Gross Domestic Product: Fourth Quarter 1993 (final), Corporate Profits: Fourth Quarter 1993 (Preliminary),* US Department of Commerce press release.

cations may create some confusion. By definition, these series are limited to the private sector—government purchases of structures and equipment are under the government purchases component. While the data are for domestic investment in the United States, equipment purchased by US businesses from abroad are included. However, capital goods produced in the United States but shipped as exports are not part of gross private domestic investment. They are entered in the GDP accounts as exports, and counting them as investment would be double-counting. By definition, all investment subcomponents in the broad category are for purchases of physical capital, that is, actual buildings, machinery, and inventories.[7]

There are a number of major components in gross private domestic investment. The first level of disaggregation is between private fixed investment and business inventory investment. Inventory investment is not considered fixed in the obvious sense that inventories are quite movable—they do not remain with a facility producing either goods or services as would structures or equipment. Private fixed investment is further divided between nonresidential and residential investment. Nonresidential investment has two major components—structures and producers' durable equipment—while the residential investment component is residential structures. Next, what are the basic concepts covered by each major component, and what are the key sources of data for estimates?

Nonresidential Structures

Nonresidential structures is the first major component of business fixed investment. This component represents expenditures made by business on structures—both farm and nonfarm. Structures covered include commercial buildings (such as office buildings), retail store structures, hotels and motels, private hospitals and educational facilities, industrial plants, warehouses, public utilities; mining exploration, shafts, and wells; and farm buildings.

Nonresidential structures investment is cyclical due to its sensitivity to interest rates and due to the need for expansion being dependent upon capacity utilization. Typically, nonresidential structures investment rises relatively late in expansion, following a rise in investment in producers' durable equipment. Structures investment is costlier than equipment and if demand falls, would significantly raise a firm's average costs. These factors help explain why structures investment usually lags that for equipment. Also, oil and natural gas prices play key roles in changes in nonresidential structures. Investment in the oil industry surged over the first half of the 1980s due to the strong run-up in oil prices but then collapsed following the OPEC oil price cuts in 1986. Similarly, natural gas exploration was depressed in the early 1990s due to the natural gas "bubble" (oversupply).

The basic source for nonresidential structures is the Census Bureau's value put-in-place data. These are used for nonfarm buildings, telecommunications utilities, and "other nonfarm structures." For "other public utilities," preliminary and annual estimates are derived from regulatory agency and trade source data. For mining, exploration, shafts, and wells, except for benchmark years, data are based on the following: for petroleum and natural gas, physical quantity times average price; for footage drilled, cost per foot from industry sources; other mining expenditures are derived from the Census Bureau plant and equipment survey. Finally, farm building investment is initially an extrapolation from Census value put-in-place data and is then later revised with annual data from Department of Agriculture surveys.

Producers' Durable Equipment

Producers' durable equipment (PDEs) is the second of the two major components of nonresidential fixed investment. This series covers purchases of equipment by private businesses and nonprofit institutions for their use in the production of goods and services. The primary subcomponents are information processing and related equipment, industrial equipment, transportation and related equipment, and "other."

In recent years, the largest subcomponent has come to be information processing and related equipment. In 1993, this subcomponent was 34 percent of nominal PDEs and 44 percent of constant dollar PDEs. The best-known category under information processing equipment probably is computers and peripheral equipment. However, it also includes diverse series such as photocopying equipment, communications equipment (telephones and facsimile machines), and scientific instruments.

Industrial equipment primarily includes equipment purchased for use by manufacturers. The transportation equipment component is led by automobiles, trucks, and aircraft.

PDEs are very cyclical due to the durability factor (purchases can be deferred during times of economic weakness) and due to their sensitivity to interest costs. Certainly, the primary factors affecting equipment investment are the cost of financial capital—interest rates—and the expected rate of return. The capacity utilization rate is generally a good indicator of the trend in expected returns. However, other significant factors affect investment, especially in equipment. Increased foreign competition leads to the need for productivity-enhancing (cost-cutting) investment. Over the 1980s, a strong dollar and increased foreign capacity spurred this type of investment in the United States in addition to investment for expansion of capacity. Over the 1970s, strong increases in labor costs encouraged capital substitution for labor. Finally, changes in pollution-control regulations and standards affect equipment investment. The amended Clean Air Act spurred significant amounts of spending on pollution-control technology in the early 1990s.

Movement in particular series in PDEs can be very interesting from a technical view. The industrial equipment component is particularly cyclical and responds to changes in manufacturing capacity utilization. For aircraft, production rates change relatively smoothly because of the long lags between order and delivery (usually four to five years), but quarterly purchases are volatile because the BEA figures are based on actual shipments of aircraft. Interestingly, transportation includes not only automobiles and light trucks purchased by businesses for their own traditional uses (such as "company cars" and delivery vehicles), but also includes motor vehicles leased to consumers. This means motor vehicles purchased by rental companies for their fleets and vehicles leased on a long-term basis by individuals as an alternative to a purchase. However, for consumers the value of the service of the leased vehicle is included in services PCEs, in contrast to durables PCEs when consumers make an outright purchase.

Occasionally, for the most recent quarterly revisions to GDP, PDEs and durables PCEs move in opposite directions due to the BEA's receiving more up-to-date *Polk* data on motor vehicle registrations. Unit estimates for motor vehicle sales are already in for all three months in the quarter for the initial GDP release, but registration data are not. As more current registration data become available, the BEA shifts motor vehicle sales between durables PCEs and PDEs (and, to a far lesser degree, also between government purchases of motor vehicles) when *Polk* data differ from their assumptions for missing months. Registration data lag figures on motor vehicle sales by two months.

Preliminary estimates and annual estimates are based primarily on several key sources. The most important source is the Census Bureau's monthly and annual surveys of manufacturers for shipments of capital goods. Since the BEA's series for PDEs only covers business purchases for capital accounts, adjustments and deletions are made to the Census shipments data for current account purchases (e.g., parts) and for purchases by government and persons. Other adjustments then are made for exports and imports of capital equipment (nonautomotive) from Census' merchandise trade reports. Exports that are shipped from manufacturers are excluded from PDEs since this is a domestic purchases concept. Similarly, imports of capital equipment are added to the Census shipments figures. Finally, a share of motor vehicle sales (in units) is allocated to PDEs. Industry data—such as from the American Automobile Manufacturers Association—are used. These are the same series the BEA carries as unit new auto sales and light truck sales. The PDEs portion is determined by *Polk* registration data and is converted into dollar values using the appropriate producer price indexes.

Residential Investment

Residential investment covers private investment in housing. Although it is often called residential structures, formally, residential structures is the larger, higher-level component of residential investment, with the other component being the little-known producers' durable equipment. However, residential PDEs is very small in magnitude and has very different subcomponents from nonresidential PDEs. In 1993, residential investment was $214.2 billion in constant 1987 dollars with structures contributing $206.8 billion and residential PDEs only $7.4 billion.

Residential structures are further broken down into components for single-family, multifamily, and "other structures." In 1993, these components were $113.1 billion (1987) dollars), $9.3 billion, and $84.4 billion, respectively. The other structures component includes mobile homes, brokers' commissions, improvements, nonhousekeeping, and net purchases of existing structures.

For improvements, data are primarily based on estimates from BLS's Consumer Expenditure Survey (CES), which is conducted on a monthly basis by Census for the Bureau of Labor Statistics (BLS). Data are obtained from a rotating panel of households. The survey covers a broad range of topics and includes questions on expenditures for improvements. The CES also obtains information on which households do not make home improvements because they do not own their house. From these responses a landlord survey is constructed by the Census Bureau, and data on their expenditures are obtained by mail. However, the landlord survey is completed only after the initial quarterly data are closed out for GDP estimates and this survey first enters estimates with annual revisions. Prior estimates are based on judgmental trend.

Residential PDEs consists of certain items purchased by owners for use in tenant-occupied housing. These include furniture (mattresses and bedsprings), other durable house furnishings, and radio and TV receivers. These items are essentially "movable" in nature and are not a "built-in" part of the structure.

In business cycle analysis, residential investment is important not only because of its highly cyclical nature but because this component tends to lead other components in the business cycle. Residential investment has these properties because it is very interest rate sensitive and is also dependent upon consumer confidence (job security and anticipated income gains). Residential investment is also cyclical because households can postpone housing purchases during recessions and/or periods of high interest rates. During these periods, demand accumulates, creating pent-up demand. When interest rates decline and expectations for economic improvement rise, pent-up demand can lead to a surge in housing activity.

While most analysts focus on short-run factors such as mortgage rate and personal income gains for predicting housing activity, long-run factors are equally important. Perhaps two of the most important long-run variables are demographics and taxes. Over the 1970s and 1980s, the maturing of the "baby-boom" generation led to a surge in housing activity. The baby-boom generation reached the critical household formation years when first home purchases are made. By the recovery and expansion of 1991 through 93, the baby-boom generation had moved past the prime years for buying a first home, and the "baby-bust" generation had assumed the role of providing most of the households in the market for a first home. Contrary to the expectations of many lending institutions, very sharp interest rate declines did not lead to a traditional housing boom in that recovery. The primary reason was that the home-buyer market was much thinner than during the 1970s and 1980s because of demographics.

Changes in tax policy can also affect housing investment. Early in the 1980s, favorable depreciation schedules and other factors encouraged construction of multifamily housing. Apartment complexes were profitable even with relatively high vacancy rates. Tax reform measures passed in 1986 removed these investment incentives, and the previously profitable multifamily sector suddenly was riddled with oversupply. This overhang in multifamily buildings carried over long enough to leave this sector out of the 1992–93 recovery and expansion for the overall economy.

The source data for permanent-site single-family and multifamily housing are the Census Bureau's value put-in-place data. Mobile home preliminary estimates are based on trade sources for physical quantity shipped, while the average retail price is obtained from the Census Bureau. For benchmark years, mobile home shipments are derived from the Census Bureau's quinquennial census. Brokers' commissions are estimated as the product of the number of houses sold, the mean sales price, and the average commission rate. Data come from the Census Bureau and trade sources. Producers' durable equipment is based on special surveys conducted by the Census Bureau.

Inventory Investment

Inventory investment is one of the key components for analyzing the strength of the economy. Its importance is likely second only to that of personal consumption expenditures. Inventory investment or changes in inventories help to keep goods production and demand in balance. Changes in inventories can portend either a weakening or a strengthening in the economy, depending on the circumstances. These conditions and methods of analysis are discussed more in the chapter on monthly business inventories. But first, what is inventory investment?

The inventory investment concept is best understood in the context of measuring GDP—an estimate of *current* production. Economists want to measure the inventory component's contribution to current output through an accounting of expenditures without double-counting. Certainly, over any given period, the dollar value of goods placed in inventory by manufacturers, wholesalers, and retailers fluctuates because inventory is sold to consumers, businesses, and government, or it is exported. But these inventories are counted as expenditures within PCEs, PDEs, government purchases, or exports. To avoid double-counting, inventories are measured on an end-of-period basis. Also, since GDP is a measure of current production, inventories already produced or existing in prior periods must be excluded. Therefore, only the change in inventories is included in the expenditure equation for adding up GDP. Inventory investment is the change in business inventories (CBI) from the previous period; it is not the level of inventories.

Typically, inventories rise and investment is positive, but if sales outstrip inventory stocking, then inventories decline and inventory investment is negative. Negative inventory investment often occurs during recession as businesses cut operating expenses during periods of weak revenues. However, the relationships between inventory change and business cycle turning points is a little more complex and are discussed in greater detail in the chapter on business inventories.

Inventory data are organized by farm and nonfarm sectors. Farm inventories are generally analyzed as a single aggregate for macroeconomic analysis, but the

CHART 13–1
Real GDP versus Inventory Change

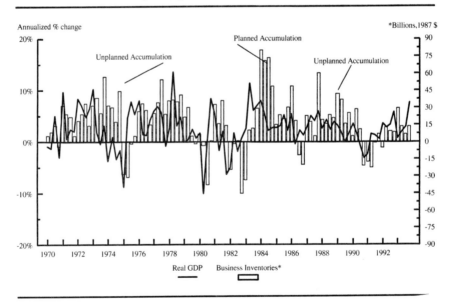

BEA has greater unpublished detail for crops and livestock. Because of the heavy seasonality of farm inventories and because inventories cannot be estimated until output is estimated, the BEA must make assumptions about current-year farm production to derive these figures. The BEA distributes estimated flows of crop and livestock output into consumption (as well as government purchases and exports) across the year. However, production estimates are very crude early in the calendar year for most crops and livestock. As the calendar year progresses and production estimates become more reliable (as crops and livestock mature), the BEA makes adjustments in its output assumptions (and others), which show up in farm inventory investment data.

Data for NIPA-based inventory levels are available for analysis even though it is the change in inventories that represents inventory investment—the figures going into GDP estimates. Levels are useful for comparing various demand concepts—such as goods GDP—to inventories. However, the change in the published nominal levels differs from nominal CBI because nominal CBI is based on end-of-period physical quantities times the average price in the period.

Source Data: Farm Inventory Investment
Farm inventories are estimated by the BEA using a commodity flow approach for crop inventories and by using US Department of Agriculture (USDA) data for livestock inventories. The constant dollar crop inventory change is based on an annual forecast for production and sales. Estimates for these are largely dependent on data from the USDA for estimated acreage planted and expected yields. For the year, the BEA produces a smooth pattern for quarterly sales of crop commodities and takes known quarterly data on Commodity Credit Corporation forfeitures and subtracts these from production projections to get an estimate of farm inventories for crops. Sales are made to all sectors but mainly to business wholesalers. For livestock inventories, the BEA generally uses USDA data directly, which include livestock on range and in feedlots.

As the calendar year progresses, changes in projections for crop production and sales are made to reflect the latest information. However, the USDA and BEA estimates for production become more reliable in the latter part of the year. Even though errors in early annual estimates for crop production and sales can be significant in some years (as during drought), quarterly inventory estimates late in the year usually are made without compensating for earlier errors in projection that are "locked in" the earlier quarter in the year. These are corrected with annual revisions made the following year.

Farm sector output for GDP is estimated in the process of deriving figures for farm inventory investment. The difference between GDP and farm output is, of course, nonfarm GDP. However, there is no allocation of farm output to various expenditure components in GDP except for farm inventories. In other words, there is no input from the farm sector in deriving expenditure components in GDP except for the farm inventory component. However, CCC purchases under federal nondefense do represent farm activity. But farm production and CCC purchases are estimated independently.

Source Data: Nonfarm Inventory Investment
Nonfarm inventory data are disaggregated into manufacturing, wholesale (merchant and nonmerchant), retail trade, and "other." Manufacturing and trade inventories are further divided into durables and nondurables although the retail trade durables data also separate automotive from nonautomotive.

Estimates for nonfarm inventory change for manufacturing and trade are based on Census Bureau surveys—including quinquennial censuses for benchmark years, annual surveys for other annual revisions, and monthly manufacturing and trade surveys for estimates following the latest annual surveys and for quarterly movement between annual surveys. Adjustments are made for data reported using different accounting methods to put into NIPA valuation. Deflators to put inventories in constant dollar format are mostly PPIs with only a few deflators being CPI-based.

Other nonfarm inventories primarily provide coverage for mining and also for various utilities such as electric and transportation. Data sources include the Internal Revenue Service, the Federal Reserve Board, the Census Bureau, and the Energy Information Administration.

What Is the Inventory Contribution to GDP Growth?

The concept of inventory contribution to GDP growth differs from inventory investment. The inventory contribution is merely the dollar value of the inventory component in dollar value growth in GDP, that is, the change in GDP. For the *level* of GDP, the inventory portion is the change in inventory levels. However, to determine the inventory contribution to GDP *growth,* one must look at the difference in inventory investment from period to period—one must subtract current period inventory change from the previous period inventory change. Inventory levels are differenced two times to get this contribution. For inventory contribution to be positive, inventories must be rising at a faster rate each period or must be falling at a slower rate. A slower rate of decline in inventories is a positive in terms of inventories' contribution to GDP growth.

Where Δ equals current period value less previous period value,

$$\text{GDP} = \text{PCEs} + \text{fixed investment} + \Delta \text{ inventories} + \text{government purchase} + \text{net exports}$$

whereas,

$$\Delta \text{ GDP} = \Delta \text{ PCEs} + \Delta \text{ fixed investment} + \Delta(\Delta \text{ inventories}) + \Delta \text{ government purchase} + \Delta \text{ net exports}$$

Government Purchases

Government purchases are not the same as expenditures. Purchases are expenditures for goods and services strictly for governments' current use. There are three primary reasons for the difference between government purchases and expenditures. First, some expenditures may actually be transferred as income to other sectors for their use. Expenditures that are transfers are not part of purchases made by the government that originally raise the revenues funding the transactions. These expenditure categories include transfers to persons, transfers to foreign governments, and grants-in-aid to state and local government. Also included in this transfer concept are net interest, subsidies, and current surplus of government enterprises.

A second difference is required to stay within bounds of the current use concept. This requires the exclusion of land purchases and financial transactions (net lending). Next, there are differences in geographical coverage: purchases exclude transactions involving US territories. Finally, there are "netting and grossing" differences between expenditures and purchases.

The timing of government purchases as entered into the GNP accounts does not always coincide with the timing of the use of the goods. For example, many military goods are purchased and stockpiled. There are no GDP components for military inventories—there is no distinction between purchases for current consumption (or use) versus inventory. Therefore, significant military activity may occur without a corresponding jump in purchases. This is what happened during the Gulf War in the first quarter of 1991. In fact, defense purchases overall fell due to the drop in purchases of fuel as allies (Saudi Arabia) contributed oil to the United States as a unilateral transfer payment.

Government purchases are broadly divided into federal purchases and state and local government purchases. Federal purchases are further divided into defense and nondefense components. For each of these series, there are subcomponents classified as durable goods, nondurable goods, services, and structures.

For defense purchases, durable goods include tanks, missiles, ships, trucks, and others. Nondurable goods include ammunition, fuel, food, and clothing. Over half of the defense services component is for compensation of employees, both military and civilian. Federal nondefense purchases are mostly made up of services, and over half of services is for compensation of employees.

Within federal nondefense purchases, significant quarterly volatility sometimes comes from the Commodity Credit Corporation (CCC) inventory change component. Purchases are made for farm price support programs. However, when these purchases swing sharply, there is usually an offsetting entry in the farm inventory component of private gross domestic investment. CCC purchases do not affect the level of current production—there is only a transfer of ownership of inventories between the public and private sectors.

In 1993, about 70 percent of state and local government purchases (nominal and real) was for services—and almost entirely for compensation of employees. Key services include education and law enforcement. Structures is still a large component and includes expenditures on highways, bridges; educational facilities, corrections facilities, and other public buildings; and waste treatment plants, among others.

For preliminary estimates, federal government purchases are based on outlays data from the *Monthly Treasury Statement* and from monthly reports of selected agencies. State and local government wages and salaries are based on the product of employment from BLS's establishment survey and earnings from

BLS's quarterly employment cost survey. The initial structures estimates at the state and local levels come from value put-in-place data from the Census Bureau. Other initial estimates for state and local government components are based on judgmental trend.

Annual estimates at the federal level are based on outlays from the *Budget of the United States* (Office of Management and Budget), the *United States Government Annual Report: Appendix* (Treasury Department), and on annual reports of selected federal agencies. Annual figures for state and local government purchases for employee compensation are derived from BLS data as well as from information from the Social Security Administration and the agencies administering social insurance programs. Census Bureau surveys of state and local governments for retirement funds also are used. For structures, annual estimates are derived from the Census Bureau's construction put in place. For components other than compensation, the two most recent years are based on judgmental trend. Earlier years are based on expenditure data from the Census Bureau's quinquennial censuses and annual surveys of state and local governments.

Net Exports

The net export component of GDP is the difference between exports and imports of goods and services. However, the net export component has been redefined to be on a GDP basis. Under the old GNP basis, exports and imports each included subcomponents for factor income (receipts from the rest of the world for exports and payments to the rest of the world for imports). On the GDP basis, net exports exclude factor income and the identity of GDP = C + I + G + X − M is valid since factor income is no longer part of exports and imports.[8]

Markets tend to discuss the foreign trade component in GDP as the net export deficit. However, the United States historically had been a trade surplus nation— at least until the bill for imported oil rose dramatically over the 1970s as both oil prices and demand for imported oil rose. Currently, the United States is in a deficit position because of high levels of oil imports. Excluding imports of petroleum and petroleum products, the nominal net export position of the United States was actually in a surplus of $22 billion in 1992, compared to an overall net export deficit of $29.6 billion. This nonoil surplus did turn back to a deficit in 1993 as import demand picked up significantly. Nonetheless, nonoil components are relatively strong in services as well as in merchandise components for foods, feeds, and beverages and for nonautomotive capital goods. Nominal services net exports were negative as recently as 1973 but have been in surplus since, widening to $67.0 billion in 1993. Now, what are the key components for both exports and imports?

Net exports is best understood by examining the export and import components separately. Each of these is broadly divided between goods and services. While discussion of trade data usually involve traded goods, services components are quite large and deserve greater attention. Also, because of comparative advantages by the United States and its trading partners, the size of various components differ for exports versus imports. Essentially, exports and imports should be analyzed from very different perspectives for merchandise and for services. Both exports and imports have components for merchandise and for services. While goods make up the majority of exports and imports, services are still important. Services in 1993 made up 30 percent of nominal exports and 18 percent of nominal imports. While the United States has run a nominal net export deficit since 1976, the services component has remained in surplus.

Merchandise and services export and import NIPA data are derived from balance-of-payments accounts data. As discussed in the chapter on monthly merchandise trade, the NIPA merchandise export and import data are primarily based on Census monthly merchandise trade data, which are put in balance-of-payments form before being adjusted to a NIPA basis. Elaboration on the individual end-use categories is also found in the same chapter.

Exports and imports on a GDP basis cover only goods and services. These categories do not include net receipts of factor income as was the case for exports and imports when the key NIPA aggregate was gross national product. Net receipts of factor income—which are divided into corporate profits, net interest, and compensation of employees—are now merely the accounting difference between GDP and GNP.

Merchandise exports and imports are divided into end-use categories—similar to the categories from monthly merchandise trade. The principal end-use categories are foods, feeds, and beverages; industrial supplies and materials; capital goods, except automotive; automotive vehicles, parts, and engines; consumer goods (nonfood) except automotive; and other merchandise. However, for imports the industrial supplies and materials component is actually presented as industrial supplies and materials, except petroleum and products. Petroleum and products imports is a separate end-use category in the NIPA data.

As in the balance-of-payments data, services exports and imports are broken down into receipts (exports) and payments (imports) for travel, passenger fares, "other transportation," "other private services," and US military transfers and direct defense expenditures abroad.

"Other transportation" covers port expenditures and freight charges for international shipments as well as operating expenses that transportation companies incur in foreign ports. "Other private services" exported and imported cover transactions not falling in categories for travel, passenger fares, other transportation, or royalties and license fees. Examples include service charges for management, professional, or technical services; lease payments, rentals, education, financial services, insurance, telecommunications, and medical services. Transfers under US military agency sales contracts cover goods transferred, not grants. US direct defense expenditures reflect expenses for maintaining armed forces abroad, including for permanent bases. US military transfers is only an export component while US direct defense expenditures abroad is only an import component. Today, military transfers are mostly cash, which foreigners use to make purchases in the United States. For direct expenditures abroad, there are offsetting entries in government purchases.

For services exports (in current dollars), the two largest subcomponents are travel and other private services, combining for over half of services exports. Next in importance are "other transportation," followed by royalties and license fees. Military transfers has slipped to under 10 percent of nominal services exports.

On the import side, nominal services is also led by travel and to a lesser degree by "other private services" and "other transportation." Direct defense expenditures abroad recently peaked in 1990 and have fallen to under 10 percent of services imports. Budgeted cuts in federal defense expenditures will likely lead to further reductions in direct defense expenditures abroad.

Within services net exports (nominal), currently the largest surpluses are for "other private services," followed by royalties and license fees and by travel. The biggest drain is direct defense expenditures abroad. The most volatile component in services exports and imports is travel, which is very sensitive to exchange rate movement. The travel net surplus position swings sharply and tends to be in deficit when the dollar is strongly valued and in surplus when it is weak.

The primary difficulty in tracking services subcomponents is that the BEA does not publish detail below the totals for these exports and imports. However, the BEA does publish the balance-of-payments equivalent series. The main differences between the NIPA and balance-of-payments data are bottom-line adjustments. The BEA takes the balance-of-payments subcomponents and then makes an adjustment for Puerto Rico and US territories and then other minor adjustments. The level of overall services exports and imports differs from the balance-of-payments data, but the primary subcomponents (excluding the adjustment line items) are basically the same for analytical purposes.

GDP Price Deflators and Price Indexes

At the economywide level, inflation is generally measured by GDP deflators. GDP deflators measure inflation across all sectors of the economy, taking into account changes in prices for consumer goods and services, business fixed and inventory investment, housing investment, government purchases, and exports and imports. While there are a number of variations for GDP deflators using different weighting and base year schemes, the two most commonly used GDP deflators are the implicit GDP deflator and the fixed-weighted GDP deflator.

The implicit GDP deflator is merely the ratio of nominal GDP to real GDP. Official GDP deflator numbers are set so that the base year deflator equals 100 rather than 1.[9] With the implicit deflator, there are no fixed weights for the components. Each quarter, each component's weight depends on expenditure patterns for that quarter. Therefore, changes in the implicit GDP deflator do not solely reflect price changes but a combination of the effects of shifts in the composition of GDP (between high- and low-priced sectors relative to the base year) and period-to-period price changes. In fact, the BEA emphasizes this characteristic of implicit deflators by not classifying implicit deflators as "price indexes." In contrast, the BEA specifically classifies fixed-weight GDP deflators as price indexes.

The fixed-weighted GDP deflator has fixed weights for the components based on expenditure shares in the base year. As such, component weights (the "basket" of goods, services, and structures) are fixed, but the relative importance of each component changes over time, depending on relative inflation rates for each component subsequent to the base year. Percentage changes in the fixed-weighted GDP deflator reflect only price changes. The drawback for this deflator is that it does not keep up with changes in expenditure patterns (the "basket") and may not be as relevant in the current year as in the base year.

Insights into the GDP Deflators

While GDP deflators measure prices for the domestic economy, it is not accurate to say that these price measures exclude the effects of import prices. Exports and imports, as well as all components of nominal and real GDP, enter the calculations for GDP deflators. Expenditures on imports technically are subtracted from both nominal and real GDP to derive deflator numbers, but imports also make their way into other expenditure measures, including PCEs, PDEs, inventories, and even government purchases. Also, import prices enter these other components with lags when the imported goods or services are inputs rather than for final consumption. It would be incorrect to say that GDP deflators are unaffected by import prices. First, imports—nominal and real—are part of the formula for calculating these deflators. Second, imports are significant portions of other goods and services components in GDP. Finally, imports provide competitive price pressure for domestically produced goods and thereby affect prices of domestically produced goods. Whether import prices show up more readily in the CPI goods component or the GDP goods deflator is an empirical question, not entirely one of definition. Table 13–2 compares the characteristics of GDP deflators to those of the CPI and PPI.

TABLE 13–2
Deflator and Price Index Comparisons

Producer Price Index for Finished Goods

- Covers consumer goods and capital equipment.
- Includes prices only for domestically produced goods.
- Fixed weights.
- Monthly periodicity.

Consumer Price Index

- Covers consumer goods and services.
- Includes prices of imported goods as well as domestically produced goods.
- Fixed weights.
- Monthly periodicity.

GDP Deflators

- Covers finished goods, services, and structures across consumer, business, government, and foreign trade sectors.
- Orientation is toward an aggregate for domestic production, but imports enter calculations directly and indirectly. Component deflators are available for imports as well as other expenditure series.
- Implicit, fixed-weight, and chain-weight series are available.
- Quarterly periodicity.

Growth in the implicit deflator can be due to either more rapid increases in prices for various components, or it can be the result of a shift in expenditures to higher-cost sectors in the economy. The higher cost is relative to the base year. However, a shift in spending between GDP expenditure components can cause unusual quarterly movement in the implicit GDP deflator. This is not a shifting to or from components with higher or lower inflation rates but to or from components with higher or lower component deflator *levels*. Of course, the effects of component price increases and sectoral shifts in GDP expenditures can have a reinforcing impact on quarterly changes in the implicit deflator or they can be offsetting.

Sharp swings in quarterly GDP deflators are often caused by changes in prices for oil, apparel, and computers as well as by annual wage increases for government employees, and occasionally by drought or other disaster affecting crops and Commodity Credit Corporation commodities. The latter two effects show up in farm inventories and federal government purchases, respectively.

Source Data for GDP Deflators

While the implicit and fixed-weight GDP deflators are aggregate price indexes, they are derived on an individual series basis. Essentially, real GDP is derived by deflating individual nominal components and then summing to get the real GDP total. Nominal and real GDP are then available to calculate the implicit deflator. Given this process, there is no one source of data for the deflator estimates—there are many sources for the deflators for real GDP components.[10]

For deflating nominal personal consumption components, the primary deflators used are individual CPI series. Also used for PCEs are foreign consumer price indexes (for expenditures abroad by US residents), price indexes maintained by private trade groups and associations for many services, and various price indexes from the BEA (such as for computers). Brokerage charges and financial services furnished without payment are deflated using an index of paid employee hours of relevant financial institutions.

Under business fixed investment, the nonresidential structures deflator is based mainly on price indexes from trade sources. Producer price series are used for a few components (for gas and petroleum pipelines and for portions of mining). For deflating producers' durable equipment, most series used are producer price indexes. Also used are import price indexes from the BLS, a BEA price index for computers, the new autos CPI for new and used autos, and trade source data for telephone and telegraph installation.

For putting residential investment into real terms, the BEA uses a Census Bureau price deflator for new one-family houses under construction, a BEA price index for multifamily housing, a PPI for mobile homes, and for improvements a CPI series is used along with Census Bureau price data. For the producers' durable equipment component of residential investment, deflation is based on PPIs.

To derive constant dollar change in business inventories, nominal inventory levels are deflated and then real inventory levels are differenced to get the inventory change. Nominal nonfarm inventories are deflated primarily with PPI series.

The BEA also incorporates data from the Energy Information Administration for petroleum stocks, BLS import price indexes for goods purchased by trade industries, a BLS price index for computers, and BEA indexes of unit labor costs for work-in-progress and finished goods in manufacturing. Farm inventories are valued in real terms directly for crops and livestock by type and are then put in current dollar terms using current prices from Department of Agriculture surveys.

For the merchandise components of net exports, deflators are based on export and import price indexes from BLS, a BLS index and other information for computers, gold prices from trade sources, and a PPI is used for transportation equipment. For services, a wide variety of indexes are used to put these components in constant dollar form. These include selected implicit price deflators for national defense purchases, BLS export and import price indexes for passenger fares, and a BEA composite index of foreign consumer price indexes for travel payments and for US government payments for miscellaneous services. Also used are CPI series for travel receipts and student expenditures and a PPI for freight and port expenditures.

For federal defense purchases, deflators are based on Department of Defense price data, a BEA earnings index, a BEA price index for computers, cost indexes from trade sources for nonmilitary structures, and PPI series for selected goods, and CPI and PPI series for utilities and communications. For federal nondefense, key series are cost indexes from trade sources and government agencies for structures, a BEA rice index and PPI for computers, and BEA earnings indexes for most services.

For state and local government, compensation deflators are derived indirectly. Constant dollar figures for compensation are based on the change in full-time equivalent employment from the base year in hours worked with an adjustment for experience for education workers. The deflator for state and local compensation can then be derived as the ratio of nominal to real compensation. For state and local structures, the BEA uses cost indexes from trade sources and government agencies to convert nominal data into constant dollar series. Deflators for brokerage charges and financial services received without payment are derived in the same manner as in PCEs. For remaining components, state and local purchases are deflated using miscellaneous CPI and PPI series and miscellaneous BEA price indexes.

EVALUATING BROAD TRENDS IN GDP

The GDP report indeed is very comprehensive and can be used for gauging the strength of many sectors. In fact, analysis of GDP trends is most productive when done at component levels. Questions regarding the sustainability of a component's contribution to overall growth and whether imbalances are developing can only be answered by looking at components.

First, for a given GDP report, one needs to discount any special, temporary factors. Most of these are discussed in the section on expenditure components.

Next, one should ask whether underlying fundamentals support current trends or whether there are temporary aberrations in growth. One can get an idea of whether current growth is excessive or not by looking at historical data over the business cycle as shown in the introductory chapter. Importantly, component growth should be consistent with other corroborating data. For example, for personal consumption, is rapid growth supported by income growth, lower interest rates (which increase consumer purchasing power), lower prices, or pent-up demand?

For business fixed investment, are interest rates and the profits outlook favorable? Is investment supported by high capacity utilization rates? For housing, are interest rates favorable, and how are demographic factors affecting the size of the market? Is there pent-up demand, and how long can it last?

For government purchases, what is planned in the federal budget, and what are the revenue projections for state and local governments?

Key imbalances often occur in the inventory component and in net exports. Particular attention should be given to these components. First, inventory investment is a by-product of production and demand trends. Inventories provide a cushion between sudden changes in demand and in production. As such, inventory investment—which is the change in inventory levels from period to period—has a planned component and an unplanned component. Businesses plan production and inventory levels to be in line with expected demand. When sales deviate from expectations, inventories change from desired levels and production is adjusted accordingly. Unexpected declines in inventories generally lead to inventories output (GDP) in the near term while unexpectedly high inventories lead to production cutbacks. These relationships are discussed in further detail in the chapter on business inventories.

Also, inventories can be evaluated by using the little-watched NIPA data on inventory levels. The BEA does release data on actual inventory levels (remember, it's the change in levels that goes into GDP) as well as a few inventory-to-sales ratios. For those not having easy access to these inventory-to-sales series, crude inventory-to-sales ratios can be constructed by creating rough estimates for sales of goods and then creating a ratio of inventories to sales to see if this ratio is "getting out of line" with recent history. Of course, services and structures are not inventoried in the same sense as goods. Using expenditure categories, rough estimates of sales might be a combination of personal consumption of durables and nondurables added with investment for producers' durable equipment. However, GDP data are available by type of goods (durable, nondurable, services, and structures), and these series are broken down between inventory change and final sales. Hence, one can add together durable and nondurable final sales for use in creating an inventory-to-sales ratio. Inventories should focus on nonfarm components.

Net exports help balance domestic demand growth and domestic production. However, corrections between domestic demand and US consumers' (and businesses') ability to pay take longer than inventory corrections. A surge in imports is usually caused by a strong dollar and strong income growth. In turn, the net export deficit widens. This is seen in growth in domestic demand (defined as GDP less net exports) exceeding GDP growth. Basically, US demand exceeds growth in domestic production. Since income is closely tied to production, when domestic demand exceeds GDP growth, a nation is consuming more than it is producing—a situation that is not stable in the long run.

Of course, imports are paid with dollars (in exchange), and as foreign holding of dollars rise, the exchange value of the dollar declines. This pushes up import prices and also reduces income growth in the United States since dollars for imports go abroad. Eventually, imports are reduced due to weaker income growth and higher import prices. In contrast, foreign growth generally picks up due to earlier strong demand and begins to buy US exports, which now cost less.

Basically, to judge the sustainability of export and import growth, one must look at growth in domestic demand relative to GDP growth over several quarters, trends in exchange rates, and income growth, both domestic and that in major trading partners.

TRACKING REVISIONS TO GDP

For the initial GDP release each quarter, not all source data are available for all months in the quarter. For the missing data, the BEA must make assumptions. The BEA releases its major data assumptions on the Department of Commerce's Economic Bulletin Board or by special request from the BEA. This table is entitled, "Key Source Data and Assumptions for the Quarterly Current-Dollar Estimates of the Gross Domestic Product."

Since this table includes actual values assumed for various key monthly series, one can track subsequent economic releases to see if actual figures are higher or lower than assumed by the BEA. Of course, one needs also to compare revisions to previously released series to get a more comprehensive picture of the likely direction and magnitude of revisions to GDP. However, a comparison of dollar values for these series—actual to assumed—does not exactly correspond to GDP revisions because the BEA also makes assumptions for series that are dependent on data sources other than the key series listed. These other sources include private industry data as well as later-received government data such as various quarterly surveys conducted by the Census Bureau. Also, many of the key series are in nominal terms and must be deflated in an often complex process, or source data series may require accounting adjustments to be in NIPA format. Nonetheless, for serious economy watchers, keeping up with the assumptions and tracking subsequent economic releases is a valuable exercise.

Additionally, the same monthly series used for tracking revisions to GDP are useful for producing one's own estimate of current quarter GDP before the advance report is released. Of course, one would have to make one's own assumptions about the missing source data in the same manner as the BEA. Table 13–3 shows the availability of key source data at the time of the initial GDP release.

Basics on the Data

Data for GDP and components on both the expenditure side (which is synonymous with product side) and the income side generally are expressed in dollar values that are at annual rates. For a given quarter, the GDP level is the dollar value of output

TABLE 13–3
Principal Source Data for GDP: Availability for the Advance GDP Release[11]

GDP Component and Monthly Series	Months Available
Personal consumption expenditures:	
Retail sales	3
Unit auto and truck sales	3
Nonresidential fixed investment:	
Unit auto and truck sales	3
Value of construction put in place	2
Manufacturers' shipments of machinery and equipment	2
Exports and imports of machinery and equipment	2
Residential investment:	
Value of construction put in place	2
Housing starts	3
Change in business inventories:	
Manufacturing and trade inventories	2
Unit auto inventories	3
Net exports of goods and services:	
Merchandise exports and imports	2
Government purchases:	
Federal outlays	2
Value of construction put in place by state and local government	2
GDP prices:	
Consumer price index	3
Producer price index	3
Nonpetroleum merchandise export and import price indexes	3
Values and quantities of petroleum imports	2

TABLE 13–4
Real GDP (Billions of 1987 Dollars, Annualized)

Year	I	II	III	IV	Annual Average
1990	4,898.3	4,917.1	4,906.5	4,867.2	4,897.3
1991	4,837.8	4,855.6	4,872.6	4,879.6	4,861.4
1992	4,922.0	4,956.5	4,998.2	5,068.3	4,986.3
1993	5,078.2	5,102.1	5,138.3	5,225.6	5,136.0

should economic activity continue at that level for an entire year. Annual figures, therefore, are averages of the quarterly annualized levels.

When analyzed as time series, overall GDP and components typically are expressed as series in percentage growth rate form. The BEA publishes them as compound growth rates, generally referred to as seasonally adjusted annualized rates, or SAAR. These calculations are properly done only by compounding. For example, the growth rate for real GDP in the fourth quarter of 1992 is calculated as:

$$PC_{SAAR} = (((5,068.3/4,998.2)^4) - 1) \times 100$$
$$= 5.7.$$

The shorthand method espoused by some analysts does not produce accurate calculations of the official growth rates but only rough approximations. The shorthand method of multiplying a simple quarterly percentage change by four produces the following:

$$PC_{S\text{-}hand} = (((5,068.3/4,998.2) - 1)) \times 100 \times 4$$
$$= 5.6.$$

Two components in GDP are usually discussed in dollar values rather than in percentage growth rates because they enter the GDP identity as a difference in dollar levels. These two series are inventory investment and net exports. Inventory investment is the change in inventory levels from period to period while net exports is the difference between exports and imports. Of course, both inventory investment and net exports are expressed as annualized dollar values.

Real GDP and components are deflated from nominal values to put into constant dollar terms. To put in real terms, a base year—usually one inclusive of a quinquennial economic census by the Census Bureau—is chosen. The year chosen does affect growth rates in real GDP as component inflation rates diverge. For example, the use of a 1972 base year for real GNP in the years following the oil price hikes in 1974 and 75 led to stronger growth estimates than would have been the case had a base year been from the late 1970s when oil had a larger share of nominal imports. The deflation of nominal oil imports to put imports in 1972 dollars lowered the adverse impact of imports within the real net export component of real GDP. Similarly, the use of a 1982 base year in the few years following the 1986 oil bust led to growth being understated relative to what it would have been in a late 1980s base year (all other being held constant). Currently, the downtrend in prices for computers since the 1987 base year is creating strong growth in real producers' durable equipment. A more current base year would reduce the overall growth rate in real PDEs and in real GDP.

TABLE 13–5

Gross Domestic Product and Components (Annual Data, Billions of 1987 Dollars unless "Nominal")

	Nominal GDP	Implicit GDP Deflator 1987 = 100	Real GDP	Total Personal Consumption Expenditures	Durables Personal Consumption Expenditures	Nondurables Personal Consumption Expenditures	Services Personal Consumption Expenditures
1960	513.4	26.0	1,970.8	1,210.8	115.4	526.9	568.5
1961	531.8	26.3	2,023.8	1,238.4	109.4	537.7	591.3
1962	571.6	26.9	2,128.1	1,293.3	120.2	553.0	620.0
1963	603.1	27.2	2,215.6	1,341.9	130.3	563.6	648.0
1964	648.0	27.7	2,340.6	1,417.2	140.7	588.2	688.3
1965	702.7	28.4	2,470.5	1,497.0	156.2	616.7	724.1
1966	769.8	29.4	2,616.2	1,573.8	166.0	647.6	760.2
1967	814.3	30.3	2,685.2	1,622.4	167.2	659.0	796.2
1968	889.3	31.8	2,796.9	1,707.5	184.5	686.0	837.0
1969	959.5	33.4	2,873.0	1,771.2	190.8	703.2	877.2
1970	1,010.7	35.2	2,873.9	1,813.5	183.7	717.2	912.5
1971	1,097.2	37.1	2,955.9	1,873.7	201.4	725.6	946.7
1972	1,207.0	38.8	3,107.1	1,978.4	225.2	755.8	997.4
1973	1,349.6	41.3	3,268.6	2,066.7	246.6	777.9	1,042.2
1974	1,458.6	44.9	3,248.1	2,053.8	227.2	759.8	1,066.8

Year							
1975	1,585.9	49.2	3,221.7	2,097.5	226.8	767.1	1,103.6
1976	1,768.4	52.3	3,380.8	2,207.3	256.4	801.3	1,149.5
1977	1,974.1	55.9	3,533.3	2,296.6	280.0	819.8	1,196.8
1978	2,232.7	60.3	3,703.5	2,391.8	292.9	844.8	1,254.1
1979	2,488.6	65.5	3,796.8	2,448.4	289.0	862.8	1,296.5
1980	2,708.0	71.7	3,776.3	2,447.1	262.7	860.5	1,323.9
1981	3,030.6	78.9	3,843.1	2,476.9	264.6	867.9	1,344.4
1982	3,149.6	83.8	3,760.3	2,503.7	262.5	872.2	1,368.9
1983	3,405.0	87.2	3,906.6	2,619.4	297.7	900.3	1,421.4
1984	3,777.2	91.0	4,148.5	2,746.1	338.5	934.6	1,473.0
1985	4,038.7	94.4	4,279.8	2,865.8	370.1	958.7	1,537.0
1986	4,268.6	96.9	4,404.5	2,969.1	402.0	991.0	1,576.1
1987	4,539.9	100.0	4,540.4	3,052.2	403.7	1,011.1	1,637.4
1988	4,900.4	103.9	4,718.6	3,162.4	428.7	1,035.1	1,698.5
1989	5,250.8	108.5	4,838.0	3,223.3	440.7	1,051.6	1,731.0
1990	5,546.1	113.3	4,897.3	3,272.6	443.1	1,060.7	1,768.8
1991	5,722.9	117.7	4,861.4	3,258.6	426.6	1,048.2	1,783.8
1992	6,038.5	121.1	4,986.3	3,341.8	456.6	1,062.9	1,822.3
1993	6,377.9	124.2	5,136.0	3,453.2	490.0	1,088.1	1,875.2

Unless specified otherwise, data are in constant 1987 dollars.

Source: U.S. Department of Commerce, Bureau of Economic Analysis.

(continued)

TABLE 13–5 (*continued*)

	Business Fixed Investment	Producers', Durable Equipment	Nonresidential Structures	Residential Investment	Inventory Investment*
1960	173.3	92.5	80.8	109.4	8.1
1961	172.1	89.8	82.3	110.1	7.2
1962	185.0	98.9	86.1	120.6	15.6
1963	192.3	105.4	86.9	135.0	16.0
1964	214.0	118.1	95.9	142.1	15.7
1965	250.6	139.1	111.5	137.3	25.1
1966	276.7	157.6	119.1	124.5	36.7
1967	270.8	154.8	116.0	120.2	27.6
1968	280.1	162.7	117.4	136.4	23.6
1969	296.4	172.9	123.5	140.1	24.8
1970	292.0	168.7	123.3	131.8	5.9
1971	286.8	165.6	121.2	168.1	20.8
1972	311.6	186.8	124.8	198.0	22.5
1973	357.4	222.4	134.9	196.6	37.7
1974	356.5	224.2	132.3	155.6	30.9
1975	316.8	198.8	118.0	134.7	−13.9
1976	328.7	208.2	120.5	166.4	25.5
1977	364.3	238.2	126.1	201.9	34.3
1978	412.9	268.8	144.1	214.5	37.2
1979	448.8	285.5	163.3	207.4	13.6
1980	437.8	267.6	170.2	164.8	−8.3
1981	455.0	272.0	182.9	151.6	24.6
1982	433.9	252.6	181.3	124.1	−17.5
1983	420.8	260.5	160.3	174.2	4.4
1984	490.2	307.4	182.8	199.3	67.9
1985	521.8	324.4	197.4	202.0	22.1
1986	500.3	323.7	176.6	226.2	8.5
1987	497.8	326.5	171.3	225.2	26.3
1988	530.8	356.8	174.0	222.7	19.9
1989	540.0	362.5	177.6	214.2	29.8
1990	546.5	367.0	179.5	194.5	5.7
1991	514.5	354.3	160.2	169.5	−8.4
1992	529.2	378.6	150.6	197.1	6.5
1993	591.8	440.2	151.5	214.2	14.3

*Change in Business Inventories.

Source: U.S. Department of Commerce, Bureau of Economic Analysis.

TABLE 13–5 (*continued*)

	Total Government Purchases	Federal Purchases (Total)	Federal Defense Purchases	Federal Nondefense Purchases	State and Local Purchases
1960	476.9	259.0	—	—	217.9
1961	501.5	270.1	—	—	231.4
1962	524.2	287.3	—	—	236.9
1963	536.3	285.7	—	—	250.6
1964	549.1	281.8	—	—	267.3
1965	566.9	282.1	—	—	284.8
1966	622.4	319.3	—	—	303.1
1967	667.9	350.9	—	—	317.0
1968	686.8	353.1	—	—	333.7
1969	682.0	340.1	—	—	341.9
1970	665.8	315.0	—	—	350.9
1971	652.4	290.8	—	—	361.6
1972	653.0	284.4	209.4	74.8	368.6
1973	644.2	265.3	191.3	74.1	378.9
1974	655.4	262.6	185.8	76.8	392.9
1975	663.5	262.7	184.9	77.8	400.8
1976	659.2	258.2	179.9	78.3	401.1
1977	664.1	263.1	181.6	81.4	401.0
1978	677.1	268.6	182.1	86.5	408.4
1979	689.3	271.7	185.1	86.6	417.6
1980	704.2	284.8	194.2	90.6	419.4
1981	713.2	295.8	206.4	89.4	417.4
1982	723.6	306.0	221.4	84.7	417.6
1983	743.8	320.8	234.2	86.6	423.0
1984	766.9	331.0	245.8	85.1	436.0
1985	813.4	355.2	265.6	89.5	458.2
1986	855.4	373.0	280.6	92.4	482.4
1987	881.5	384.9	292.1	92.9	496.6
1988	886.8	377.3	287.0	90.2	509.6
1989	904.4	376.1	281.4	94.8	528.3
1990	932.6	384.1	283.6	100.4	548.5
1991	946.3	386.5	281.3	105.3	559.7
1992	945.2	373.0	261.2	111.8	572.2
1993	938.9	354.9	242.4	112.5	584.0

Source: U.S. Department of Commerce, Bureau of Economic Analysis.

TABLE 13–5 (*continued*)

	Real Net Exports	Real Exports	Real Imports	Nominal Net Exports	Nominal Exports	Nominal Imports
1960	−7.6	88.4	96.1	2.4	25.3	22.8
1961	−5.5	89.9	95.3	3.4	26.0	22.7
1962	−10.5	95.0	105.5	2.4	27.4	25.0
1963	−5.8	101.8	107.7	3.3	29.4	26.1
1964	2.5	115.4	112.9	5.5	33.6	28.1
1965	−6.4	118.1	124.5	3.9	35.4	31.5
1966	−18.0	125.7	143.7	1.9	38.9	37.1
1967	−23.7	130.0	153.7	1.4	41.4	39.9
1968	−37.5	140.2	177.7	−1.3	45.3	46.6
1969	−41.5	147.8	189.2	−1.2	49.3	50.5
1970	−35.2	161.3	196.4	1.2	57.0	55.8
1971	−45.9	161.9	207.8	−3.0	59.3	62.3
1972	−56.5	173.7	230.2	−8.0	66.2	74.2
1973	−34.1	210.3	244.4	0.6	91.8	91.2
1974	−4.1	234.4	238.4	−3.1	124.3	127.5
1975	23.1	232.9	209.8	13.6	136.3	122.7
1976	−6.3	243.4	249.7	−2.3	148.9	151.1
1977	−27.8	246.9	274.7	−23.7	158.8	182.4
1978	−29.9	270.2	300.1	−26.1	186.1	212.3
1979	−10.6	293.5	304.1	−23.8	228.9	252.7
1980	30.7	320.5	289.9	−14.7	279.2	293.9
1981	22.0	326.1	304.1	−14.7	303.0	317.7
1982	−7.4	296.7	304.1	−20.6	282.6	303.2
1983	−56.1	285.9	342.1	−51.4	276.7	328.1
1984	−122.0	305.7	427.7	−102.7	302.4	405.1
1985	−145.3	309.2	454.6	−115.6	302.1	417.6
1986	−155.1	329.6	484.7	−132.5	319.2	451.7
1987	−143.0	364.0	507.1	−143.1	364.0	507.1
1988	−104.0	421.6	525.7	−108.0	444.2	552.2
1989	−73.7	471.8	545.4	−79.7	508.0	587.7
1990	−54.7	510.5	565.1	−71.4	557.1	628.5
1991	−19.1	543.4	562.5	−19.6	601.5	621.1
1992	−33.6	578.0	611.6	−29.6	640.5	670.1
1993	−76.5	598.3	674.8	−63.6	661.7	725.3

Sources: U.S. Department of Commerce, Bureau of Economic Analysis. *Survey of Current Business*, August 1993, and press release, *Gross Domestic Product: Fourth Quarter 1993 (Final), Corporate Profits: Fourth Quarter 1993 (Preliminary)*, March 31, 1994.

TABLE 13–6
Real Gross Domestic Product (Levels and Percent Changes, SAAR)

		Billions 1987 $	Percent			Billions 1987 $	Percent
1960	Q1	1,976.9	7.4	1972	Q1	3,037.3	8.3
	Q2	1,971.7	−1.0		Q2	3,089.7	7.1
	Q3	1,973.7	0.4		Q3	3,125.8	4.8
	Q4	1,961.1	−2.5		Q4	3,175.5	6.5
1961	Q1	1,977.4	3.4	1973	Q1	3,253.3	10.2
	Q2	2,006.0	5.9		Q2	3,267.6	1.8
	Q3	2,035.2	6.0		Q3	3,264.3	−0.4
	Q4	2,076.5	8.4		Q4	3,289.1	3.1
1962	Q1	2,103.8	5.4	1974	Q1	3,259.4	−3.6
	Q2	2,125.7	4.2		Q2	3,267.6	1.0
	Q3	2,142.6	3.2		Q3	3,239.1	−3.4
	Q4	2,140.2	−0.4		Q4	3,226.4	−1.6
1963	Q1	2,170.9	5.9	1975	Q1	3,154.0	−8.7
	Q2	2,199.5	5.4		Q2	3,190.4	4.7
	Q3	2,237.6	7.1		Q3	3,249.9	7.7
	Q4	2,254.5	3.1		Q4	3,292.5	5.3
1964	Q1	2,311.1	10.4	1976	Q1	3,356.7	8.0
	Q2	2,329.9	3.3		Q2	3,369.2	1.5
	Q3	2,359.8	4.8		Q3	3,381.0	1.4
	Q4	2,364.0	1.1		Q4	3,416.3	4.2
1965	Q1	2,410.1	8.0	1977	Q1	3,466.4	6.
	Q2	2,442.8	5.5		Q2	3,525.0	6.9
	Q3	2,485.5	7.2		Q3	3,574.4	5.7
	Q4	2.543.8	9.7		Q4	3,567.2	−0.8
1966	Q1	2,596.8	8.6	1978	Q1	3,591.8	2.8
	Q2	2,601.4	0.7		Q2	3,707.0	13.5
	Q3	2,626.1	3.9		Q3	3,735.6	3.1
	Q4	2.640.5	2.2		Q4	3,779.6	4.8
1967	Q1	2,657.2	2.6	1979	Q1	3,780.8	0.1
	Q2	2,669.0	1.8		Q2	3,784.3	0.4
	Q3	2,699.5	4.6		Q3	3,807.5	2.5
	Q4	2,715.1	2.3		Q4	3,814.6	0.7
1968	Q1	2,752.1	5.6	1980	Q1	3,830.8	1.7
	Q2	2,796.9	6.7		Q2	3,732.6	−9.9
	Q3	2.816.8	2.9		Q3	3,733.5	0.1
	Q4	2,821.7	0.7		Q4	3,808.5	8.3
1969	Q1	2,864.6	6.2	1981	Q1	3,860.5	5.6
	Q2	2,867.8	0.4		Q2	3,844.4	−1.7
	Q3	2,884.5	2.3		Q3	3,864.5	2.1
	Q4	2,875.1	−1.3		Q4	3,803.1	−6.2
1970	Q1	2,867.8	−1.0	1982	Q1	3,756.1	−4.9
	Q2	2,859.5	−1.2		Q2	3,771.1	1.6
	Q3	2,895.0	5.1		Q3	3,754.4	−1.8
	Q4	2,873.3	−3.0		Q4	3,759.6	0.6
1971	Q1	2,939.9	9.6	1983	Q1	3,783.5	2.6
	Q2	2,944.2	0.6		Q2	3,886.5	11.3
	Q3	2,962.3	2.5		Q3	3,944.4	6.1
	Q4	2,977.3	2.0		Q4	4,012.1	7.0

TABLE 13–6 (*continued*)

		Billions 1987 $	Percent			Billions 1987 $	Percent
1984	Q1	4,089.5	7.9	1989	Q1	4,817.6	3.2
	Q2	4,144.0	5.4		Q2	4,839.0	1.8
	Q3	4,166.4	2.2		Q3	4,839.0	0.0
	Q4	4,194.2	2.7		Q4	4,856.7	1.5
1985	Q1	4,221.8	2.7	1990	Q1	4,898.3	3.5
	Q2	4,254.8	3.2		Q2	4,917.1	1.5
	Q3	4,309.0	5.2		Q3	4,906.5	−0.9
	Q4	4,333.5	2.3		Q4	4,867.2	−3.2
1986	Q1	4,390.5	5.4	1991	Q1	4,837.8	−2.4
	Q2	4,387.7	−0.3		Q2	4,855.6	1.5
	Q3	4,412.6	2.3		Q3	4,872.6	1.4
	Q4	4,427.1	1.3		Q4	4,879.6	0.6
1987	Q1	4,460.0	3.0	1992	Q1	4,922.0	3.5
	Q2	4,515.3	5.1		Q2	4,956.5	2.8
	Q3	4,559.3	4.0		Q3	4,998.2	3.4
	Q4	4,625.5	5.9		Q4	5,068.3	5.7
1988	Q1	4,655.3	2.6	1993	Q1	5,078.2	0.8
	Q2	4,704.8	4.3		Q2	5,102.1	1.9
	Q3	4,734.5	2.5		Q3	5,138.3	2.9
	Q4	4,779.7	3.9		Q4	5,225.6	7.0

TABLE 13–7
Analyzing the News Release: Key Questions

- For personal consumption, the chapter on personal income has a separate list of detailed questions for monthly personal consumption expenditures from which the quarterly data are averaged directly.
- For business fixed investment, how is growth or decline allocated between the two major components—producers' durable equipment (PDEs) and nonresidential structures?
- For PDEs, is investment spurring domestic production, or does a significant share appear to be imported?
- Was a rise in PDEs caused by a spike in motor vehicle purchases by leasing companies? Is it due to fleet building or to incentives for consumers to make long-term leases instead of making outright purchases?
- Are purchases of computers inflating real PDE figures more than usual, thereby overstating the impact on the economy?
- Was residential investment (construction) speeded up or hindered by unseasonable weather?
- Did residential investment get a boost from additions and alterations?
- If inventories rise sharply, how much appears to be planned for expected stronger domestic demand or for a near-term rise in export shipments?
- If inventories are drawn down, is it due to an unexpected surge in current demand, or is it due to weaker expected demand?
- If inventories rise significantly and appear to be unplanned, how much appears to be in goods that are generally imported?
- If inventories decline, will rebuilding be met with domestic production or imports?
- How much of the change in business inventories is in the nonfarm component and how much is in the farm component?
- Does the change in farm inventories reflect the yearly trend that is consistent with estimates for growth in farm output, or was there a temporary aberration (e.g., a shift in inventory ownership between the private sector and the government sector—Commodity Credit Corporation)?
- Are exports temporarily boosted by a surge in aircraft exports—which are discrete and volatile.
- Are overall imports raised by a temporary restocking of oil inventories?
- Were services exports and imports—travel components in particular—affected by personal safety issues caused by conflict abroad?
- Do changes in the exchange value of the dollar portend a change in the travel components of services net exports?
- Have services net exports been affected by a change in the level of US military activity abroad?

NOTES FOR CHAPTER 13

1. US Department of Commerce, *News: Gross Domestic Product: First Quarter 1993 (Final)*, June 23, 1993, p. 1.
2. Carol Carson, "Replacing GNP: The Updated System of National Economic Accounts," *Business Economics*, July 1992, pp. 44–48.
3. Carol Carson, "GNP: An Overview of Source Data and Estimating Methods," *Survey of Current Business*, US Department of Commerce, July 1987, p. 105.
4. For US accounts, the sum of expenditures GDP and sum of incomes differ by a series known as the "statistical discrepancy." Also, there is the question of whether or not all income is properly reported even though expenditures from unreported income often are measured. A related question would be whether there are significant (illegal) expenditures that are missed. The BEA's policy has been not to estimate such activity.
5. The BEA also provides GDP by Industry, but these data are available only on an annual basis. Annually, GDP by Industry in current dollars is equal to the sum of incomes. However, in constant dollars, GDP by Industry is based on largely independent deflation and differs from constant dollar GDP by the deflated statistical discrepancy and by the "residual.' For further information on GDP by Industry, see the May 1993, "Gross Product by Industry, *Survey of Current Business*, 1977–90," pp. 33–54.
6. Exports and imports of certain goods, primarily military equipment purchases and sold by the federal government, are included in services.
7. Transfers of financial assets generally are not included in the GDP accounts since GDP measures income and expenditure *flows*—not asset levels—as a basic objective. Exceptions include grants-in-aid (sometimes to foreign countries) when transfers are in kind and a change in ownership of Commodity Credit Corporation (CCC) inventories between the federal government and private corporations.
8. See the earlier discussion on the switch in emphasis from GNP to GDP for further elaboration on factor income.
9. Official deflator levels are rounded to one decimal place. Hence, published percentage changes for implicit GDP deflators may vary slightly from percentage changes derived from the ratio of nominal GDP to real GDP, which are not rounded in this manner.
10. U.S. Department of Commerce, "Annual Revision of the US National Income and Product Accounts," *Survey of Current Business*, July 1992, Table 8, pp. 37–42.
11. Daniel Larkins, Larry R Moran, and Ralph W Morris, "The Business Situation," *Survey of Current Business*, US Department of Commerce, July 1992, p. 2.

BIBLIOGRAPHY

Carson, Carol S. "GNP: An Overview of Source Data and Estimating Methods." *Survey of Current Business*. US Department of Commerce. July 1987, pp. 103–26.

Carson, Carol S. "Replacing GNP: The Updated System of National Economic Accounts." *Business Economics*. July 1992, pp. 44–48.

U.S. Department of Commerce. "Annual Revisions of US National Income and Product Accounts." *Survey of Current Business*. July 1992, pp. 6–42.

———. "The Comprehensive Revision of the U.S. National Income and Product Accounts: A Review of Revisions and Major Statistical Changes." *Survey of Current Business*. December 1991, pp. 24–42.

———. "Gross Domestic Product as a Measure of US Production." *Survey of Current Business*. August 1991, p. 8.

CHAPTER 14

THE COMMERCE DEPARTMENT'S INDEX OF LEADING INDICATORS AND OTHER COMPOSITE INDEXES

INTRODUCTION

The index of leading indicators is one of a family of cyclical indicators published and maintained by the US Department of Commerce. In particular, the index of leading indicators is important because it is considered a recognizable leading barometer of recession or recovery. While economists and financial analysts usually gain early insight into developing business cycle changes by tracking many indicators, the leading index is most understood by the public and many policy makers as a reliable indicator. There are three composite indexes—leading, coincident, and lagging indicators—which are designed to track turning points in the economy. They use what is generally referred to as the cyclical indicators approach in identifying peaks and troughs. Specific time series are studied to see whether they historically tend to lead, coincide, or lag broad movements of the business cycle. These historical relationships are then used to identify the turning points in a current business cycle.

> Each index measures the average behavior of a group of economic time series that show similar timing at business cycle turns but represent differing activities or sectors of the economy. The series that tend to lead at business cycle turns are combined into one index, those that tend to coincide into another, and those that tend to lag into a third.[1]

The indexes are put into composite form and are considered to be superior to individual series because they represent a broad spectrum of the economy and because in different business cycles, some individual indicators may perform better than others. In particular, the components that perform best in each cycle may vary, and there would likely be little foreknowledge of which of these would be better for each turning point. Using a composite index reduces some of the risk of tracking the economy with the wrong component or wrong few components. Also, a composite index reduces some of the monthly measurement error normally associated with a given cyclical indicator.

Historically, the system of composite indicators originated with the work on business cycles by Arthur F Burns and Wesley C Mitchell while they were at the National Bureau of Economic Research, Inc. (NBER).[2] Their first list of cyclical indicators was published in 1938. In 1961, the Department of Commerce began publishing monthly reports of the NBER's indicators, which were classified as leading, coincident, or lagging. In 1968, the department first published the composite indexes of cyclical indicators. The NBER and Commerce Department still consult in evaluating and improving these composite indexes and in developing new cyclical indicators.

To be included in the composite indexes of the Commerce Department, components are evaluated according to seven major characteristics[3]:

1. Cyclical timing.
2. Economic significance.
3. Statistical adequacy.
4. Conformity to business cycles.
5. Smoothness.
6. Prompt availability.
7. Revisions.

This means: (1) cyclical indicators are grouped in terms of whether they lead, coincide, or lag business cycle turning points; (2) indicators are judged on how well they quantify some aspect of the economy in a theoretically meaningful way—the components in each index are chosen to represent various facets of the economy; (3) the indicators chosen must be reasonably accurate statistically; (4) the leading, coincident, or lagging tendency of a given component should be generally consistent across business cycles; (5) an indicator should not be volatile so as to give conflicting signals from month to month; (6) the indicator should be available to the public soon after the occurrence of the actual economic activity; and (7) a component series typically should not be subject to large monthly revisions.

Traditionally, the BEA has grouped cyclical indicators by economic process and even published composites for each economic process. Over the years, however, the different categories have changed. Until the end of 1991, seven categories of economic processes were in use.[4] Originally, the economic processes were defined so as to have some commonality in terms of economic behavior or theory. Currently, the categories no longer are clearly defined as economic processes but do represent diverse facets of the economy with the BEA delineating 14 groups for individual cyclical indicators and two groups for composite indicators.

The index of leading indicators is broadly representative of the economy as its components are drawn from six separate (BCI) groups of cyclical indicators. Those covered are: (1) labor force, employment, and unemployment; (2) sales, orders, and deliveries; (3) fixed capital investment; (4) prices; (5) personal income and consumer attitudes; and (6) money, credit, interest rates, and stock prices. Groups that the leading index does *not* draw from are: (1) output, production, and capacity utilization; (2) inventories and inventory investment; (3) profits and cash flow; (4) wages, labor costs, and productivity; (5) saving; (6) national defense; (7) exports and imports; and (8) international comparisons. The sectors not drawn from do not have series that exhibit good leading characteristics.

The Commerce Department's composite indexes are released to the public in news release form generally the last week of the month following the reference month or early the first week of the month thereafter. The news release is entitled *Composite Indexes of Leading, Coincident, and Lagging Indicators.* More detailed data are published in the Business Cycle Indicators section of the *Survey of Current Business.* With each monthly release, the BEA provides an initial value to the latest month plus revisions for the previous five months. Monthly revisions are not made to earlier periods even if data from original sources are revised further back historically. However, annual revisions pick up changes in seasonal factors and other minor changes missed earlier. Annual revisions usually occur with the September release and generally cover the previous five calendar years plus data already released in the current calendar year. Comprehensive revisions are irregular. All three composite indexes currently have a base year of 1987 being set equal to 100. The latest comprehensive revision was released in December 1993, with the initial release of data for the statistical month of October 1993.

THE COMPOSITE INDEX OF LEADING INDICATORS

The composite index of leading indicators is the most closely followed of the three indexes because it typically foreshadows changes in the direction of the economy. Policy makers, players in the financial markets, and business persons can use these data as a valuable input into key decisions dependent on the state of the economy. The next few sections of this chapter focus on the leading index by first explaining the meaning and importance of each of the 11 components. Following sections discuss how well this index forecasts turning points and how the composite index should be used for predicting turning points. Finally, the methodology in deriving the leading index from its components is reviewed in moderate detail.

Most of the components of the three composite indexes are seasonally adjusted prior to inclusion in the indexes. The stock price index and the index of consumer expectations are not in seasonally adjusted form. Also, a few minor subcomponents of the price series for sensitive materials are not seasonally adjusted.

Although a few very minor changes were made in the components that are included in the composite indexes with the 1993 comprehensive revision, the 1989 revision is the primary basis for components currently included in the composite indexes. Table 14–1 summarizes the components in each composite index (the January 1989 revised indexes) with their prior versions. Although more complete details are discussed in the section on the 1993 comprehensive revision, the primary difference between 1993-based components and 1989-based components is the changing of constant dollar series to 1987 constant dollars from a 1982 constant dollars.

Average Weekly Hours of Production or Nonsupervisory Workers in manufacturing. The average workweek in manufacturing usually changes direction before the economy because, first, the manufacturing sector itself is very cyclical; second, because of the uncertainty that is prevalent close to turning points, busi-

TABLE 14–1a
Components of the January 1989 Revised Indexes and Previous Composite Indexes'

Composite Index of Leading Indicators	
1989 Revised Components	*Previous*
Average weekly hours of production or nonsupervisory workers, manufacturing.	Same.
Average weekly initial claims for unemployment insurance, state programs (inverted).	Same.
Manufacturers' new orders in 1982 dollars, consumer goods and materials industries.	Same.
Contracts and orders for plant and equipment in 1982 dollars.	Same.
Index of new private housing units authorized by local building permits.	Same.
Index of stock prices, 500 common stocks.	Same.
Money supply, M2, in 1982 dollars.	Same.
Vendor performance, percent of companies receiving slower deliveries; same title as previous component but incorporates improved data source for recent years.	Vendor performance.
Change in sensitive materials prices, smoothed; same title but based on revised methodology and consistent data for entire period.	Change in sensitive materials prices, smoothed.
Dropped.	Change in business and consumer credit outstanding.
Dropped.	Change in manufacturing and trade inventories on hand and on order in 1982 dollars, smoothed.
Change in manufacturers' unfilled orders in 1982 dollars, durable goods industries, smoothed.	Not included.
Index of consumer expectations.	Not included.

nesses initially prefer to change the hours worked than to hire or lay off workers. Also, changing hours worked is less costly and faster in the short run than changing the size of the labor force. This component is originally released in BLS's monthly employment report.

TABLE 14–1b
Components of Current and Previous Composite Indexes

Composite Index of Coincident Indicators

1989 Revised Components	*Previous*
Employees on nonagricultural payrolls.	Same.
Personal income less transfer payments in 1987 dollars.	Same.
Index of industrial production.	Same.
Manufacturing and trade sales in 1982 dollars.	Same.

Composite Index of Lagging Indicators

1989 Revised Components	*Previous*
Average duration of unemployment in weeks (inverted).	Same.
Ratio, manufacturing and trade inventories to sales in 1982 dollars.	Same.
Average prime rate charged by banks.	Same.
Commercial and industrial loans outstanding in 1982 dollars.	Same.
Ratio, consumer installment credit outstanding to personal income.	Same.
Change in index of labor cost per unit of output, manufacturing, smoothed.	Index of labor cost per unit of output, manufacturing—actual data as a percent of trend.
Change in consumer price index for services, smoothed.	Not included.

Average Weekly Initial Claims for Unemployment Insurance, State Programs (Inverted).   This component measures the number of people filing for unemployment benefits. As the economy enters recession, the number of people asking for benefits rises because of layoffs. Prior to recovery the number of initial claims declines. Obviously, this component moves in the opposite direction as does the economy; thus, this component is inverted (multiplied by negative one) before entering the calculations of the overall index. The BLS tabulates the data from the state programs and releases the data on a weekly basis. This series is different from the US Labor Department's civilian unemployment rate, which is derived from its national survey of households. While both the initial claims series and civilian unemployment rate generally lead peaks in the business cycle, the unemployment rate is classified as lagging following troughs, and the claims indicator is coincident relative to troughs.[5] In late 1992, the initial claims series was redefined to include initial claims made under the July 1992 Emergency Unemployment Compensation amendments.[6] The emergency claims program was separate from the regular state programs, and there often were incentives for workers to file under the emergency program rather than the regular unemployment insurance program.

Contracts and Orders for Plant and Equipment in 1987 Dollars.   This investment indicator acts as a leading indicator from two major perspectives. First, an increase (decrease) in business capital investment suggests that firms are more (less) optimistic about the economy. More importantly, as the actual investments are made (equipment being manufactured or plants built), changes in employment and income occur. Changes in this component of the leading index suggest that businesses foresee turning points in their own business activity and then the production that is related to the investment brings about further changes in other sectors. The new orders data in current dollars come from the Census Bureau's M3 report (*Current Industrial Reports: Manufacturers' Shipments, Inventories and Orders*) while the construction contract figures are from Dodge/McGraw-Hill. Deflators for the orders are derived by the BEA, and the construction contracts are put into constant dollars using deflators from the Census Bureau reports, *Construction Put In Place.*

Index of New Private Housing Units Authorized by Local Building Permits. Housing activity itself is very cyclical since consumers can generally postpone home purchases until the business cycle is in a period of relatively low mortgage rates and high consumer confidence. Low mortgage rates typically occur during later stages of a slowdown or the early stages of recovery, since total credit demands have not yet built back up to the point of putting pressure on rates. These lower rates enable more households to purchase housing while rising consumer confidence makes them more willing to purchase. Builders, being aware of more favorable conditions, usually take out more building permits to build both speculative and nonspeculative housing stock. Housing construction generally leads a recovery and the issuance of permits precedes construction. Also, permits generally decline during the latter stages of expansion (that is, just before the onset of recession) because, typically, rising interest rates and increasing consumer concern about the strength of the economy slow housing purchases, lead to a rise in housing inventory, and cause a decline in permits issued. This component in the leading index is based on standard Census data from the monthly housing permit release (the C40 report) but is in index form such that 1967 = 100. Also, this index incorporates late received data not included in the initial housing permit release for a given month.

Manufacturers' New Orders in 1987 Dollars for Consumer Goods and Materials Industries.   The placement of orders with manufacturers is the first step in the production process for consumer goods (as well as for other goods). Once there is an increase in orders, production rises, and, in turn, employment and income increase. The reverse is true for a decline in orders. Hence, the orders indicator tends to lead the economy. This component is derived from the Census Bureau's monthly report on new factory orders (the M3 report), and nominal dollar values are deflated using a variety of producer price indexes from the BLS and other sources.

Change in Sensitive Materials Prices, Smoothed.   Some very basic materials prices are very sensitive to cyclical changes in demand. When demand starts to rise prior to recovery, prices of these goods will accelerate as manufacturers bid for relatively fixed supplies; during recession, inventories often are worked down. Similarly, price increases will decelerate or even fall as demand for inputs tapers off before the onset of recession. This leading index series itself is a composite of the individual components of two series previously published in the Commerce Department's *Business Conditions Digest*, or *BCD*, which was last published for March 1990 as a cost-cutting measure. These two series are the index of producer prices for sensitive crude and intermediate materials and the index of spot market prices, raw industrial materials; in the past they have been referred to as BCD series #98 and #23, respectively.

These and other BCD series are now referred to as BCI series (for the Business Cycle Indicators section in the Survey of Current Business where they are published by the Business Cycle Indicators Branch of the BEA). BCI #98 is produced by the Bureau of Labor Statistics and includes cattle hides, lumber and wood products, news wastepaper, mixed wastepaper (NSA),[7] corrugated wastepaper, iron and steel scrap, copper base scrap, aluminum base scrap, other nonferrous scrap (NSA); sand, gravel, and crushed stone; raw cotton, and domestic apparel wool. BCI #23 is compiled and copyrighted by Commodity Research Bureau, Inc., New York. This index includes copper scrap, lead scrap, steel scrap, tin (NSA), zinc (NSA), burlap (NSA), cotton, print cloth (NSA), wool tops (NSA), hides (NSA), rosin, rubber, and tallow. BCI series 99 is not a direct composite of series 98 and 23 because some subcomponents overlap. For these subcomponents, each is given half the weight of the other subcomponents, which are equally weighted.

A Digression: What Is Smoothing of Some Components?   Some economic time series have irregular short-term fluctuations that can make cyclical movement difficult to discern. Smoothing is a way of discounting the irregular movement and focusing on cyclical trends. While smoothing does eliminate some of the noise in the data, the trade-off is that some of the lead in the data is lost. There are numerous smoothing techniques, but the one used by the BEA is a special autoregressive (based on past values) moving average technique developed by Statistics Canada. It replaces the simple weighted moving average method used prior to the 1989 revisions to the composite indexes.

The moving average previously used took the most recent four values of the series being smoothed; assigned weights of 1, 2, 2 and 1, respectively; divided the sum by 6 to get a weighted average; and placed this smoothed value at the end of the time span. That is, data for September, October, November, and December were weighted and averaged to the smoothed value for December.

The smoothing technique developed by Statistics Canada reduces the amount of lead time given up to get the smoothed value.

The filtered [smoothed] series F is derived from the actual series A by applying the following formula:

$$F_t = 0.134 * A_t + 1.451 * F_{t-1} - 0.586 * F_{t-2}$$

The result is similar to a weighted average of series A with weights for the current month and the 6 preceding months equal to 0.134, 0.195, 0.204, 0.182, 0.145, 0.104, and 0.036, respectively.[8]

The actual value in the initial observation is treated as the filtered observation. This smoothing technique is used for all smoothed series in the composite indexes.

Index of Stock Prices, 500 Common Stocks. This component is the well-known Standard and Poor's index of 500 common stocks and is a monthly average taken directly from S&P's publication, *The Outlook.* This index is a measure of expected profitability since markets price stocks on profit potential rather than solely on past earnings. The competitive nature of the stock market forces traders not to wait on actual earnings reports but to bid for stocks based on knowledge of general economic conditions as well as factors affecting earnings potential for specific firms. If the stock market participants expect profits to improve as a result of an impending recovery, then stock prices are bid upward prior to a rise in actual earnings. If a recession is expected, profits are projected to weaken, and bidding for stocks is less aggressive or participants begin to sell stocks to lock in profits or to minimize losses.

Money Supply, M2, in 1987 Dollars. This financial indicator leads the economy for several reasons. In the short run, a rise in the real money stock will typically lower interest rates and stimulate demand for durables both for consumers and businesses. Lower interest rates also boost housing sales. For businesses, inventories are cheaper to finance and this increases demand for goods. Eventually, production increases and income rises to give further support to the economy. Should the money supply decline, interest rates would typically increase and have effects to the opposite of the above. Nominal money supply data are produced by the Federal Reserve Board of Governors and are deflated by the BLS's all urban consumer price index to derive a constant dollar series.

Vendor Performance, Slower Deliveries Diffusion Index. This component is from a monthly survey of national manufacturers produced by the National Association of Purchasing Management. This survey covers many facets of manufacturing activity—such as production, orders, and employment—in addition to vendor performance. The data are from responses to a question pertaining to whether supplier (vendor) deliveries are slower, unchanged, or faster. The idea is that when business increases, supplier firms are not able to make deliveries as promptly as when orders are slack. Slower deliveries generally are viewed as a positive indicator of improving economic conditions. That is, more manufacturers report supplier deliveries as slower than the month before because of a pick-up in economic activity. Data from the National Association of Purchasing Management are used only from the period beginning in 1976 to the present. Prior to 1976, the data came from a similar survey produced by the Purchasing Management Association of Chicago. The more recent data were substituted due to their broader national coverage but were not available prior to 1976.

Index of Consumer Expectations. Changes in consumer attitudes often lead the economy. The theory behind the leading nature of a consumer confidence index is that consumers as workers are aware of economic conditions at the workplace. A general belief that conditions are improving—such as reflected in new orders at work or increased production schedules—lead to higher consumer confidence. Similarly, consumer confidence declines as company or plant financial prospects appear to deteriorate. In turn, consumer willingness to spend or make financial commitments is affected. For example, consumers are more (less) willing to purchase a new car or buy a new house if work prospects are improving (worsening). Another theory behind the leading nature of this component is that the index reflects consumers' awareness of other indicators discussed in the news that affect the economy. These other indicators allegedly include interest rates, unemployment rates, layoff notices at major companies, and the stock market. The index of consumer expectations is compiled monthly by the University of Michigan's Survey Research Center. The base period is the first quarter of 1966, which equals 100.

Change in Manufacturers' Unfilled Orders in 1987 Dollars, Durable Goods Industries, Smoothed. Beginning in 1989, this component (although in 1982 dollars at that time) replaced the previous series for the change in inventories on hand and on order. Essentially, the earlier component was derived from unfilled orders data for the "on order" portion and from inventory data for the "on hand" portion. Because of the late tabulation of inventory data, this leading index component was not available for initial releases. This lack of inclusion in the initial release was one of the primary reasons for dropping it from the leading index because missing data in the initial release were the primary source of large revisions for later months. However, the "on order" portion of inventories is carried over to the current version of the leading index. The current unfilled orders series includes the orders portion of the change in inventories on hand and on order. However, the earlier version did not include capital goods and defense products, whereas the current component covers all durable goods.

This component is based on Census Bureau data from its M3 advance monthly report on durables factory orders, inventories, and shipments. Basically, this component focuses on some of the M3 data that exhibit the greatest sensitivity to business cycles and have long production periods. Many new orders series in the Census report are based on shipments data either because of difficulty in obtaining new orders data or simply because some industries generally fill new orders the same month. In effect, for some durables industries (and nondurables, but they are not as cyclically sensitive and are not relevant for this discussion) new orders have no information content for future production plans—just for current production and shipments. This is one reason why only unfilled durables orders are used in this leading index component. Unfilled orders definitely are suggestive of future production, whereas new orders include both shipped orders and unfilled orders. For the facet of the economy covered by this component, the unfilled orders data scored higher than the new orders data in predicting turning points. Durable goods orders also are more cyclical than nondurable goods. Financing conditions—which are sensitive to the business cycle—are often more of a factor for durables than nondurables. Finally, durable goods frequently have longer production cycles than nondurables and for durables the orders information provides a longer lead on production trends. One example would be for aircraft, which has a very long production cycle.

COMPREHENSIVE REVISIONS IN 1993

The latest comprehensive revision to Commerce's composite indicators took place with the December 1993 release of October data. This revision had two major features:

(1) The incorporation of revised data for the index components, partly to reflect the results of the 1991 comprehensive revision of the national income and product accounts (NIPAs), and (2) improvements in the methodology for calculating the composite indexes, mainly a change in the weighting of the index components and the elimination of the trend adjustment for the indexes.

The 1993 comprehensive revision was not as broad in scope as the 1989 comprehensive revision. The 1989 revision involved significant changes in the composition of the indexes. The 1993 revision had only minor changes in composition and primarily focused on updating data and improving the methodology for calculating the three indexes. The improved methodology was based on earlier experimental calculations described in Green and Beckman's article in the June 1992 *Survey of Current Business*. As will be discussed in greater detail later, revisions included changes in component standardization factors, a change in the base period for the indexes, and two changes in index formulas—the component weights and the dropping of the use of index trend adjustments.

Changes in Components

There were only a few changes in component definitions. For the leading index, the revised index has four constant dollar series changed to a base year of 1987 from the previous base year of 1982. The new orders component had a minor change in definition and the sensitive materials prices components now uses a revised formula for creating its composite from subcomponents. The following summarizes the changes in the leading, coincident, and lagging indexes.

Component Changes with 1993
Comprehensive Revisions

For components with no changes, no mention is made.

Leading Index

1. Manufacturers' new orders for consumer goods and materials.
   * Changed to 1987 base year from previous base year of 1982.
   * New orders component revised to include all nondefense durable goods not classified as capital goods (involved the addition of three minor durable goods categories and elimination of minor duplication with the contracts and orders component).
2. Contracts and orders for plant and equipment.
   * Changed to 1987 base year from previous base year of 1982.
3. Change in sensitive materials prices.
   * Now based on a revised formula for composite indexes—this series is a composite of many price subcomponents.
4. Change in manufacturers' unfilled orders, durable goods industries.
   * Changed to 1987 base year from previous base year of 1982.
5. Money supply, M2.
   * Changed to 1987 base year from previous base year of 1982.

Coincident Index

1. Manufacturing and trade sales.
   * Data prior to 1977, which were in 1982 dollars, were rescaled to link with 1977 data and subsequent data, which are in 1987 dollars.

Lagging Index

1. Ratio of manufacturing and trade inventories to sales.
   * Data prior to 1977 are revised to incorporate the rescaling of data to 1987 dollars.
2. Commercial and industrial loans outstanding.
   * Changed to 1987 base year from previous base year of 1982.
3. Change in index of labor cost per unit of output, manufacturing, smoothed.
   * Effects of year end 1992 bonus payments (included in the latest annual NIPA revision) on this index are smoothed prior to the usual smoothing technique.

As usual with comprehensive revisions, various statistical factors for the calculation of the three indexes were revised. These include new component standardization factors, new index standardization factors, and the dropping of the use of trend adjustment factors in the calculation of the indexes, a change in the base year from 1982 to 1987 being set equal to 100, and changes in index formulas.

Some of these changes are discussed in further detail in the section on deriving component net contributions.

For a complete understanding of the 1993 comprehensive revisions, a look at the 1989 comprehensive revision is useful. The 1989 revised indexes are the basis for the current version of composite indexes—with the minor component changes incorporated in 1993 as discussed earlier. This also provides historical perspective. Table 14–1 compares pre-1989 revision index components with those inclusive of the 1989 revision for leading, coincident, and lagging composite indexes.

LEADING INDICATORS: HOW GOOD A FORECASTING TOOL?

Before going into detail about some guidelines for using the index of leading indicators to forecast, one should look at one of the more popular "rules-of-thumb" for predicting changes in the economy: the three consecutive declines or increases rule. By analyzing the problems with this technique, one can better understand a more comprehensive approach in using this index.

The Three-Month Rule-of-Thumb (Does the Index Really Forecast?)

Many business analysts use the common guide that a turn in the economy must be preceded by three consecutive declines in the index of leading indicators before a recession, or three consecutive increases prior to recovery. Of course, there are rules for two or four consecutive months, but the three-month rule is the most commonly used. The primary question is: How good is this rule in predicting turning points in the economy? Table 14–2 shows business cycle peaks and troughs since the end of World War II and the number of months of lead (or lag) time that the three-month rule precedes the turning point (based on current revisions to the index). At the bottom of Table 14–2 are the dates that the three-month rule made false predictions for turning points. As shown, the three-month rule suggests that some problems exist with this index being used as a forecasting tool. A few basic problems are apparent: (1) the index at times provides false signals; (2) leads prior to recovery are often negative (after-the-fact);[10] and (3) leads prior to recession are variable and can be short at times. These shortcomings, however, are not as severe as one might first think.

First, were the false signals really misleading? According to the three-month rule, using the most recent data revisions, five recessions were predicted in which no recession occurred for at least two years thereafter. While there were no official recessions following these signals, real GDP growth did slow significantly within two quarters of the leading indicator's warnings in 1951, 1962, 1966, and 1984. Manufacturing output in particular declined and other sectors slowed. From a definitional point of view, the index signals were false on these occasions: from a practical perspective, the index was an accurate predictor of either a downturn in manufacturing or of a growth slump overall. The index is a better forecaster for turning points in manufacturing than for the economy overall. Only did the late

TABLE 14–2
Lead Times of the Three-Month Rule-of-Thumb for the Index of Leading Indicators,
Using 1989 and 1993 Revisions

Peak	Months Lead Time of Signal Using Revision of		Trough	Months Lead Time of Signal Using Revision of	
	3/89	12/93		3/89	12/93
November 1948	+2	+2	October 1949	+1	+1
July 1953	+2	+2	May 1954	+1	+1
August 1957	+6	+6	April 1958	−1	−1
April 1960	+1	+8	February 1961	+5	−1
December 1969	+5	+5	November 1970	−2	−2
November 1973	+3	+6	March 1975	−2	−2
January 1980	+12	+12	July 1980	−1	−1
July 1981	−4	+5	November 1982	0	0
July 1990	+12	+12	March 1991	−1	−2
Average lead for 9 peaks	+4.3	+6.4	Average lead for 9 troughs	0.0	−0.8

False Signals of Recession	False Signals of Recovery
February 1951–August 1951*#	None over 1948–1993[12]*#
April 1962–June 1962*#	
April 1966–December 1966*#	
May 1984–October 1984*	
March 1984–October 1984#	
October 1987–December 1987*	
October 1987–January 1988#	
October 1991–December 1991#	
June 1992–September 1992#	

*Using Revision of March 1989.
#Using Revisions of December 1993.
Peaks and troughs are dated as determined by the National Bureau of Economic Research (NBER).
Pluses indicate number of months prior to turning point and minuses indicate months following the turning point.

1987 data signal neither an actual recession, a downturn in industrial production, nor a slow-down in real GDP growth.

Posing another problem for the three-month rule is the fact that frequent data revisions may "overturn" what originally was a three-month change in trend. Table 14–2 is based on revised data for the leading index. Since the overall index is based on 11 components, most of which are revised for two or three months (and longer for some) following the original estimate of the leading index, revisions in the overall index is a fact to be lived with. Sometimes, a three-month rule may be invoked only for later revisions to turn into a two-month decline followed by a small rise. Hence, frequent data revisions make the indicator more difficult to interpret. For example, when the index for September 1984 was released, figures for June, July, and August were revised to show three consecutive declines.[11] Disagreement arose within the economic community over whether this meant that a recession was imminent. In hindsight, no recession developed in terms of an actual decline in economic activity. But were the revised data misleading?

To answer the first question briefly: the indicator did presage a sharp deceleration in real GDP growth in the first half of 1985 from very rapid growth in the early stages of recovery. Specifically, the manufacturing sector was very weak.

As shown in Table 14–2, the leads of the leading index are highly variable and sometimes even after the fact relative to official turning points. Also, data for a given month are released about four weeks after the reference month. That is, data are available for forecasting one month after the economic event, and this further reduces the lead time of the index in terms of real time availability to a user. Business decisions based on the information in the index are not timely as one might prefer. The question, then, is, Is the index useful for forecasting?

On a qualified basis, the index indeed is very useful for forecasting. In terms of predicting recoveries, the index is not as timely as in predicting recessions. From a business perspective, being a little late recognizing a recovery is considerably more tolerable than not foreseeing a recession. In terms of lead times, the

CHART 14–1
Leading Index versus Real GDP

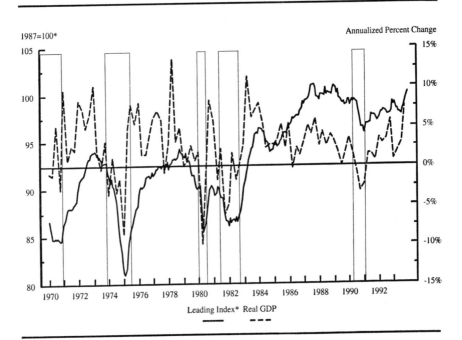

Source: US Department of Commerce.

index has longer leads than other popular economic series—such as real GDP (which really helps to define the cycle), the unemployment rate, or retail sales. When reported, all of these series also have a one-month lag or longer relative to the reference month and also do not have any "leading" information. While the index of leading indicators occasionally has a very short lead prior to recession, actually knowing, or at least being very confident, that a recession is underway is still very important information. Even if there is no lead in some recessions, this index is still the best indicator for confirming the onset of recession or at least very weak economic growth. Recognizing that the economy has just peaked allows for better planning in anticipation of a further weak economy.

The Three Ds

Apparently, the three-month rule can pose problems for a forecaster. Should one wait to see if data are revised before analyzing changes in the index? To do so would certainly reduce the predictive value of the index, since lead times are already short for some business cycles. To predict turning points in the economy, economists at the NBER and BEA have suggested for a long time that the focus should not be on the duration facet of changes in the index. Three consecutive declines (increases) are just not enough information on which to base a prediction of recession (recovery). For example, what if three very shallow declines are followed by a sharp rebound? Or what if only two or three components are pulling down the overall index due to special, temporary factors? These questions lead to the "three Ds": depth, diffusion, and duration.

Simply put, the significance of changes in the index depends on how strong the percentage changes are, how widespread the changes are among the various components, and for how many months the reversal in trend has continued. The three-month rule only focused on the duration facet. The "three Ds" approach helps to eliminate some of the uncertainty created by data revisions. For example, a three-month decline in June through August 1984 (in the version released October 31, 1984) obviously met the three-month rule. Furthermore, later revisions could be interpreted still to forecast weakness in the economy—or at least in manufacturing. Current versions of the data (as of April 1994) indicate the index fell eight consecutive months beginning in March 1984 with decreases ranging between 0.1 and 0.6 percent, yet no official recession occurred. Nonetheless, industrial production fell over the September through December 1984 period, thereby suggesting that the original data correctly predicted a weakening in the economy even though there was no official recession. By looking at the depth and diffusion of the original changes, one could see that pending temporary weakness was the correct way to interpret the original signal, even though the three-month rule was not met.

Another occasion in which looking at the three dimensions of the leading index would have helped to interpret the status of the economy was in late 1987. The October through December 1987 period was a false signal of recession using the simple three-month rule. This period included and immediately followed the October 1987 stock market crash. Importantly, the three declines in the composite index were led by sharp drops in financial variables—the S & P 500 component and real M2—along with consumer expectations. There was no clear signal from the other components. In fact, two orders components were up in two of the three months, along with vendor performance. Other components were little changed. Essentially, component analysis suggested that a recession was not certain given that weakness was concentrated in the financial sector. Weakness in consumer expectations probably reflected concern over financial markets specifically. A more in-depth look at the leading index once the three-month rule was met would have indicated that a wait-and-see attitude was still appropriate in terms of gauging whether a recession was imminent.

Deriving Component Net Contributions to the Index

Net contributions are an important focus of analyzing changes in the leading index, since the breadth of gains or losses across components is of interest in determining if the economy is strengthening or weakening. Net contributions are how components are analyzed. Net contributions can be derived from raw data for components that are put into either symmetrical percent change form or in first differences. Component data are then adjusted for component weights and for index standardization. Before looking at these calculations in detail, what are the concepts that are involved?

Monthly Symmetrical Percentage Changes and First Differences
The percent changes used in deriving component contributions are symmetrical percent changes using both the current month and previous month for the denominator. This has the desirable quality of producing percent changes of equal magnitude when a component rises and then falls (or falls and then rises) by the same absolute amount. Standard percentage changes are biased in the sense that decreases tend to be smaller than increases, since the base period for decreases is naturally larger than for a subsequent increase (this bias also holds for increases that are followed by a decrease). Symmetrical percent changes are defined as the difference between the current month, M_0, and the previous month, M_{-1}, divided by the sum of the two months and then multiplied by 200.

$$PCsymmetrical = \frac{(M_0 - M_{-1})}{(M_0 + M_{-1})} * 200.$$

First differences (the current month less the previous month) are used for series that contain zero or negative values or that are already in percentage change or ratio form. For the index of leading indicators, the two components put in first difference form are change in unfilled durables orders in 1987 dollars and change in sensitive materials prices. For the coincident index, all components use symmetrical percent changes, while for the lagging index, first differences are used for two of the seven series: the change in index of unit labor costs and the change in consumer prices for services. In the previous version of the composite indexes, first differences were also used for leading indicator components for vendor performance and for consumer confidence and lagging index components for the business inventory-to-sales ratio, the prime rate, and the ratio of consumer installment credit outstanding to personal income.

Component Weights

Component weights are derived from component standardization factors that are constrained so that the sum of component weights for each index is 1 for each index. What are component standardization factors?

Components are standardized because they have varying degrees of volatility. Some series have significantly larger monthly percent changes (without regard to sign) than others. Without standardizing components, those with larger mean absolute percent changes would dominate the overall composite indexes. The component standardization factor is the long-run average (absolute) of the series' percent changes. This means that the average of the absolute values of the standardized components equals one over the long-term period used for the calculation. Component standardization factors are revised only with comprehensive revisions; there are no annual revisions to these factors.

Component weights are calculated separately over the 1948–77 and 1978–89 time periods since the data behaved very differently over these time periods. Table 14–3 shows data for the more recent period.

Index Standardization Factors

In order to make the movement in the three composite indexes consistent with each other, the weighted averages calculated in the preceding step for the leading and lagging indexes are standardized. This is done so that the long-run averages (without regard to sign) of their component percent changes equal that of the coincident index. The ratio of the average weighted changes (from the previous step) of the leading index components to the corresponding average weighted component changes in the coincident index is the leading index standardization factor. For the lagging index, the index standardization factor is calculated similarly. For the leading index, the index standardization factor as currently calculated over the 1948–89 period is 0.850; for the lagging index, 1.161. These values below 1 indicate that before standardization, these indexes had greater monthly volatility than the coincident index. For the coincident index, the index standardization value, of course, is 1.000.

The result of the revisions to the formulas for calculating the indexes is that the current indexes have smaller cyclical amplitude than the old indexes, thereby reducing some misleading signals from the indexes.

An Example of Calculating the Net Contributions and Index Percent Change

For an example of calculating the net contribution for a component, we can use the initial claims data in the initial release for the statistical month of December 1993 as shown in Table 14–3. December initial claims were 311,000 while November's were 334,000. First, the symmetrical percent change is calculated:

TABLE 14–3
Calculation of Composite Indexes: Leading Indicators

Component	Raw Data Nov. 1993	Raw Data Dec. 1993	Percent Change or 1st Difference	Component Standard-ization Factor	Weight	Index Standard-ization Factor	Net Contri-bution To Index
Average workweek, manufacturing (hours)	41.7	41.7	0.000	0.420	0.156	0.850	0.00
Initial claims (thousands)	334	311	−7.132	4.347	0.015	0.850	0.13
New orders, consumer goods and materials (billions 1987 $)	112.51	114.05	1.359	1.973	0.033	0.850	0.05
Vendor performance (diffusion index, %)	50.7	51.7	1.953	4.318	0.015	0.850	0.03
Contracts and orders, plant and equipment (billions 1987 $)	40.94	40.66	−0.686	5.539	0.012	0.850	−0.01

Housing permits, (index 1967 = 100)	109.6	117.7	7.127	5.520	0.012	0.850	0.10
Change in unfilled orders, durables (billions 1987 $)	-2.85	-2.69	0.178*	0.416	0.158	0.850	0.03
Change in sensitive materials prices (percent)	-0.06	0.27	0.330*	0.162	0.405	0.850	0.16
Stock prices, S & P 500 (index 1941–43 = 10)	462.89	465.95	0.659	2.883	0.023	0.850	0.02
Money supply, real M2 (billions 1987 $)	2,765.2	2,764.0	-0.043	0.417	0.158	0.850	-0.01
Consumer expectations (index 1966 Q1 = 100)	70.3	78.8	11.402	5.067	0.013	0.850	0.17
					Percent change in index		0.7

*For these series, first differences are used rather than symmetrical percent changes. With the latest revision, vendor performance and consumer expectations are on a symmetrical percent change basis rather than first differences.

$$((311 - 334)/(311 + 334)) * 200 = -7.132.$$

The symmetrical percent change is then multiplied by the component weight (0.015) and then divided by the index standardization factor (0.850):

$$(-7.132) * (0.015)/0.850 = -0.13.$$

The -0.13 would be the net contribution for the initial claims series except that it must be inverted (multiplied by -1) to take into account that a decline in claims is a positive.

Basically, each component's net contribution is derived by (1) taking the appropriate symmetrical percent change or first difference, (2) multiplying this by the component weight, and (3) dividing by the index standardization factor.

To get the percent change in the overall index, the net contributions are summed as shown in Table 14–3 (discounting any rounding error). In contrast with earlier versions of the leading index, no trend adjustment factor is added to the sum of the net contributions.

What Were Trend Adjustment Factors?   The trend adjustment factors for the leading, coincident and lagging indexes were derived in earlier versions of the composite indexes to make their trends equal to the trend for real GNP. The long-term growth rate in real GNP was the target trend, and the trend adjustment factor was defined as the target minus the trend in the raw index. The raw index was an index derived from converting symmetrical percent changes of the component contribution sums to normal percent changes. These were then used to create raw index levels. In the immediate pre-1989 versions of the composite indexes, the target trend was the average of the trends of the components of the coincident index. The switch to targeting the trend in real GNP was made because economists generally focus on real GNP as a measure of long-run economic activity.[13] The current version of composite indicators does not use a trend adjustment factor because the trend adjustment factor tended to temporarily mask turning points at the peak of a business cycle—the trend adjusted leading index would still be positive while the raw index might be declining.

The Coincident and Lagging Indexes: Dating the Business Cycle

The coincident index is primarily used as a tool for dating the business cycle. The lagging index plays an ancillary role also. For determining cyclical peaks and troughs in the United States, the NBER is generally acknowledged by economists as the official arbiter. While there are no set rules for "measuring" turning points, historical decisions by this group strongly suggest rules-of-thumb that involve the coincident index.

Once monthly economic data are persuasive that a recent turning point has occurred, the appropriate NBER committee meets. Each economist on the committee presents his or her argument for the specific month for the turning point based on various economic indicators. If there is disagreement over the month, then there is further discussion leading to a compromise position. Importantly, the economic indicators used in this evaluation are primarily those in the coincident index, even though others can and do enter into the debate.[14] Specific attention is usually given to the movement in the coincident index.

Generally, in the post-World War II period, business cycle peaks and troughs have been officially pegged to peaks and troughs in the coincident index, although historical revisions have shifted turning points in the coincident index by one month in several cases. Historically, a turning point has been pegged as official when a given peak or trough in the coincident index is followed by six consecutive months that are a reversal of the previous trend.

If there is not a reversal of trend for six consecutive months, then usually movement in real GDP (or real GNP prior to 1992) is the other primary consideration. Two consecutive *quarterly* reversals of trend in real GDP are then the complementary determining factor to movement in the coincident index. A peak is usually placed in the last quarter with positive real GDP growth, and similarly a trough is put in the last negative quarter before the reversal of trend. If there are six consecutive months of reversal of the coincident index, then there is no compelling need for either two quarters of reversal in real GDP nor a need to place the peak or trough in the same quarter that real GDP peaked or troughed.

If a recovery is weak and wavering, then the committee usually waits to date a trough after the level of economic activity (usually in terms of real GDP) surpasses its previous peak. Once real GDP exceeds the previous peak, any subsequent downturn would be classified as a separate and new recession. The NBER announced the March 1991 trough on December 22, 1992, when it was apparent that real GDP for the third quarter of 1992 exceeded the peak of the second quarter of 1990 and would not be revised down below this level.

The main reason that the coincident index, not real GDP, may turn one quarter is that the coincident index is still dominated by manufacturing components, while real GDP has a greater share in nonmanufacturing sectors (services and construction), which can keep growth positive if the manufacturing sector is only mildly negative. The coincident index does have components other than industrial production, but for employment and personal income, manufacturing still creates the greatest cyclical movement. This also is somewhat true for business sales.

On a final note in the determination of peaks and troughs, the NBER also looks at leading and lagging indicators (the composites and components) to see if they, respectively, have peaked (troughed) prior to and after the prospective peak (trough) of the coincident index. If the coincident index is well bracketed, this helps to confirm and define business cycle turning points. Essentially, the primary purpose of the lagging index is to help confirm turning points in the business cycle.

KEYS TO ANALYZING THE MONTHLY REPORTS

First, one should remember that the leading index is designed to predict turning points—it is not a good measure of the strength of the economy. In fact, there is very low correlation between percent changes in the index and percent changes in real GDP, even after taking lags into account. However, there is a strong correlation between the coincident index and real GDP as measured with quarterly growth rates. One of the primary reasons that the coincident index does reasonably well in this regard is the inclusion of real personal income (excluding transfers) in the coincident index. Personal income is a large component of GDP on the income side of the ledger for the national income and production accounts.

The leading index is primarily useful during times of uncertainty. However, in order to judge if a turning point is imminent, one should not focus solely on the number of months of decline or rebound. One should use the "three Ds"—depth, duration, and diffusion—to see if a change from trend is widespread and significant in magnitude. To examine these factors, one can look at component contributions to see whether a turning point is likely. As discussed earlier, component contributions take into account normal differences in the size of monthly percent changes between the various components.

As is shown in Table 14–2, the leading index has a shorter lead in predicting turning points in recovery than in downturns. Therefore, whenever the index strengthens, one should expect to see improvement in the economy relatively quickly.

Finally, the leading index is a better indicator for turning points in manufacturing than for real GDP. This is due to the inclusion of leading indicators for manufacturing (the orders series, the manufacturing workweek, vendor performance, and sensitive prices), the lack of indicators covering services, plus the fact that manufacturing is more cyclical than real GDP.

TABLE 14–4
Interpreting the News Release: Key Questions

Leading Index

- Does the latest figure for the index represent a continuation of a trend, or is it near a possible turning point? Over how many months has the current trend continued?
- How large was the change in the index?
- How many components moved in the same direction?
- Has recent movement in the overall index been dominated by just one or two components (perhaps the stock market component or money supply), or are most components moving together?

For Defining a Turning Point

- Has the leading index had six consecutive moves in the direction opposite the most recently established trend *or* has real GDP reversed course for two consecutive quarters?
- What month is the turning point for the coincident index?
- To help define the turning point, for the apparent peak or trough as depicted by the coincident index, does the lagging index turn similarly within the following twelve months?

NOTES FOR CHAPTER 14

1. Barry Beckman and Tracy Tapscott, "Composite Indexes of Leading, Coincident, and Lagging Indicators," *Survey of Current Business,* US Department of Commerce, November 1987, p. 24.
2. Gary Gorton, "Forecasting with the Index of Leading Indicators," *Business Review,* Federal Reserve Bank of Philadelphia, November/December 1982, p. 16.
3. Beckman and Tapscott, "Composite Indexes," p. 24.
4. These categories were (1) employment and unemployment; (2) production and income; (3) consumption, trade, orders, and deliveries; (4) fixed capital investment; (5) inventories and inventory investment; (6) prices, costs, and profits; and (7) money and credit.
5. The NBER and BEA give ratings (in terms of being leading, coincident, or lagging) to each cyclical indicator relative to (1) peak, (2) trough, and (3) overall. If the ratings for peak and trough activity differ, then a series is given an overall rating of "unclassified." This is discussed further in the Business Cycle Indicators section of Commerce's publication, *Survey of Current Business.*
6. See *Composite Indexes of Leading, Coincident, and Lagging Indicators,* September 1992, US Department of Commerce, p. 1. Release date: November 3, 1992.
7. NSA = not seasonally adjusted.
8. Marie P Hertzberg and Barry A Beckman, "Business Cycle Indicators: Revised Composite Indexes," *Survey of Current Business,* US Department of Commerce, January 1989, p. 25.
9. The Commerce Department's composite indexes were first released in their current form for the January 1989 release on March 3, 1989. See Marie P Hertzberg and Barry A Beckman, "Business Cycle Indicators: Revised Composite Indexes," *Survey of Current Business,* pp. 23–28.
10. However, the actual turning point of the leading index did precede that of the coincident index on all four of these late three month rule-of-thumb forecasts. The turning point comparison is basically a one-month rule.
11. The latest historical revisions (as of September 1992) show consecutive declines in the index of leading indicators from May 1984 through October 1984. Earlier revisions—using the old 12 component composite—actually changed the data so that there were no three consecutive declines.
12. Earlier versions of the leading index did have a greater incidence of false signals. See Gary Gorton, "Forecasting with the Index," p. 20.
13. The March 1989 comprehensive revision to the composite indicators occurred prior to the BEA's completion of the December 1991 benchmark revision of the national income and product accounts, which included a shift in emphasis from gross national product to gross domestic product as the key measure of aggregate production.
14. For more detailed discussion of the considerations involved, see Geoffrey H Moore, *Business Cycles, Inflation, and Forecasting,* 2nd ed., 1983, pp. 5–9.

BIBLIOGRAPHY

Beckman, Barry A, and Tracy R Tapscott. "Composite Indexes of Leading, Coincident, and Lagging Indicators." *Survey of Current Business.* US Department of Commerce. November 1987, pp. 24–28.

Gorton, Gary. "Forecasting with the Index of Leading Indicators," *Business Review.* Federal Reserve Bank of Philadelphia. November/December 1982, pp. 15–27.

Green, George R, and Barry A Beckman. "Business Cycle Indicators: Upcoming Revision of the Composite Indexes." *Survey of Current Business.* US Department of Commerce. October 1993, pp. 44–51.

————. "The Composite Index of Coincident Indicators and Alternative Coincident Indexes." *Survey of Current Business.* US Department of Commerce. June 1992, pp. 42–45.

Hertzberg, Marie P, and Barry A Beckman. "Business Cycle Indicators: Revised Composite Indexes." *Survey of Current Business.* US Department of Commerce. January 1989, pp. 23–28.

Moore, Geoffrey H. *Business Cycles, Inflation, and Forecasting.* 2nd ed. Cambridge, Massachusetts: Ballinger Publishing Company, 1983.

Ortner, Robert, and Theodore S Torda. "Leading Index: A Useful Guide but Not an Automatic Indicator." *Business America.* August 6, 1984, pp. 22–23.

Ratti, Ronald A. "A Descriptive Analysis of Economic Indicators." *Review.* Federal Reserve Bank of St. Louis. January 1985, pp. 14–24.

US Department of Commerce. Bureau of Economic Analysis. *Handbook of Cyclical Indicators, A Supplement to the Business Conditions Digest,* 1984.

INDEX